SOUL SURVIVORS

SOUL SURVIVORS
Stories of Women and Children in Cambodia

by
Bhavia C. Wagner

photography by
Valentina DuBasky

foreword by
Jack Kornfield

WILD IRIS PRESS
Eugene, ❀ Oregon

Soul Survivors
is published by Wild Iris Press

Acknowledgments
With deepest gratitude to the Cambodians who generously shared their life
stories, our interpreter Cheam Kosal, Paul Strasburg, the Lyman Fund,
Linda Hartke, Church World Service, Maryknoll, Khemara, Cambodian
Women's Development Association, Indra Devi, Global Exchange, Arial,
Alan Brewer, the cyclo drivers, and our many friends who supported the
development of this book.

For further information about Cambodia or Soul Survivors,
and to schedule talks about Cambodia contact:

Wild Iris Press
PO Box 5231, Eugene, OR 97405
cambodiaedu@hotmail.com
(541) 343-3782
www.friendshipwithcambodia.org

ISBN 978-0-9753951-0-3
Previously published as ISBN 0-88739-391-8
Library of Congress Catalog Number 2002101294

Printed in the United States of America and the United Kingdom

Dedicated to the children of Cambodia,
non-violence, and loving kindness.

Table of Contents

Soul Survivors

This man walked in from the countryside to sell his clay pots on a street corner in Phnom Penh. The juxtaposition of the poor farmer against the modern office building illustrates the inequalities in wealth and the class resentment that helped fuel the creation of the Khmer Rouge.

"Only loving kindness can free us"
Message from Maha Ghosananda

The United Nations held a conference to discuss the future of Cambodia in 1981. During that time, we held a Buddhist ceremony for peace. At the end of the ceremony, a Khmer Rouge leader came up to me, very cautiously, and asked if I would come to Thailand to build a temple at the border. I said that I would.

"Oh!" thought many people. "He is talking to the enemy. He is helping the enemy! How can he do that?" I reminded them that love embraces all beings, whether they are noble-minded or low-minded, good or evil.

Both the noble and the good are embraced because loving kindness flows to them spontaneously. The unwholesome-minded must be included because they are the ones who need loving kindness the most. In many of them, the seed of goodness may have died because warmth was lacking for its growth. It perished from coldness in a world without compassion.

I do not question that loving one's oppressors—Cambodians loving the Khmer Rouge—may be the most difficult attitude to achieve. But it is a law of the universe that retaliation, hatred, and revenge only continue the cycle and never stop it. Reconciliation does not mean that we surrender rights and conditions, but means rather that we use love in all our negotiations. It means that we see ourselves in the opponent—for what is the opponent but a being in ignorance, and we ourselves are also ignorant of many things. Therefore, only loving kindness and right-mindfulness can free us.

Maha Ghosananda, Cambodia's spiritual leader, is a highly esteemed Buddhist monk and founder of the Cambodian movement for peace and non-violence. Reprinted from Step by Step: Meditations on Wisdom and Compassion (1992) *by Maha Ghosananda with permission of Parallax Press, Berkeley, California.*

1

A rural woman grinds rice into flour as she talks with her neighbor. Twenty-five percent of the households in Cambodia are headed by women, most of whom are widows. In 1979, at the end of the Khmer Rouge regime, sixty-five percent of Cambodia's population were women.

Foreword

The tales you hold in your hand of the women and children of Cambodia make a moving and inspiring book, both devastating yet necessary. The eloquence of their stories and the heartbreak they depict become ennobling because of the spirit that carries them. They are stories that have to be told, that have to be held up to the light of humanity. For the sorrows of Cambodia have not ended. They have been repeated in greater or lesser forms in Rwanda and Bosnia, in Colombia, and continue even now in our history.

What can we say in the face of such human tragedy? How can it be held, and how can it be healed?

Maha Ghosananda, the Buddhist elder, used to lead peace marches through the embattled territory of his beloved Cambodia even though his life was threatened, chanting the words of the Buddha, the Blessed One: "Hatred never ceases by hatred but by love alone is healed. This is the ancient and eternal law." And heal we must. The soul demands it.

It was in the first years of the refugee camps in my own work with Maha Ghosananda that the life force and the soul of the Cambodians became visible to see. The camps were on a desolate piece of border land, dry and barren in the hot season, holding hundreds of thousands of people enclosed by barbed wire and UN mandated guards.

The Cambodian holocaust had allowed only parts of families to survive—a mother and three children, an old uncle and two nephews—and each was given a little bamboo hut about four feet wide, six feet long, and five feet high. In front of each hut was a tiny patch of land no bigger than one square yard. Yet after only a few months of camp life, next to most of the huts in these little squares of ground, people had planted gardens. They had squash plants with two or three small squash on them, or a bean plant, and other vegetables. The plants were very carefully tended, with little bamboo stakes for support. The tendrils of a bean plant would wind around the stake and up over the roof of the house.

Every day the refugee family would have to walk a mile and stand for nearly an hour in a long line at the pit well at the far end of the camp to carry back a bucket of water for their plants. It was an amazing thing to see these tiny gardens in the middle of this barren camp in the dry season, when you could barely believe that anything would grow. With these gardens the Cambodians were also rekindling their indomitable spirit.

Martin Luther King Jr. spoke of this spirit during the days of bombings and death that were the darkest period of the civil rights struggle. He said, "We will match your capacity to inflict suffering with our capacity to endure suffering. We will not hate you, but we will meet your physical force with soul force."

In their extraordinary way, Bhavia Wagner and Valentina DuBasky have entered the heart of sorrow to bring forth this spirit and let it speak to us.

I bow to their courage to tell these tales.

I bow to the brave hearts of these women and children who offer their stories here.

I bow to that eternal spirit that shines through us all.

With blessings,

Jack Kornfield
Spirit Rock Center

SOUL SURVIVORS

A child plays with a ball on his porch. His family is considered well-off by Cambodian standards because their house is made of wood and has a tile roof, instead of being constructed from bamboo and thatch. His family's income comes from making and selling water storage jars. Only thirty percent of Cambodia's families have access to safe drinking water, which is the primary reason why nearly 60,000 children die each year before reaching age five, according to UNICEF.

Drawn to Cambodia

My sweat-soaked clothes stuck to the vinyl seat of the bus as I absent-mindedly watched a woman selling pungent durian fruit and wondered if our driver would succeed in getting us across the border into Cambodia. It was 1991, and I was traveling by land from Ho Chi Minh City to Phnom Penh in a hired minibus with twelve Americans, including photographer Valentina DuBasky. We had just finished a citizen diplomacy mission in Vietnam—a peace walk to protest the US trade embargo and offer friendship to the Vietnamese people. Curiosity drew us to Cambodia. We wanted to see for ourselves what this internationally ostracized country was like.

Our driver told the border officials that we were health care workers and we were given permission to enter Cambodia. I felt relieved as we moved forward and turned my attention to the scenery as we bumped our way down Highway 1. The rural Cambodian landscape appeared deserted. It was completely underwater except for the road and a few houses on stilts. Severe floods had destroyed that year's rice crop. We caught the last *salaang* (ferry) of the day across the great Mekong River with only minutes to spare.

The sun set behind ominous dark clouds, and it was close to midnight before we reached Phnom Penh and checked into the historic Le Royal Hotel. The grand old building was crumbling in disrepair, and bats flew ahead of us down the looming corridor, past empty rooms with the name plates of foreign aid organizations that once had offices here. The place felt abandoned, and I was dismayed to find that the door to my room didn't even have a lock.

The following morning, we walked through the empty streets of Phnom Penh. People cautiously avoided us, and only a group of barefoot begging children in tattered clothes hovered near us. Although it had already been twelve years since the genocidal Khmer Rouge left, it was clear that the city and its residents had not recovered from the trauma and destruction when nearly two million people died from execution, starvation, or disease. "Shell-shocked" came to my mind as my first impression of Cambodia.

Kris, a member of our group, had been to Cambodia before and had worked in the refugee camps in Thailand in the early 1980s. It was through her contacts that we found Saroan. We were happy to meet a Cambodian who could speak English and were delighted when Saroan agreed to be our guide.

Slowly, over the next few days, Saroan told us his story—of how he was sent to a Khmer Rouge labor camp as a child and, soon afterward, heard that his parents had been killed by the Khmer Rouge. He described how he escaped to Thailand, traveling alone through the jungle at age twelve. After living in a refugee camp in Thailand, Saroan managed to emigrate to the United States and stayed with several foster families before finding a home. He worked his way through college and graduated with a degree in computer programming. Saroan then decided to return to Cambodia because he wanted to help his people. He had been back three months when we met him.

I listened intently to Saroan's story. I had never met anyone who had experienced so much suffering, and I was amazed that he had retained so much goodwill toward humanity. His story touched me deeply, and I carried it in my heart when I returned to the United States.

In 1992, I went back to Cambodia and started working with women's organizations, helping them market their handicrafts in the United States. I came to know the gentle yet strong Cambodian women and heard their equally incredible stories of trauma and recovery.

I could see that Cambodia was changing rapidly. All five warring factions, including the Khmer Rouge and the Cambodian government, had signed a peace accord in the fall of 1991. Soon afterward the United Nations Transitional Authority arrived with its entourage of 22,000 soldiers and personnel to oversee disarmament, repatriation of refugees, and elections. Saroan was now working for the United Nations. The formerly empty streets of Phnom Penh were choked with white UN Land Rovers, and the bustling city had a new feeling of guarded optimism. There was even an air of celebration during the Water Festival, as the parks along the Mekong River filled with families who came to picnic and watch the boat races.

The following year I had a chance meeting with photographer Valentina DuBasky, whom I hadn't seen since my first trip to Cambodia in 1991. As we walked down a country road in western Massachusetts on a dark summer night under a bowl of stars, the idea to create this book dropped down on us. After brief consideration, we knew without a doubt that we should take on this project. The stories of Cambodian women and children, their sorrow and their hope, needed to be shared with the rest of the world.

Each step of the way, a door opened to help this book materialize. The grants and support we received felt like a shadow of the Divine assistance and protection that many of the Cambodian survivors experienced. When Valentina and I arrived in Cambodia in August of 1994 to begin our work on this book, the war was underway again. The Khmer Rouge had refused to participate in the national elections and instead was fighting the new Cambodian government.

We found ourselves living under a death threat from the Khmer Rouge, a terrorist measure directed against all Americans, French, and Australians due to our governments' support of the newly established Cambodian government. Widespread violence made it dangerous to travel in most of Cambodia's rural areas, and when I did, I nervously pulled a *kramar* (traditional Cambodian scarf) over my head in a feeble attempt to be less conspicuous.

Just before we arrived in Cambodia, three foreigners were kidnapped from a train and held for ransom. Months later they were found dead, and King Sihanouk warned tourists not to come. We learned to use caution, and we shared with Cambodians the underlying fear and tension that accompanies the perpetual threat of violence by the Khmer Rouge. Not long after our visit to Angkor Wat, the Khmer Rouge paid poor peasants $8,000 and a few water buffalo to ambush and kill an American couple who were exploring temple ruins.

Worried but not intimidated, we proceeded with our project. Through my friends, previous contacts, and the generous help of humanitarian organizations including the Cambodian Women's Development Association, Indra Devi, Khemara, and Maryknoll, I found just the right people to interview.

I invited a brilliant and caring woman, Cheam Kosal, a language teacher at the University of Phnom Penh, to be my interpreter. Kosal helped bridge the cultural and language barriers and was a tremendous asset to this project.

About two-thirds of the way into my research I arrived at a point where I couldn't stop crying. The profound sadness that the Cambodians carried was more than I could bear. I wept for days and wondered if I'd have to give up the project and go home. Finally, Divine Grace took me to a place of peace and understanding. I could see that beneath the pain of their losses was a foundation of hope. Life continues. People keep struggling to survive, to improve their lives, and most beautifully, to help each other.

As I worked on this book I realized that my own life was also a story of loss and recovery, though not of the same magnitude as the Cambodians. At some point in our lives, each of us loses something very precious and dear. It was inspiring to meet these courageous people who rebuilt their lives after serious losses.

The survivors' accounts included in this book offer a window to Cambodian history and culture from the perspective of women and children. But more than that, they carry a message of hope for humanity. They demonstrate how goodness is more powerful than evil, and that no matter how much brutality and torture people endure, they still carry the capacity and the will to offer kindness to others. These stories are testimony to the strength and goodness of the human spirit. It is my pleasure to share them with you.

Bhavia Wagner

SOUL SURVIVORS

Take off your shoes and enter the homes and lives of Cambodian women and children.

Cambodia's Trauma and the Khmer Rouge

The principles of Buddhism are enshrined in the hearts of each Cambodian: Nothing is ever permanent. We accepted, and that was how we let go of the pain and had the strength to rebuild each day for the future. In each breath, we inhale hope, life, and loving-kindness, and we exhale the sorrow and pain."
—Mu Sochua, founder of Khemara, a Cambodian women's development organization

Cambodia's recent history has a period of tragedy and brutality similar to the Holocaust of World War II. Out of Cambodia's seven and a half million citizens, close to two million died from execution, starvation, or disease during the genocidal rule of the Khmer Rouge from 1975 to 1979. How could something this horrendous happen?

The Khmer Rouge grew out of the Cambodian communist movement of the 1940s, which sought to break the country free from French imperialism. The movement was fueled by deep-seated anger and resentment toward long-term injustices in Cambodian society, such as government corruption and a wide gap in wealth between poor rural peasants and relatively rich urban residents. Cambodian college students studying in France met to discuss Marxist socialist ideals and formed the Cambodian communist movement. One of the students was Saloth Sar, who later changed his name to Pol Pot and became the leader of the Khmer Rouge. "Khmer" means Cambodian and "Rouge" is red in French, referring to communism.

Upon Cambodia's independence from France in 1954, the communists focused on improving conditions for the country's poor peasants. Violence in Cambodia began in 1967 with the outbreak of an armed communist revolution against King Sihanouk. Two years later, the Vietnam-American war spilled into Cambodia when the United States started illegally bombing neutral Cambodia in a futile attempt to destroy North Vietnamese hiding there. King Sihanouk was over-thrown in 1970 by Cambodian General Lon Nol, and the Khmer Rouge started fighting the new US-backed military government. Millions of people were forced to leave their homes and farms and hundreds of thousands were killed or wounded. War refugees flooded Phnom Penh.

On April 17, 1975 the Khmer Rouge defeated the Lon Nol govern-ment. Leaders of the Khmer Rouge with differing political ideologies vied for power and it was Pol Pot who won control—an extremist who viciously set out to create a class-free society by eliminating all traces of foreign contamination. It is difficult to imagine why Pol Pot, who grew up in Cambodia, studied in France, and taught in a Phnom Penh high school, would want to exterminate all the educated people in Cambodia. He was a rigid ultra-nationalist, and in his mind anyone tainted by foreign or capitalist influences was the enemy.

The Khmer Rouge received support from China because both were enemies of Vietnam and the Soviet Union. Envisioning a nation of Maoist agrarian communes, the Khmer Rouge declared "Year Zero" and pro-ceeded to brutally dismantle Cambodian society. The new government immediately evacuated the cities, forcing all at gun point to leave their homes and walk to the rural areas. Schools were closed, books destroyed, and seventy-five percent of the teachers were murdered.

Children were taken away from their parents, and everyone over four years old was forced to live in work camps and perform hard man-ual labor. Food rations were desperately insufficient, and helpless mothers watched their own children die from starvation.

The Khmer Rouge shut down the hospitals and systematically exe-cuted the doctors; only fifty physicians remained in 1979. Proper med-ical care was eliminated and many people died from untreated illness-es. The Khmer Rouge outlawed spiritual practice, destroyed Buddhist temples, and killed the monks. People targeted for extermination and taken away to be murdered included the educated class, former urban residents, and ethnic Cham, Vietnamese, and Chinese. Bodies piled up, filling mass graves in rural areas that came to be known as the killing fields. Very few families escaped being touched by death, and Cambodia became a land of traumatized widows and orphans.

Pol Pot and the secret committee at the top of the Khmer Rouge were driven by a vision of complete equality, hatred toward perceived oppressors, and a desire to hold power at any cost. They used fear to control people and lived in a climate of growing paranoia. The Khmer Rouge kept expanding its definition of "class enemies" to the point where comrades suspected of dissent were also executed.

The Khmer Rouge chose peasants to be local leaders and execu-tioners. Those who harbored anger toward the rich were ruthless, while others were more sympathetic. Malleable young people were designated as supervisors and spies. The Khmer Rouge brought out the darkest side of human nature and allowed the forces of fear, anger, hatred and revenge to govern. The tactics of terror spiraled out of control.

Wanting to reclaim Cambodia's ancient territory, the Khmer Rouge undertook a series of border attacks against Vietnam and Thailand in 1977. These clashes continued until 1979 when the Khmer Rouge was driven out of Cambodia by the Vietnamese army.

The Khmer Rouge fled to Thailand and Cambodia crumbled into chaos. Mothers searched neighboring villages for their missing children and then walked the long journey home, to the place they had lived before the Khmer Rouge period. Upon arrival, they usually discovered that all their possessions had been stolen, and often their houses were destroyed. Many families returned to damaged rice fields or farms underlain with landmines and rendered useless. Not enough rice was planted in 1979, and there were shortages of seed, farming equipment, and draft animals, so millions went hungry.

Women constituted sixty-five percent of the population in post-Pol Pot Cambodia, and the demographic imbalance made it difficult for widows to remarry. Single women who couldn't find husbands worried about what would happen when they became old and needed help, since they wouldn't have children to look after them. In a traditionally male-dominated society, more than half of the households were run by women, mostly widows, who struggled to feed and support their own children along with the orphaned children of relatives. Many widows found it difficult to earn an income because they lacked marketable skills, credit, or land. The loss of relatives eliminated their traditional family support system, so they had no one to help share their psychological burdens or material needs. Consequently, many women committed suicide.

Cambodia was slow to recuperate from the extreme devastation. Meanwhile, the ousted Khmer Rouge set up bases in Thailand near the Cambodian border and with the support of China, Thailand, and the United States started guerrilla warfare against the new Vietnamese-backed government. The war depleted Cambodia's remaining resources and consumed forty percent of the national budget, leaving scarce funds to rebuild the country's infrastructure, hire teachers, train medical personnel, or assist farmers. Most of the physically able men, including boys as young as twelve years old, were conscripted into the military. Women worked almost as hard in the 1980s as they had in the forced-labor camps of the Khmer Rouge.

Intensifying the cruelty of the period, the United States led a world economic embargo against Cambodia between 1979 and 1992 in an effort to collapse the government. Cambodia had become an enemy of the United States because it was being supported by Vietnam. The

United States also saw to it that all UN development aid was denied, even donations of shovels or other agricultural tools. Soviet-bloc communist countries provided limited aid.

At the end of 1991 the Cambodian government and the three warring resistance factions, including the Khmer Rouge, signed a peace accord. The international economic embargo was finally lifted, and assistance from the West started arriving, although virtually none of it reached Cambodia's poor peasants. Most of the aid was channeled to UN activities, including election preparation and repatriation of 370,000 Cambodians who lived in refugee camps in Thailand. Many returning refugees ended up in urban slums, for lack of farmland free of landmines.

Cambodia's newly elected government was a coalition of the political party associated with the former Vietnamese-backed government, led by Prime Minister Hun Sen, and the royalists' political party, led by King Sihanouk's son, Prince Ranariddh. The Khmer Rouge broke the peace accord by refusing to disarm, not participating in the election, and starting a war against the new government. This new surge of fighting forced over 50,000 people to flee from their villages, and these internally displaced citizens became the poorest of the poor.

Up until 1997, the Khmer Rouge controlled about fifteen percent of Cambodia, had thousands of soldiers and waged guerrilla warfare against the Cambodian government. The insurgents were supported through the sale of Cambodian gems and timber, with help from the Thai military who also profited. Peasants collaborated with the Khmer Rouge because soldiers came into their villages and killed them if they didn't cooperate. The Cambodian army was poorly managed, underpaid and ineffective in its efforts to defeat the Khmer Rouge.

In 1997, the year before the national election, Second Prime Minister Hun Sen ousted First Prime Minister Ranariddh in a coup, destabilizing Cambodia and causing many countries to withdraw their aid in disapproval. Later that year, the Khmer Rouge publicly humiliated Pol Pot in a mock trial. In 1998, the United States attempted to extradite Pol Pot for an international trial, but he died the day before he was to be turned over to Thai officials. Thousands of soldiers defected from the Khmer Rouge between 1996 and 1998 significantly reducing its strength.

The national election in 1998 was stained with political intimidation and human rights violations prior to election day. However, the ballot casting and counting was deemed free and fair by UN election monitors. After months of dispute over election results, Hun Sen assumed the role of Prime Minister. The new government faced the Khmer Rouge legacy, a devasated nation.

One government report summarized the problems facing Cambodian women as unemployment, prostitution, AIDS, a shortage of day-care centers, domestic violence, landlessness, illiteracy, a lack of education and vocational training, under representation in politics and government, and high rates of maternal and child mortality. Undaunted, Cambodian women continue struggling to overcome these obstacles.

In 1999, two Khmer Rouge leaders, Khieu Samphan and Nuon Chea, were allowed to re-enter Cambodian society, while two others, Ta Mok and Duch, were captured and charged with genocide, finally bringing thirty years of violence to an end. The US-funded Cambodia Genocide Program gathered evidence for a UN-organized international tribunal to bring justice to Cambodia by putting the Khmer Rouge on trial for the deaths of nearly two million people. The trial began in 2008.

In the following chapters, fourteen Cambodians share their personal stories, describing their tragic losses during the murderous rule of the Khmer Rouge and how they rebuilt their lives in the subsequent years. Photographs offer a glimpse of who they are today. These women and children are diverse in age, ethnicity, occupation, and experiences. What they have in common is that they are all survivors who are working to improve their own lives and the lives of others.

Sam Ol's dance teacher adjusts her position as sunshine pours into the royal palace's dance pavilion. In ancient times mythical apsara dancers delivered messages from the gods to the king. Originally reserved only for the king, classical dances are now performed before foreign dignitaries and tourists. Classical dance is one of the oldest and most beautiful art forms in Cambodia.

Sam Ol ❀ Classical Dancer

Sam Ol's story is an adventurous tale of a twenty-year-old classical dancer who secretly fled Cambodia in 1975 when the Khmer Rouge came to power. Her cleverness, courage, and charm helped her survive and escape from the Khmer Rouge many times, but when she finally reached the Thai border she decided to stay in Cambodia and suffered under Pol Pot. In 1978, Sam Ol became seriously ill, but her life was saved when the community held a special magical ceremony for her "spirit teacher," with most unusual cooperation from the Khmer Rouge. Sam Ol was one of four dance students from her class of twenty who survived and returned to Phnom Penh after the Khmer Rouge was forced out. Today she works as a classical dancer at the royal palace and supports her widowed mother, sisters, and nephews.

It was a hot and humid morning when I met Sam Ol in the burned-out shell of the Bassac Theatre on the banks of the flooded Bassac River, down the street from the enormous Cambodiana Hotel. The theater had been the rehearsal and performance stage of the Ministry of Culture's Art Department until a fire destroyed it in 1994. The government didn't have funds to rebuild it, so the dancers and musicians practice in what's left of the lobby, partially exposed to the elements.

As I waited for Sam Ol, I watched the graceful women dancing to the sweet Cambodian music. Their movements were slow and controlled, perfectly synchronized and flowing. The ethereal music and the soft motion of the dancers transported me into a peaceful meditative state, convincing me that Cambodian classical dance is truly from the heavenly realm.

Sam Ol greeted me with a friendly smile. She agreed to an interview and to teach private dance classes to a group of novice foreigners, including me. Through my weekly dance lessons, I became friends with Sam Ol and came to know her winsome, free-spirited personality. I also enjoyed her humorous cousin Pov who always accompanied her.

I felt comfortable around Sam Ol because she was open and honest with her emotions, which was unusual for typically reserved

Cambodians, and especially women, who are taught to be quiet and "ladylike." She shared her sadness about the past, her frustrations at work, and her concerns for the future.

"If it weren't for my spirit teacher helping and protecting me, I would have died during the Khmer Rouge regime," Sam Ol explained. Today she helps heal Cambodia's wounds by bringing the lovely art of classical dance to the shattered souls of Cambodia.

Sam Ol:

I love to dance. I started dancing when I was ten years old, and went to class every Thursday after school. My mother saw that I was graceful and had ability, so she put me on the waiting list to study at the Arts School in Phnom Penh, and I was admitted at age fifteen. I enjoyed dance class in the morning but wasn't much interested in my general studies in the afternoon.

Not long after I started attending Arts School in 1970, the Khmer Rouge began shelling Phnom Penh. We were terrified, and for our safety my father moved my family to the Air France office where he worked as a guard and messenger. It was too dangerous to travel across the city, so for the next five years I lived near my school at a relative's house and just went home on the weekends to see my family.

When the Khmer Rouge took over Phnom Penh in April 1975, the soldiers forced us all to leave our homes. I was pushed into a crowd of people walking southeast on Highway One and couldn't go to the Air France office to find my family. When we reached the village of Areiksat in Kandal Province, the Khmer Rouge ordered us to start digging irrigation canals.

I missed my family and longed to be with my parents, so after working for a month and a half I escaped. I slipped away one night when no one was watching and the next day I blended in with the people who were returning on foot to their native provinces. On reaching the border of Kompong Cham Province I was overjoyed when I ran into my sister Oeun and my cousins Sophin and Chanthy. They persuaded me to run away with them to Laos or Thailand because there was so much killing in Cambodia.

We were all in our early twenties and felt daring. We created false travel permits, which worked well because most of the Khmer Rouge couldn't read. They stopped us many times as we traveled north toward Laos and told us that we had to start working for Angka, the government. We would stay a short time in each place and sneak away at night.

After a few weeks of traveling through Kompong Thom Province we reached mountainous Preah Vihear Province, where the weather was cold. We met a villager who told us that if we wanted to go through Preah Vihear we would have to know how to climb a tree to escape from wild animals and we couldn't say anything bad to the spirits that lived in the trees. He said the spirits could see us but we couldn't see them, and if we cursed they would hear us and get angry. Then the spirits would make a wild animal appear, like a tiger or snake, and we would become terrified or sick.

Preah Vihear sounded too scary, so we turned toward Siem Reap. At that point we were traveling in a group of twenty women and men, and among us were a pilot, a doctor, an artist, and an athlete. Usually we traveled only at night, but when we came to a stretch of road that was quiet and didn't have villages, we walked during the day. Unfortunately, we were stopped by Khmer Rouge soldiers who asked where we were going. When we said we were going to Battambang Province they became angry and told us that the time to travel to one's native village was over and we should start working.

They ordered us to stay in a house with a soldier and his mother. I knew that single people were sent to work in remote areas, so I pretended to be married. But when it was time to go to bed I went to sleep in the room with the other women and my "husband" went to sleep in the room with the men. The soldier's mother realized I wasn't really married. I worried that she would report us the next day and we'd be punished, so we decided to escape that night.

I went out the front door, pretending I had to go to the bathroom, while the others climbed out the windows. We met on the road and quietly slipped away. We broke into small groups, and I went with my sister and two cousins. The night was very still. After an hour or two we heard the sound of a horse and saw the light of a bike, and realized that the Khmer Rouge soldiers were coming after us. We hid behind a mound of dirt next to a deep hole. It was very dark and Chanthy fell into the hole. We had to pull him out. The soldier on horseback rode past and didn't see us. We were glad when we saw the soldier on a bicycle go straight ahead at the corner where we had turned left.

We continued traveling through the night. At dawn, I stayed near the road to keep watch while the others slept in the forest. An older couple with a cart came by and I learned that they were traveling to Siem Reap Province. I had the idea that if we could get across the provincial border with their help, the Khmer Rouge from Kompong Thom Province wouldn't follow us.

At first I told the couple I was from Battambang Province because I wanted them to think I was returning home, but they said, "No, you are not. Your accent is different." Then I told the truth and asked if we could join them. They wanted to know if I was traveling in a group of nine men and women because the Khmer Rouge had announced that they wanted to arrest this group. I told them that there were only two women and one man with me. The couple agreed to let us join them and added us to their travel permit by changing the number. They wanted to reach the Thai border just as we did.

We arrived in Siem Reap Province in September and said goodbye to the older couple. We were happy when a few days later we met up with some of our former travel companions. They told us that two people from our group had been captured the night we all escaped from the soldier's house. The man who had pretended to be my husband stole a chicken and was cooking it with another man. The Khmer Rouge saw the smoke and arrested them.

We continued to walk toward Thailand, but the Khmer Rouge came by and stopped us on the road. They sent us to a place called Policam Village. It was just a big field and not many people lived there. They gave us a knife and a hoe and told us to build a house. We were supposed to make a palm leaf roof, but we were city people and we didn't know how, so we gave some of our extra clothes to a farmer in exchange for the roof. We pretended to build the house.

We traded more clothes for pumpkin and made a dessert, which we traded for rice. We met two men from Phnom Penh who were kind to us. We knew they were also trying to leave Cambodia, although we never asked them directly. They had a plan for escaping and wanted to help us, but we knew that there are two ways of helping, the good way and the bad way. We were young women, old enough to marry. We weren't sure about their intentions, but we decided we had no choice but to escape with them.

The next day, the two men looked for a way to cross the Krowline River to Battambang Province. Other people asked if they could go with us, but we told them it was better to travel in a small group. After dark, we left in a pouring rain, glad because the Khmer Rouge were too lazy to follow us in the rain through rice fields and banana groves. During the night we became lost in the forest, but at dawn we found the river. The men cut down banana trees and tied them together to make a raft. They put all our things on it and took Chanthy across the river and left him on the bank with our bags. Then they came back, picked up my sister, my cousin, and me, and took us safely across.

We walked past rice fields and through a forest until we reached Tmorpok District. I was very tired and hungry and we didn't have any food. Chanthy asked if I would take a few clothes into the village to trade for food, since I was the only one who was brave enough. I told my companions that I wanted to live in that village because I was tired of traveling. I hated sleeping on the ground and using a stone for a pillow every night.

My companions wanted to go on to Thailand, but I told them I wanted to stop. I knew there were tigers and wolves in the forest, and I didn't know how to climb a tree to escape. I could see that they were angry with me. My sister begged me not to leave the group, but I said goodbye. They didn't want us to become separated so everyone, including the two men, followed me into the village.

When we came to the community kitchen, we were surprised to see Khmer Rouge soldiers there. We decided we had better enter and apologize, otherwise they might kill us. We planned to tell them we had made a big mistake and had just been traveling. The soldiers asked us a lot of questions—where we came from and who we were. I told them I was a seller. They opened my bag and took out my photos, perfume, and necklace and said these belong to capitalists. Those items made them despise us.

The soldiers told the cook to prepare lots of rice for us as well as dessert, even though everyone else was eating watery rice porridge. At that point I didn't know that they intended to kill us, so I ate happily while the others hardly ate at all and looked miserable. We couldn't talk with each other because we were being watched. After eating we felt sleepy and wanted to rest, so the women got down from the stilt house and took a nap in an ox cart with a roof, while the men stayed in the house. We slept until sunset.

We were then escorted through the dark by soldiers on horseback, in front and behind us. I was glad they didn't tie us up. By then I realized they intended to kill us, and I wanted to run into the forest, but couldn't. There was no way to escape. The people we passed felt sorry for us. They had seen many students killed, as well as government workers, educated people, and market sellers.

The Khmer Rouge took us to the meeting house in the center of the village where a lot of people were gathered. The soldiers instructed us to wipe our feet and go in. The Khmer Rouge leader started to interrogate us. Where did we come from? Why did we arrive so late? What did we do? Everyone else in my group was speechless. I told him that we were from Phnom Penh but we were returning to our native village in Battambang Province, and that my occupation was a seller. The leader was kind to us and told us we must start working. We couldn't believe they didn't kill us.

We were sent to work in different places and saw each other only a few times a year. I wanted to stay in Cambodia but my friends still wanted to go to Thailand. The two men who helped us cross the river didn't know how to farm, and when they were told to plow they were terrified and felt sick because they knew people from the city were killed. They tried to escape several times but were always caught. One day the Khmer Rouge came and told them they were being taken away to be ox cart drivers, but everyone knew they were taken away to be killed. I was very sad because they were like brothers to me. I felt guilty because if they had not followed me into the village that day, they might have survived.

No one had enough rice to eat, and I was full of grief when I heard that my cousin Chanthy had died of hunger. I learned how to trick and steal to survive. I made friends with the kitchen staff and with a guard who stole rice for me at night. I ate wild leeks and sweet potato leaves. I wanted to live so I could see my parents again.

We toiled every day. One day after work, our camp celebrated the Khmer New Year. The cooks butchered a pig and prepared special dishes, including dessert. For the first time, we were allowed to eat until we were full. That night people sang and danced, using a bucket and spoons for instruments. A few people in the village had learned dances from a Khmer Rouge dance group that mimed fighting with guns and working hard. In the dance they rolled up their pant legs and pretended to dig canals. I thought it was disgusting and didn't want to watch.

I felt hopeless because I feared I would never leave that place. I imagined that I'd never even see the main road again. We didn't have a radio and were totally cut off from the rest of the country. There wasn't enough food, and people became weaker and weaker. No one dared to go against Angka, the government, because we knew we would be killed if we did. My despair grew when the Khmer Rouge sent me to build a dam far away.

I became sick and was demoted to "second strength," the weaker work force, which meant I was given even less rice to eat. I developed a high fever and was carried back to the village in an ox cart. There was no modern medicine to treat me, and no one thought I would recover. Nine traditional healers came to see me. The first gave me a tea made from bark, the second gave me traditional medicine pills, and the third steamed me, accidentally scalding my leg. The next healer burned little pieces of cotton on my nose, forehead, and temples, which left scars on my face.

I was seriously sick for three months and everyone said I was incurable. When I acted insane and tried to run into the forest or jump into the river, people followed me and brought me back. I stayed with my cousin Sophin, but I remember feeling all alone, without parents, brothers, or sisters.

One day a former monk who knew traditional medicine came to see me. He believed there was an unhappy spirit inside me. The monk took a small stick like the kind they use to beat ghosts and while he was hitting me the spirit in me told the monk, "If you want to beat me, take the branch of the banana tree because it will hurt me." The branch of the banana tree is very soft, but I started bleeding when the monk hit me with it. I drifted in and out of consciousness and was sometimes aware of the spirit speaking through me. I could hear it like an echo in my ear.

The monk asked who I had been in the past, and my cousin told him I was a dancer. In Cambodia we believe that each artist has a *kru*, a spirit teacher, inside her who helps her. The monk thought I might have done something to wrong my spirit teacher.

Before the Khmer Rouge took over the country, I regularly prayed with the other dancers to our spirit teachers and offered food and incense. It had been almost four years since I had done that, which may have been the reason I got sick. The monk said we needed to make an offering to my spirit teacher, and he found an old villager who knew how to prepare the ceremony.

First the villagers made the *bay seiy*, a special centerpiece, by rolling banana leaves into fingers and placing them around a tall green banana stem. They decorated the nine levels with jasmine flowers and incense, and put eggs and candles on the top. Then they arranged special foods on the table, like logan fruit because it signifies wealth, but not custard apple because it represents poverty. The Khmer Rouge leader allowed the villagers to use an ox cart to bring the heavy musical instruments.

They put me in the middle of a circle of people in front of a house, and at sunset the ceremony began. At first they played Khmer music, which was the wrong music. When they changed the music to *pin piet*, which is the classical dance music, my spirit started to recover. Between three and four in the morning I began to know myself and was able to sit up. I asked for a dance costume, and they brought me a blouse, a *compun* (dance skirt), and everything I requested. I put the clothes on and began to dance. It was nearly dawn.

The next day I felt well enough to eat rice and regular food. Up until then I could only eat bananas and drink orange or coconut juice. People were amazed by my improvement and told me I changed color seven times during the ceremony.

I couldn't believe the villagers helped me like that, at a time when people thought only about getting enough food and their own survival. I must have done good deeds in a past life and that allowed their goodness to come forward and help me when I was sick. The villagers there knew how to have the ceremony for spirits because Prince Sihanouk used to have similar ceremonies at a temple in that area before the war. The prince came to pray at that particular temple because it had a reputation for being effective.

The Khmer Rouge leadership changed during the time I was sick. It was the end of 1978 and leaders from the eastern part of the country were sent to the west. Our new district leader was from a higher class than the former, who was a farmer. He didn't kill anyone and instead was compassionate and allowed the villagers to hold the ceremony to help me.

After I felt better, I asked permission to work at the dam where my sister was working. There I met another cousin, Sophon, who had worked in a textile factory in Phnom Penh before 1975. The Khmer Rouge made her continue working at the factory until mid-1978, when they sent her to work in Battambang Province.

The Vietnamese invaded in late 1978; we heard a lot of shelling and saw the Khmer Rouge leave. I fled northeast to the city of Siem Reap with my sister and two cousins. When we reached Siem Reap, I found my old friend Date, and we stayed with her while the fighting continued. Date was a singer, and she earned enough rice to feed everyone. I picked vegetables that had been planted during the Khmer Rouge regime and traded them for rice, which I then traded for clothes. Rice was used for currency. After a couple of months the fighting ended and it was safe to travel. We left for Phnom Penh by car, stopping in Kompong Cham Province for a week to visit Date's family.

I arrived in Phnom Penh on July 7, 1979 and went directly to my parents' house. I was sad to find no one there. I went to the Ministry of Culture and was given a job as a classical dancer. Thirty out of fifty professional classical dancers survived the Khmer Rouge regime, and only four dance students returned from my class of twenty at the art school. Fortunately, most of the important teachers survived.

I performed in the Royal Palace and was appointed to teach in the public schools that requested a classical dance teacher. During summer vacation, ten-year-old girls came to the palace, and I taught them Choun Por, the welcoming dance.

In 1980, I was filled with happiness when my mother, brother, two sisters, and four nephews returned from Site Two refugee camp in Thailand. But I became very sad when I learned that my father had starved to death. I was his favorite child. My mother told me that my oldest brother was also dead. He had been a Lon Nol soldier, and at first the Khmer Rouge asked him to be a driver, but later they murdered him. I cried when I heard that five of my nieces died of hunger.

My father always wanted me to marry a European so I would have a secure life. He thought foreigners treated people well and didn't look down on workers, even office cleaners. I wanted to get married, but because my father was dead I needed to take care of my mother and support my brother, sisters, and nephews.

It is difficult being the head of a family. It feels like a big responsibility on my shoulders. I have a sister who lives in the United States and helps us by sending money occasionally. My salary as a classical dancer is only $12 per month, and I earn $1 at each performance.

Between 1979 and 1991, I taught during the day, and in the evening I performed for guests of the government, such as ambassadors and other foreigners. I went home exhausted. I didn't like putting on and taking off heavy make-up every day and was worried that it would age my skin prematurely. In 1981, I traveled to the Soviet Union to perform. Since then I have danced in East Germany, India, Thailand, and Australia. When Prince Sihanouk returned to Cambodia in 1991, his wife wanted to help the dancers increase their income, so now we perform only once a week and we give private lessons to earn more money.

The government doesn't pay attention to the dancers or give us much support. Sometimes there is favoritism given to some of the dancers. I think the government should look after all the dancers until they retire, like a mother looks after her children until they are grown up. My hope is that I can work until I am 50 or 55.

I worry about Cambodia. I had hoped for peace in 1979 when Pol Pot left, but the Khmer Rouge started fighting the government. After the peace agreement was signed in 1991 and Prince Sihanouk returned, I expected peace again, but the war didn't end. Now we have a new government, and I hope the fighting is over. I wish that Cambodia could survive on its own and not depend on other countries, but we lack expertise.

It doesn't bother me that I didn't marry, because I don't think I would be happier with a husband. It is nice to be independent. I tried to go back to school, but I couldn't study because there were too many problems at home. My mother worried too much, and in 1984 she became weak with a fever and died at age fifty-seven. In 1985, my brother was accused of being a member of the Son San opposition party and was put in jail for a year.

Now I help my divorced sister raise her four boys. She is a fruit seller, and her educational level is low. She has many difficulties and doesn't always take responsibility for the children. I take care of the boys when they are sick, and my other sister, who is a part-time waitress, helps them with their studies.

My cousin Pov came to live with us in 1991, when her mother moved to America. We are her only relatives in Phnom Penh. She and I go everywhere together because it is safer, and we keep each other company. According to our custom, it's not good for a woman to travel alone. Pov used to work with the Central Women's Association as a mobile educator, teaching about women's health and child care. She quit when she got sick, and now she is a freelance writer and photographer.

In 1987, Pov started wearing men's clothes because women in Cambodia are looked down on by men. Sometimes children think Pov is a man, but they realize she is a woman when she uses "cha," the Khmer word for "yes" that women use, instead of "ba," which men use.

Classical dance was created for the king and is very proper. It's close to perfection, which is why I like it. Classical dance is always in my mind, and I love it very much. There are about thirty dances, but we only perform a few. People laugh because we always repeat the same ones. My boss says they are new to the foreigners, so we keep doing them over and over instead of practicing and performing different ones.

I am afraid some of the dances will be forgotten and lost. Two of our important teachers died recently, and there is only one left who knows the old dances. We don't have enough special costumes for the dances that have animal roles. I would like to see all the dances survive as an important part of Cambodia's cultural heritage.

Before the Khmer Rouge we used to create new dances. The Queen loved classical dance, and she would gather all the dancers and the song writers together and give them a poem from which they would create a new dance.

The Queen died in 1975, and no one supports classical dance as much as she did. She used to help the dancers by obtaining materials from other countries to make the costumes.

Not many Cambodians have seen Khmer classical dance or understand it, which is unfortunate. Most of our performances are for private groups, and the only time we perform for the public is on *Om Touk*, the boat racing holiday, and *Chaul Chhnam*, the Khmer New Year. We have youth clubs where volunteer dancers train the children, but I think dance should be included in every school curriculum instead of only a few schools.

An Australian humanitarian organization invited me to teach dance to the very poor children who pick through garbage and try to sell the plastic bags and cans. When I saw their situation I didn't think about the money because I knew I wanted to help. I enjoy teaching them how to dance. I hope they will have a better future.

If it wasn't for my spirit teacher helping and protecting me I would have died during the Khmer Rouge regime. I saw so many graves. Now I make an offering of incense and fruit to my spirit teacher every Thursday with the other dancers.

My spirit teacher communicates to me through my dreams and shows me when I am in danger or when something is going to happen. I remember my dreams and recognize the symbols. If I dream of reaching the top of a mountain I will succeed, but if I can't reach the top I will fail. I know I will have good luck when I dream of my parents coming to see me, of building a new house, or of wearing a dance costume. If I dream that I am fat or drowning, it is a warning that I will become sick. Most importantly, my spirit teacher helps me dance well.

Sam Ol's cousin Pov gives her a lift, passing by an expansive city park in Phnom Penh. Motorbikes are a common form of transportation in urban areas. Most Cambodians cannot afford a car.

In her free time, Sam Ol volunteers at a program for former street children. She teaches young gymnasts how to incorporate classical dance moves into their floor routines. Very little attention is given to the arts in Cambodia, since most people are busy just trying to survive.

Cambodia's glorious Angkor Wat crumbles, as a child, representing today's dire poverty, quietly begs from foreign tourists. The classical dance that Sam Ol performs dates back 1,000 years to the golden age of Angkor Wat, when mythical apsara dancers were carved in stone on the walls of temples. The magnificent buildings were constructed by slaves, and some Cambodians believe the oppression that built the empire has returned in the form of the Khmer Rouge, as punishment according to the law of karma.

Ratha presents an AIDS education program in a rural village as a TV camera man from Phnom Penh tapes her. AIDS is a growing problem in Cambodia and prevention is practically non-existent. Indra Devi, the women's organization started by Ratha, received a grant to inform Cambodians about the danger of AIDS.

Ratha ❧ Teacher

It was April 18, 1975, the day after Pol Pot seized power, when Ratha's husband, an employee of the Department of Agriculture, was "called to a meeting." A few days later Ratha heard that he had been executed. She was now alone, left to raise five young children. Ratha barely survived the Khmer Rouge regime, and at one point she skillfully persuaded a Khmer Rouge leader not to kill her. In 1979, she resumed work as a teacher and struggled to support her children. Ratha was frustrated with the corruption in Cambodia's government and education system, and in 1993 she formed Indra Devi, a women's organization that works for peace, justice, and human rights.

I took a *cyclo* (bicycle taxi) over to meet Ratha at the Indra Devi office in central Phnom Penh, near the embassy district. I often chose cyclos over motorcycle taxis because the cyclo drivers are so poor; most are farmers from the countryside who look as worn-out as their clothes. They always smiled so gratefully when I paid them a generous fare of 1000 riels, about forty cents.

Indra Devi's simple two-room office was staffed by dedicated volunteers. Ratha had just returned from a meeting with other human rights groups to discuss how to respond to the recent assassination of a newspaper editor who had criticized the government. I felt admiration for Ratha and her colleagues who put their lives on the line each day as they stood up for justice in Cambodia. I noticed that Ratha was a master at putting on a pleasant face, in spite of what was happening, and I found her to be a skilled orator. Her stories were always filled with descriptive drama, and she spoke to me honestly and directly about the political and economic situation in Cambodia.

Ratha is always in the middle of the action, attending human rights conferences, walking in peace marches, or collecting signatures to ban landmines. She also is a gracious host. One day she invited me, photographer Val DuBasky, and a few others for an excursion into the countryside. She arranged for the sons of her friends to take us on their motorbikes. Very few Cambodians can afford to buy motorbikes, much less cars.

First we stopped in a small village and watched women weaving beautiful cloth on looms under their houses on stilts. Then we took a boat to an island in the Mekong River and enjoyed Khmer music and a dance performance. On the way home we stopped to have a picnic lunch of cold chicken, pickled radish, cucumber salad, custard apple fruit, and, of course, rice. It was a very pleasant day, just the lift our spirits needed, and a nice antidote for Ratha's serious human rights work.

Ratha:

Since I was very young my father taught me to have the heart to help other people. He didn't want to be rich, but to only have enough, because he said that when we die we don't take anything with us. "Please, only do good," he told me. "After you are gone people will remember your name. Reputation is the only thing that cannot be stolen. It is different from material wealth, which can be easily destroyed."

My father was an orphan and a person who loved justice. Even when he was working in top-level positions as the governor of Pursat Province, the deputy of Kompong Chhnang Province, or the minister of culture for Cambodia, he still paid attention to poor people and tried to help them. When my father met an orphan who didn't have enough money to go to school, he supported him. He lived modestly and rode a bicycle to work, so most people didn't realize he was a high-ranking official.

Usually parents with only two children tend to spoil them, but my father always told me I would have no inheritance and I needed to be self-reliant. He made me work and wear ordinary clothes without much jewelry. In contrast, my mother loved jewelry very much. My parents each had their own ideas, and in our house my mother's room was furnished with modern imported furniture, whereas my father's room was furnished with traditional handmade Cambodian furniture. My father observed the Buddhist precepts so rigidly that my mother said he should become a monk.

Before the Khmer Rouge regime, I was a primary school teacher in Battambang, and my husband worked for the Department of Agriculture in forest management. My husband and I loved children, and we had five.

On April 18, 1975, the Khmer Rouge called my husband to Phnom Penh for a meeting. Later I learned that he had been brought there to be killed with other government workers. The next day, the Khmer

Rouge ordered everyone to leave Battambang city. I carried my baby and my father held the hands of my two older children, while my mother and my domestic helper took the other two. There were a lot of people walking in the street, and we were afraid of losing each other. When we arrived in the countryside the Khmer Rouge directed us to live in remote Wiel Trea Village in Autaki District. The land was barren and there were no trees.

The Khmer Rouge made everyone in the village eat together, and they gave each person only one small bowl of rice porridge twice a day. Sometimes we would have soup, but never with meat or fish. When I looked down into the bowl, I could only see water and vegetables. If we wanted more to eat, we had to find it ourselves, and we ate nearly everything we could get hold of, even uncooked shrimp. Many people had health problems due to lack of good nutrition, and swelling was common. We ate inappropriate things, like leaves, which gave us diarrhea.

My children were all young, aged one to six. We were ordered to live in a house with several other widows, and my parents were sent elsewhere. The Khmer Rouge taught us to cut off loyalty to our families and to only watch out for ourselves. People frequently quarreled because there was not enough food to go around. If people stole even small things, the Khmer Rouge killed them. A woman or man who committed adultery was executed. I saw many people buried.

I was heart-broken when the Khmer Rouge killed my father. They knew that he was educated and guessed that he was a former government employee. The following year, I was very sad when my mother died from an illness.

I am alive today due to luck. When the Khmer Rouge made us leave home, I took our medicine, including penicillin, vitamins, and my husband's dysentery medicine, a big can of a thousand tablets. Often I was able to trade the medicine for fish or rice. The Khmer Rouge told us to be honest and show everything we had, but I had a strategy and gave some and hid some. I knew I needed to play a game to survive.

When it came time to plow the rice fields, the Khmer Rouge made us women be the oxen. It took twelve women to replace two oxen. Later, we were forced to build a dam, and I watched the Khmer Rouge beat the people who carried soil too slowly. Everyday I worked from early morning until ten in the evening, with only a half-hour rest after dinner. My two oldest children had to work as well.

Next, the Khmer Rouge sent us to transplant rice. They told my work group to make eighty bundles of rice per day. In some fields it was easy to make eighty bundles, but in others it was very difficult. They didn't take the conditions into account, so my co-workers asked me to talk to the Khmer Rouge leader about this. When I did, the leader told us to just follow orders and not make comments. Afterward, they searched my house to find out if I was involved in a group working against them.

When we harvested rice they assigned ten people to harvest one hectare, 100 meters square, and we had to work until it was finished, sometimes late into the night. Everyone wanted to be in my group because I worked quickly. I used to be an athlete and play basketball and handball, which helped me work efficiently.

One evening the Khmer Rouge called everyone to a meeting at which a woman was accused of stealing soap and trading it for rice. The Khmer Rouge leader announced that she was guilty of giving rice to the enemy. That woman had helped me once, so somehow I found the courage to stand up and say, "She wanted that food for her children, not the enemy. She is not the only one who trades things to get food. Everyone trades. If you take her, then you should take all of us to jail." I was so glad when they let her go.

One morning, while I was harvesting rice, the Khmer Rouge came for me. They walked me like a prisoner three kilometers back to the village because they had decided to kill me and my children. They didn't say why, but I assumed it was because they knew I was educated. Before they took us away, the head of the village, who was about sixty years old and a kind man, gave us a good meal, a special soup, and rice. He asked how many children I had reported to the Khmer Rouge government. "Five," I answered. "If you had told them less, I could have kept some from being killed," he said to me, placing his hand on each child's head before we were taken away.

Armed Khmer Rouge soldiers drove us away in a cart pulled by a motorbike, while the head of the village followed on his bicycle. People cried when they saw us, knowing that my father and husband had already been killed. The Khmer Rouge took us to a compound of several houses surrounded by barbed wire. We were escorted into a wooden stilt house.

I saw the head of the village arrive, put his bicycle under a tree, and go into the office to ask for my release. He was appointed village head by the Khmer Rouge, but he didn't act like the Khmer Rouge and instead was humane and never ordered killings. Everyone in the village loved him. He came out of the office with a sad face, and when he went to his bicycle I called to him, "Father, are you leaving me now?" He couldn't say anything and just nodded.

The soldiers guarded us. My youngest child saw an orange on the table and cried for it. I asked if the child could have it, and the soldier gave it to me. Then the Khmer Rouge chief came and told me I could bathe before dinner. When we sat down to eat, we were brought a big bowl of rice, pork soup, sardines, fried fish, sauce, and bananas. I hadn't seen food like that for two years; it was like going to a restaurant. The servants told us to eat until we were full, but they had pity in their eyes. I could see it, because I had been a teacher.

After dinner the soldiers took us to another house, and I noticed that we had eaten the same meal as the Khmer Rouge chief, on the same nice dishes. The chief handed me a lamp and a shovel and explained that if during the night I wanted to use the toilet, I needed to take the lamp so I would not be mistaken for the enemy. I felt sleepy after that big meal and fell asleep with my five children all squeezed together under one mosquito net.

That night, I prayed in my heart that all my ancestors would come help me and make the Khmer Rouge take pity on us. Praying was something I started doing in 1975, when the Khmer Rouge came to power.

At sunrise, the Khmer Rouge took me to work with the youth group, and I had to leave my children behind. A soldier watched me from a dike. No one dared talk to me because when someone was considered guilty, anyone who spoke to that person was also suspected of being guilty. I worked alone while the others worked together, harvesting rice and tying it in bundles, until ten in the morning when another soldier came to take me back. For lunch we were given only rice porridge with salty fish, but we were allowed to eat until we were full. After we finished the guards said, "Prepare to leave, the car is ready."

As we passed through the village I asked the soldier to stop the car at my friend's house because I wanted to get another sleeping mat and mosquito net. My friend was the aunt of a high-ranking Khmer Rouge leader in Phnom Penh, and I had known her before 1975. She had helped me over the past year by sending me food, and I kept my gold and silver at her house because I figured the local Khmer Rouge wouldn't dare search it.

I knelt before her, which is how we show respect to an older person, and asked for a mat and a mosquito net. I wanted to stop at her house because I thought I might never see her again, but since I was there I decided to get my gold and put it in a small bag around my waist, like a belt, in case the Khmer Rouge leader would accept a bribe. "Why are you taking so long?" the soldier called to me. My friend told me to go, and I couldn't find the words to say good-bye.

"Here's my house," I said as we drove past, but the soldier didn't stop. I began to worry that they really would kill me, or else punish me by making me work very hard breaking stone. We can't see when the time to die will come, I thought. They confined me in another compound surrounded by barbed wire. At about three in the afternoon they took me to meet the top Khmer Rouge leader, the one who had arrested my father.

The Khmer Rouge leader told me to come in alone, but I carried in my youngest child, hoping it would make him feel some sympathy.

When I sat down in a chair, he accused me of being upper class and asked who my husband was. I told the truth because I figured he already knew and just wanted to see if I would answer honestly. He hated the upper class and was very rude to me. He called me the enemy and said city people were betrayers. I apologized. He accused me of not struggling enough.

I asked to have a chance to say a few words before I was killed. He consented. "I didn't expect the others to help me, only you," I said. "If I have done something bad, I ask you to forgive me. I promise I will be honest to Angka (the government), and if I do anything wrong in the future, you can sentence me. I ask you, father, to release me." Miraculously, he had pity on me and merely confined us for fifteen days. The soldier who led me away said I was very lucky. Later, when one of my friends was taken to the same man, he ordered the soldiers to kill her immediately. Maybe God helped us.

A few months later, the Khmer Rouge arrested a man who accidentally released fish from a trap. That evening they called everyone to a meeting. The Khmer Rouge tied the man's hands behind his back, stood him in front of the room and declared that he was guilty of stealing. Then they took a knife and cut open his belly and cut out his liver. I was shocked and felt sick. I could not eat after seeing that, and I thought of what the Khmer Rouge had said before, "We don't profit if we keep you, and if you are taken away we don't lose anything." They considered us worthless.

As for me, I survived those times by not thinking too much. I had to train my heart to not think about the bad, even though I saw a lot of people dying. I only thought about working, eating, and sleeping, because that was enough. Still, I felt sorry for my children. I was weak, but I found the strength to keep working.

One day, my work group was told to transplant forty bunches of rice, but when the leader saw us finish early she increased it to eighty bunches. We tried to work fast and complete the work by three in the afternoon so we could look for food, like snails or snakes, on the way home. When we did, the leader changed our assignment to 120 bunches. We talked among ourselves and decided our strategy didn't work, because even if we finished early and could gather some food, we would have spent too much energy working hard. We decided to work at a normal pace in the future.

My work group was smart enough to develop a secret system of trade which we used occasionally. One person would go off to be the trader, and the rest of us gave her gold jewelry to exchange for rice, palm sugar, fish, or potatoes. On the way back from trading she played a trick on the Khmer Rouge and acted like she was going fishing. She carried a bucket that had the trade goods in it, covered with leaves.

Once the trader was caught, and she was confined for fifteen days and fed watery porridge. When she finally came back to work and told us that everything was gone, we just said, "That's OK." She had to be extremely careful after that because if she were caught again, she might be killed.

By the end of 1978, the Khmer Rouge had become even more mistrustful and frequently investigated everyone. Many people were killed. We could not get extra food by trading because we were watched all the time, day and night. I became very skinny and bony, as did my children. No one was trusted, and the Khmer Rouge comrades started betraying and killing each other.

The Khmer Rouge kept asking me about my background, and I told them I was a teacher. When they registered the women whose husbands used to be government workers, the head of my village felt compassion for me and my children and didn't put me on the list. He told me to hide that day, so no one would notice that I didn't register. I worried day and night, and whenever the Khmer Rouge soldiers looked in my direction, I asked God to conceal me. One day I heard a rumor that I was supposed to be killed, but I told myself I didn't need to think about it because worrying wouldn't change anything.

I was relieved when Vietnamese soldiers arrived and the Khmer Rouge ran into the forest. I was released from the Khmer Rouge. I was free! I took my children and began walking home to Battambang City, which was a long journey. People who had older sons or daughters with them were able to carry rice to eat along the way, but all my children were young, so we only ate sugar cane.

The next day, to our disappointment, the Vietnamese soldiers escorted us back into the rural area. On the way we found unripe fruit and ate it since we hadn't had fruit in years. It tasted delicious. The soldiers treated us very badly, and after a week we realized they were Khmer Rouge wearing Vietnamese uniforms. We made a plan to escape and sent two women to find out if there were any Khmer Rouge behind us. The women pretended to be digging forest potatoes. When they came back and reported that it was safe, some of us escaped that night and headed toward the city of Battambang.

When we finally arrived in Battambang, in January 1979, we learned that only the Vietnamese were allowed to live in the city, so we stayed in the outskirts. At the end of August there was a call for teachers, and I applied. I was hired and attended a short five-day refresher course. I celebrated my graduation by eating stir-fried vegetables with meat and rice, since food was what I was lacking under the Khmer Rouge. I was so happy to be employed.

The school I was assigned to work in was eight kilometers from where I lived. Only Vietnamese leaders and communist party members were allowed to travel in the city, but the son of a friend of my father arranged permission for me to pass through the city on my way to work.

As I rode my bicycle on a quiet street along the river, I could see that the Vietnamese were collecting and taking away everything that had value. I saw a building full of sewing machines and another full of generators. There were big government trucks filled with goods, especially furniture. The Vietnamese took anything they could sell, even window glass.

They went into people's homes with metal detectors to try to find where the gold was buried. After the Vietnamese had taken all the valuables, they let people come into the city. The formerly rich people didn't get their homes back because the new government leaders had taken the nice houses for themselves and their relatives.

I discovered that my wooden house in Battambang had been taken apart for the materials, so I continued to live with other homeless families near a temple. I decided to go to Phnom Penh to see about getting my grandfather's house, and I made arrangements with a friend to watch my children. I was afraid I would have to pay a bribe in order to get permission to go, but an official took pity on me and put my name on his travel form so I could go with him. The truck trip to Phnom Penh was very expensive, forty dollars per person.

Just outside Phnom Penh, I got down from the truck to go to the toilet, and it left without me. The local police came up to me and asked if I had permission to be there. When I told them what had happened, they accused me of being a smuggler and took me to the district authorities. I relaxed when I walked into the office and saw that the district leader was my husband's former boss. He gave me a permit to be there.

It was December 1979 when I arrived in Phnom Penh, and the city was very quiet. I felt nervous when anyone stopped me. I asked permission to visit my grandfather's house, and as I walked up to it I saw that it was occupied by Vietnamese. I asked to have a look inside and found it to be just a skeleton of a building with nothing in it. It had been stripped clean, even the wooden walls were gone. The Vietnamese asked me where the valuables were hidden. "Don't worry," they said. "We can share them." I was worried because it was so quiet there. They could have killed me and no one would have tried to help me.

Next, I went to Kandal Province, to the house my mother and I built on my great-grandparents' property. When I arrived I saw that the land had been divided among many people, and most of the fruit orchards, including the mango and coconut trees, had been cut down. Only 200 *pnew* fruit trees remained. I could not hold back my tears when I remembered my great-grandparents. The house was now being used as a government office, but I found my cousin living in a room on the second floor. When I wanted to get a coconut from a tree next to the house, my cousin said I would have to ask the government for permission. I was upset because I was not even allowed to eat my own family's coconuts.

Since I had no other house, I decided to bring my children to live with me on the porch of the second floor of the house in Kandal Province. I wanted to be near my ancestors' graves so that I could offer food and incense each year, according to our custom. When the rainy season came, I asked the government for permission to move into an empty room. The government workers always made noise on the first floor of the house because they didn't want me living there. I told them that I wanted the field with the 200 fruit trees, but the officials said it belonged to the government and to all of the people. When I protested they agreed to give me a small piece of land near the fruit trees.

After moving into "my house" I applied to the government in Kandal for a teaching position. They didn't hire me, and said they had to investigate me, to see if I was associated with the enemy. Fortunately, one of my aunts who worked for the Ministry of Education helped me get a job as trainer of primary school teachers in Phnom Penh. I moved there and kept that position for three years.

There were a lot of Vietnamese experts working with us in the Education Department. We disagreed with them about the curriculum. The experts wanted us to use the Vietnamese curriculum that said Prince Sihanouk was the enemy of Cambodia. They eliminated the history of Cambodia and replaced it with the history of communism. Geography was only about Cambodia, not the world. Russian and Vietnamese were the only foreign languages taught, while English and French were forbidden.

I disregarded their rules and secretly taught French out of my home for extra income until the vice-president of the Education Department accused me of being involved with the enemy and started to investigate me. Luckily, the second vice-president was a friend of mine, and she advised me to change jobs and teach at Phnom Penh High School. I attended a course on teaching high school math and then started in my new position.

My salary only covered the cost of food for my children, so after school each day I tutored the children of government officials to earn extra money. I even planted vegetables for my family on the school grounds. Inflation was very high, and the value of the riel kept dropping. I taught from 6 A.M. until 7 P.M. every day of the week until I became so exhausted that I was hospitalized with a lung problem.

In 1986, I saw corruption begin in the Ministry of Education, especially during final examinations. Male students over sixteen years old who didn't pass the exam were forced to join the army and fight the Khmer Rouge. All parents worried about this. Even I, a teacher, was afraid when my son took an exam. Parents who didn't want their son in the army would pay a bribe so that their son would "pass" the exam. If they didn't have money, their son had to hide. Other parents started giving bribes so their children could get jobs.

Children of government officials always passed the exams. Their parents just sent a letter that said "This is my child" and had an official stamp on it. Some school administrators and teachers became very rich. Corruption made students lazy. Most of them didn't study or respect the teachers, who became discouraged and just filled up class time without concern about the quality of their teaching.

The situation horrified me. Our education system taught corruption to the children and didn't allow the good students to pass. I didn't want to participate in administering the exams, because I didn't want to destroy our country's future, so I told the school officials that I was sick and asked to be excused.

Corruption was all through the government. Officials lied to the public. They said that a bribe would assure that a young man would become a policeman instead of a soldier, but after training for three months, the young men were then sent off to the battlefield. The government took men to cut down trees in the jungle "so the enemy wouldn't have a place to hide," but then the timber was taken to Vietnam for export. Our country became deforested.

Farmers were forced to sell their harvest of corn, beans, and rice to the government for very low prices. If they didn't sell it to the government, they were accused of hiding it for the enemy. Some farmers took their grain to sell in the market to get a better price, but on the way they often were arrested. The farmers could buy their release by paying the police with gold or jewelry. The big houses around Kandal market were used to store government rice and beans before it was taken to Vietnam by boat or truck.

We were heavily controlled by the government. If a young man didn't have a student ID, he was taken to join the army. Some of my friends were accused of being the "enemy" without reason, and were kept in jail for two or three years. One friend was arrested and put in jail just because a guest slept in her house for one night before traveling to Thailand. I was afraid of many things: my son being taken into the army, the government accusing me of being the enemy, and not being able to support my family. Everyone was afraid, even children who were excellent students. Corruption made people act abnormally.

I felt very angry and tried to think of a way to protest this situation. Although I was a person who didn't like to write, I decided to compose a poem about it. I wrote that students who pass by bribery will not be good leaders in the future and will just create more corruption. I wrote about my sympathy for the teachers and for the homeless people who had such sad stories. I wrote about how downhearted I felt because I thought my country would collapse. In my poem, corruption was the field that grew bad people. I said the government should correct itself and stop seeing black as white.

I read my poem to a friend. I wanted to put it in the newspaper, but that belonged to the government. I was afraid and hid it in my closet. The next week, I asked one of my colleagues to take it to the newspaper office, but not tell them who wrote it. I signed my name as "The woman who cares about her country." My poem was edited and published, but no one really paid attention and the corruption continued to increase.

If the Ministry of Education was corrupt, I imagined that the other ministries were even more so. I began writing more poems, especially late at night. My heart was depressed, and the poems helped release my sadness. I prayed for someone to come and help my country. Many of my friends thought I was crazy. "You don't need to think about those things," they said. "Just pay attention to what's in front of your face, like supporting your family."

Corruption was the worst in 1991, at the time of the peace talks between the government and the other warring groups. Government officials were afraid that they wouldn't be able to get bribes after the peace agreement was signed and the United Nations took over. The big houses were sold and half of the proceeds went to the government and half to the officials. No one dared protest about the land being taken by the leaders.

It made me angry when I heard that my land in Kandal Province had been given to the governor and he intended to sell my house. I had been living in Phnom Penh for many years, but I still considered that to be my land. A friend of mine advised me not to protest because they could easily hire a person to kill me. Everyone else was afraid, but I was furious.

I became sick and had to rest for six months. One of my sons peddled a *cyclo* (bicycle taxi) to earn money to support our family. I continued to write. I wrote a poem about the government taking my land and my house. I said that years ago the king took land from the people, but this government is worse than the king. When I sent the poem to the governor of Kandal Province, he became very angry and ordered police to guard the land and had the 200 fruit trees cut down and made into charcoal.

I filed a complaint with the Ministry of Property Control. In my letter I asked why my land, which used to belong to the government, was now owned by the governor. "Can only government officials own land and houses?" I asked. They replied that since I moved away, I didn't have a right to the house or the land. "The governor never lived there so how did he get the house and the land?" I demanded. "My husband was killed by Khmer Rouge, and you are the second Khmer Rouge that has continued to destroy the achievement of my ancestors. I just want a small part of the land, as a symbol of my great-grandparents. Every family needs to keep something for the next generation. You owe me a favor because I am the brake on the motorbike that stops you from wanting more and more, which then makes the people more and more angry. You will create a revolution," I warned.

The officials tried to deceive me and claimed the land had been given back to the government, but I saw that the harvest continued to go to the new governor, the son-in-law of Prime Minister Heng Samrin. I could see that all the government officials were in cahoots with each other. But after I filed my complaint, other people did too.

Before the 1993 election there were a lot of killings and assassinations. People were found dead but we didn't know who killed them. The country was in chaos. Before one of my sons moved to a distant province, he begged me give up my land dispute. "All of us rely on you," he said. I decided to stop wasting my time and instead to focus on earning money since my standard of living was so low.

The United Nations Transitional Authority of Cambodia (UNTAC) came in 1992 as the temporary government and started preparing for elections and setting up a court system. At that time an organization to protect human rights was formed by some people who had just been released from prison after being wrongly accused. Most people were afraid of being affiliated with the new human rights association, but as soon as I heard about it I rode my bicycle directly from school to join. "Aren't you afraid of being killed?" asked my school principal and friends, but I didn't listen to them and encouraged other people to join also. I was one of eight people who attended a course on human rights offered by the association. I was pleased to be part of a group that was working for justice.

The association wanted women to attend an international meeting in Thailand called Women Overcoming Violence. I volunteered to go and the president of the association volunteered his wife, but she didn't attend. She and her children moved to France because they were afraid they would be killed if they stayed in Cambodia.

I was eager to attend the meeting because they were going to discuss the rights of women. I was amazed that they dared to speak out about human rights. My school would not give me permission to leave and claimed it was inappropriate. I decided to go anyway, but I didn't tell anyone because I was afraid I might be arrested. I left at four in the morning and traveled to Bangkok by taxi, even though it took a couple of days, because I could not afford to fly. I was sick and worried, but brave enough to take part in the meeting. I was the only Cambodian who attended the conference.

When I arrived back in Cambodia, I was glad to hear that my second son had passed the test for becoming an interpreter at UNTAC. I was also hired by UNTAC and worked with the French in public security. I was an interpreter and kept documents about non-governmental organizations. I was pleased because UNTAC was concerned about my security and gave me a lift home every day to protect me.

I realized that I, as one person, was not as strong as an organization, so I asked others to form an association with me for the purpose of helping people, especially women, in Cambodian society. On March 27, 1993, we established Indra Devi, named after an important woman in Cambodian history. Indra Devi has members, but most of them are poor widows who don't have time to volunteer.

The kidnappings and killings in Cambodia continued in 1993. A few weeks before the election there was a conference about justice in Cambodia. None of my seven board members dared to attend, so I went and took my youngest daughter. When I was invited to speak I proposed an international meeting for women to share their ideas on how to strengthen peace in Cambodia.

We organized a political forum, and over 300 people attended, which was more than I expected. I invited three monks and ten nuns, and I seated them in a prominent place in the room to remind us of being peaceful. I was the moderator, and we presented 12 questions to the 21 political parties, including a question about how they planned to help women and children.

My board members feared that the government would think we were accusing them of not providing justice, so they left early to avoid the possibility of trouble and didn't stay to help me clean up. Prior to the meeting, I had asked UNTAC to come and guard us, but they said Saturday and Sunday were their days off. I had applied to the district authority for protection, and they sent four policemen who stayed for five minutes and then left. I was relieved when there were no incidents of violence and I arrived home safely.

Over the next year I went to several more international conferences. The Asia Foundation invited me to attend the International Women in Development conference in the United States. Next, I went to a conference in the Philippines, and I traveled to Japan on a speaking tour. I spoke frankly about the problems in Cambodia and tried to help the world understand the situation facing women. Sixty-five percent of Cambodia's population is women, but in our National Assembly there are only five women out of 120 members. We have never had a woman minister and even the Minister of Women's Affairs is a man!

This is the first time I have been head of an organization, and some Indra Devi members say they want a different president. They accuse me of making decisions without them, and they think other members of the organization should travel to international conferences instead of me. There is a lot of jealousy in Cambodian society. They think that I am too honest and outspoken and are afraid that one day the government will put us all in jail.

In the months preceding the election a lot of people who were associated with FUNCINPEC (the royalists) and Son San (the capitalists) political parties were shot dead, but the incidents were reported as robberies. I don't know who did the killings; some say it was the former Vietnamese-installed government that became the Cambodian People's Party (CPP). There had been a lot of corruption during the last twelve years and people were not happy with that government, so CPP was afraid of losing the election.

Many of us were afraid that if CPP lost, war might break out because the majority of the soldiers were CPP. Shortly before the election, Maha Ghosananda, a Buddhist monk, led a peace walk from the city of Siem Reap to Phnom Penh. He asked all people and all political parties to have peaceful hearts, especially on election day.

Not everyone walked the entire distance of 300 kilometers, but many participants walked the length of their province. People all along the route served food to the peace walkers, even if they were very poor. In Kompong Thom Province the peace walk was shelled, but luckily the bombs did not explode.

I went on the peace walk with my daughter. She had been an excellent student in high school, but she failed the entrance exams for medical school and the economics institute, maybe because of corruption, so she became a airline flight attendant. We wore white clothes on the walk, because white is a symbol of peace and a good heart, and we carried lotus flowers which represent purity and softness. Eighty percent of the peace walkers were women. We begged Cambodian society to end the divisions and the civil war, and stop creating widows and orphans.

I walked in support of peace for three days through the streets of Phnom Penh with thousands of other people. People stood in front of their houses and waved at us. They set out bowls of water so the monks and nuns could sprinkle the water and give a blessing. We prayed for peace and security. I was tired and had blisters on my feet by the time we ended at the royal palace. But I felt very happy to be part of the effort to awaken people's desire to stop the violence. King Norodom Sihanouk and his wife came out of the palace and warmly received us.

We waited seven days for the election results. During that time, CPP became more angry and cruel, so Maha Ghosananda held a special ceremony for three days at Wat Phnom, our city monument, and then for another three days in front of the royal palace. At the ceremonies, monks spoke about ark hengsa (non-violence) and not being angry. Finally, the results showed that neither party won the election, so CPP and FUNCINPEC agreed to share power. We were relieved that war did not break out.

The conditions in Cambodia used to make me feel angry and helpless, but when I met people working for human rights I became inspired and my attitude changed. I decided to do something to help my country, to help women and poor people, and to bring peace to Cambodia. I don't have a lot of knowledge and I often have memory problems, but I am brave enough to face difficulties and challenges and do my best.

Ratha holds photos of her father, who was killed by the Khmer Rouge because he was educated, and her mother, who died from an untreated illness during the Khmer Rouge's cruel rule. The memory of her father's compassion survives in the form of Ratha's humanitarian work.

Like this young woman, Ratha worked as a teacher. School expenses including fees, books, and clothes are one of the largest yearly expenditures for a rural family. The drop-out rate in primary school is about fifty percent. Many families are too poor to educate all of their children, so they usually choose to put their sons through school and keep their daughters home to tend younger siblings and do the household chores. By twelfth grade there are three times more boys than girls.

Chath holds a blow fish brought to him by these children. He and other volunteers travel to rural villages giving landmine awareness programs in an effort to help reduce the number of injuries. Cambodia has an average of two to three victims a day from landmines and unexploded ordnance. Demining is slow, dangerous, and very costly.

Chath ❀ Refugee and Human Rights Worker

Chath was a child without a childhood. At age five, the Khmer Rouge took him away from his parents and put him in a work camp. As he dug irrigation canals and planted rice in leech-infested paddies, all he could think of was missing his mother. During the chaos following the Khmer Rouge regime, Chath and his brother fled to a refugee camp in Thailand. A year later they emigrated to Denver, Colorado. There Chath faced the US version of poverty, violence, and racism. It wasn't until one of his high school teachers recognized his potential and put him in a special international studies program, that Chath began to blossom. After graduating from college, Chath taught about AIDS in the inner city. In 1994, he returned to Cambodia to work for human rights.

I met Chath in San Francisco through my volunteer work at Global Exchange, a non-profit organization that promotes international understanding. Chath wanted to know more about our work in Cambodia, so I arranged to meet him over lunch. He reminded me of a wise sage in a young man's body, an old soul with a deep connection to the Divine. Chath is a good-natured, caring person who is sensitive, thoughtful, and altruistic.

We became friends and Chath introduced me to San Francisco's Cambodian community. He took me to the Buddhist temple in the pink house where the orange-robed monks live, and I met his adopted grandmother Yea, an old nun. We visited Cambodian families living in crime-ridden neighborhoods. I talked with a gang member and a woman whose son was shot dead, an innocent victim of drug-related racial violence.

In March, I attended the big Cambodian New Year's celebration and watched Chath perform traditional dances. He had a lead role and was one of the best dancers. Chath is also a marvelous poet.

The next time I saw Chath was in Cambodia. He was writing grant proposals for a Cambodian human rights organization, and in his spare time he taught English to neighborhood children. His presence was a gift to Cambodia because he offered so much kindness to the people he met. I could see that the difficult conditions in Cambodia sometimes depressed Chath, but he chose to stay and do what he could.

Chath told me about the day he almost stepped on a landmine. This close encounter with death convinced him that his life has a purpose. He believes he lived so he could do something for others. Chath is fulfilling that purpose through his humanitarian work and by just being his naturally compassionate self.

Chath:

When I was a young child my mother took me with her to the temple and taught me about Buddhism. She was very religious. She told me to be kind to other people and to not kill animals. I usually only killed fish, because fish was the food that sustained our lives, but under the Khmer Rouge I was told to slaughter a chicken. I was afraid that God would see me and something bad would happen to me, so I first asked permission from the chicken.

When the Khmer Rouge arrived in Battambang Province in 1975 they carried guns and were dressed in Lon Nol soldiers' uniforms. They came to our house and told us to get ready to leave the next morning. I didn't understand what was happening because I was only five years old. My mother stayed up late that night, preparing food to take with us. We left our house just before sunrise, and I carried two live chickens in my arms. Our whole family was together, including my five brothers, three sisters, mother, and stepfather. My father had been a Lon Nol soldier and was killed when I was a year old. My two oldest brothers were married, so their wives and children were with us too.

We stepped into chaos in the street. I saw armed soldiers and people rushing in every direction. There were children crying and I heard gunshots, noisy livestock, and cookware banging. Soon it was very hot and dusty. We became separated from my oldest brother and his family, but we had to keep walking because it was impossible to find anyone in that crowd. Lost children were picked up by new families. We didn't know where we were going, and by the time we stopped for lunch people had begun to camp along the road.

We walked for five days. Each time we came to a village we stopped to get water and fruit, and we fished if there was a pond. We arrived at a village where my mother knew some people, and we stayed with them for a month, until the Khmer Rouge forced us to move on.

The next village we stopped in we were allowed to stay for a few months, but we had to fend for ourselves and sleep outdoors on the ground. My mother traded her jewelry and all our extra clothes for food until we had only the clothes we wore. Soon we were out of food and had nothing to eat for days. I was very hungry and thought I would die. I ate leaves, which gave me diarrhea. Then the Khmer Rouge started giving out a small ration of rice, only one cup for each family per day.

The Khmer Rouge told us their plans for agrarian reform, and said they wanted the children, ages eight to twenty-five, to go and work in their parents' native village and improve it so their parents could live there. One of my older brothers volunteered to go, against my mother's wishes, and was taken away in a truck.

The rest of my family was sent to Kop Kmum Village, where we built a little house with a thatched roof next to a pond. Early each morning we went to a stream and caught fish, shrimp, and crabs with our hands, and we dried them to trade for rice and salt. I hated wading into that cold water, but my older sister Sarouen was ready to hit me in the head if I held back. A few months later, my stepfather developed digestive problems and his belly swelled up. He died because there was no doctor to treat him.

As the weeks passed we started hearing about people being killed by the Khmer Rouge, and we became scared. A woman was ordered to speak in front of a group meeting, and everyone heard her Vietnamese accent. The next day she disappeared, and was murdered. My older brother kept his identity a secret, because he would have been killed by the Khmer Rouge if they knew he was a former Lon Nol soldier. My mother was put on a list of bad people when someone reported that she had discussed the past. We couldn't trust anyone. The Khmer Rouge turned everyone against each other, even children against their parents.

The next month, the Khmer Rouge announced that all the children would have to go to training school. We realized that it was propaganda when we arrived at the work camps. The rain dripped through the thatch-roofed building I slept in, and I shivered in the cold because there were no blankets. I had only the black pants, black shirt, and red checkered scarf given to me by the Khmer Rouge. Kids peed in their beds and it smelled terrible.

We were ordered to take turns patrolling at night, to make sure no one ran away, and they made us get up at dawn every day and march to the fields chanting, "Jayo, jayo, Angka," which meant "Victor, victor, Angka." I had no idea who Angka was until another kid told me it meant "the government."

I dug trenches and moved dirt, without knowing what I was building. The elephant grass cut my legs, and my bare feet were bruised. I transported little rice plants from one field to another, and then stood in water all day as I transplanted the rice seedlings and pulled leeches off my legs. Later, when the grain was almost ripe, I banged on buckets to scare birds out of the rice fields. Every day we worked until sunset.

The work was hard, compared to what we were fed. We were given only one meal a day, usually just plain rice, but sometimes with a little fish, salt, or soy sauce. I was so hungry that I grabbed anything that moved, like a little crab, and ate it raw. I climbed tamarind trees and ate the fruit, which made me sick. There was a big grove of orange trees nearby, but the Khmer Rouge wouldn't let us eat the oranges. We didn't steal them because we were afraid of what they might do to us if we were caught, maybe torture us. Everyone suffered, even upper-class Chinese ate rats like the rest of us. One of my friends became sick with a high fever and died, because there was no medicine.

Every two weeks the Khmer Rouge had big meetings, supposedly to boost our spirits. They called us "comrades" and encouraged us to work harder. We knew that if we didn't work hard enough they would assign us extra work as a punishment. The Khmer Rouge made us stand up and confess our errors and report everything we saw. If I didn't like someone, I could have made something up about him, and he would have been killed.

I remember walking home from one of those meetings at night when it was raining and storming. It was completely dark, and we couldn't see a thing. I was holding on to the other children and crying when we all fell into a ditch filled with cold water.

All I could think about was my mother. I missed her and worried about her, because she was old and had a limp. Our parents are very important to us, and we are taught to care for them when they are older, so I felt responsible for my mother and wanted her to be safe. Most of the Khmer Rouge were young, only about fifteen to eighteen years old, but they were in positions of power and they lacked love and compassion. I think they feared for their own lives, which turned them into someone else. There was one Khmer Rouge leader who was nice to me and let me visit my mother in the "hospital," which was actually a temple where they put sick people. That was the only time I saw my mother in two years.

Suddenly, one day in 1979, when we were working in the fields, we heard bombs and watched the Khmer Rouge leaders escape. The Vietnamese had come, and we ran to find our parents. When I arrived in the village it was silent and empty. I was scared. I reached my mother's house, but only my three-year-old sister was there. I picked her up and ran toward the fields where I was glad to find my mother threshing rice.

My family was reunited, except for two of my brothers. We walked home to Battambang Province, and along the way my mother asked people if anyone had seen Pieroun, my oldest brother. One day someone told us the Khmer Rouge killed Pieroun when they discovered he was a former Lon Nol soldier. His wife killed herself, and his children and mother-in-law starved to death. My other brother, who was taken away by the Khmer Rouge when he volunteered to improve a village, still hadn't returned.

When we reached our village, we saw that our house was gone and now there were two new houses built on our land, so we moved into one. My sister Sarouen and I scavenged for food, picking up rice left in the fields after the harvest. One day we were out collecting bamboo shoots during the rainy season and were shocked to find the body of a dead girl floating in the water. Another time we heard someone scream and went over to see what was the matter. Everyone was staring at a man with his head cut off, an executed Khmer Rouge.

Later in 1979, when I was nine years old, I was out gathering food and I almost stepped on a landmine. I noticed the string just in time. I felt that I had almost died, and it made me accept the idea of fate. I figured I was not meant to die, otherwise I would have starved to death or stepped on that mine. I felt I must have a purpose and believed I was supposed to live so I could do something for other people.

A couple of months after we returned home, my brother became a guide and led people through the jungle across the dangerous border into Thailand. One day, my sister Sarouen came up to me and told me we had to leave because mother wanted us to go to Thailand with my brother. She explained that our mother would join us later, after my missing brother returned, so we set off.

We were with a small group of people, and it took us two days and two nights to cross the border into Thailand. The second night, as we were walking quietly, we heard men speaking Thai, and then there was shooting. Everyone in our group scattered and ran because we knew the men were thieves. I hid in a bush and feared I would be left behind. It was pitch dark, but by a miracle my older brother found me and my sister. We hid until everyone had left, not saying a word, and then we crossed safely into Thailand. I felt sure someone was watching over and protecting me.

We were glad to arrive in Aranyaprathet refugee camp because there was enough food and we felt safe. We applied for resettlement in the United States, because we had distant relatives there, and we also applied to France because my brother spoke French. One day, we got word that my mother wanted us to return to Cambodia, but we didn't go because we were terrified to cross the border again. My mother stayed in Cambodia with my two brothers and two sisters, and I never saw her again.

Six months after we arrived at the camp, my sister Sarouen moved to the United States to live with relatives. I stayed in the refugee camp for a year and a half with my brother and sister-in-law. There I played soccer, grew a vegetable garden, and studied French. We watched La Cont, the Cambodian opera, and saw movies about germs and diseases. I went to a Bible school taught by an American man who spoke fluent Khmer, and we performed a play about Jesus.

One day, I made a kite out of newspaper and bamboo. I glued it together with cooked rice and decorated the tail with colorful cloth. Then I climbed through the barbed wire fence and out of the refugee compound to fly it. Sometimes I went to the forest to make charcoal to sell for cooking fuel, or I went honey hunting and smoked out the bees with cigarette smoke.

I had a dog named Pay who followed me everywhere. One day he was hit by a car, and some people cooked him and ate him. I was shocked. Before the Khmer Rouge regime, my family had two dogs to guard our house from robbers. They were our pets, and we never thought about eating them.

We went through an interview process at the refugee camp in which they asked about our health history and what my brother and his wife did for a living. We knew we had to be careful to answer the questions correctly so we could get permission to leave. They asked me to write my name. The officials didn't believe we were brothers, so I changed my name from Uy Boun Thouen to Bou Thouen and was adopted by my brother in 1981. We were happy when we heard that we had been accepted by the United States.

First we were sent to Bangkok for a week, where we were packed into a small building and treated poorly by the Thai government officials. Then we went to the Philippines and lived for six months at a refugee camp in the mountains. I liked that camp. There was a river to swim in and a miniature model of Angkor Wat made out of cement.

After school, we played soccer with a flat ball in the rain, and we bathed under a waterfall. I saw the movie *Superman* and really believed he could fly. One day, I slipped out of camp and walked down to the ocean, where the black people live. I'd never seen black people before. I took cans of food rations, like beans, that we didn't want to eat because they weren't part of our traditional diet, and traded them for fruit.

The plane ride to the United States seemed like a dream. People looked different from us and I felt like I was on the wrong planet. I couldn't eat the food because I had never seen bread and butter, and I felt airsick. My sister and relatives met us at the airport in Boulder, Colorado. As we drove home I looked at all the cars and buildings and thought it was nothing like my village.

When we arrived, my relatives told me to take a shower, so I went to the bathroom but didn't know what to do because I had never used a shower or a flush toilet before. Later, we went to the thrift store to buy used clothes, and, on the way, my sister told me how traffic lights worked.

It was summertime and regular school was not in session, so I started attending an English language school. My teacher, Mrs. Brunot, was so kind and patient. In the fall I was very excited about starting fifth grade, but it turned out to be difficult because I didn't know enough English. One day I felt sick and didn't know how to tell the teacher, so I crawled under the table and laid down on the floor. She found me and drove me home. I think my body was adjusting to the new situation.

A few months later, we moved to Denver because my brother found a job at a typewriter ribbon factory. We lived in a poor inner-city black neighborhood, where my brother was beaten up and we were robbed. No one would talk to me on the school bus, and I didn't have any friends. When they picked teams for sports I was always chosen last.

The black kids and the Mexican kids picked on me and said my breath smelled bad and my hair was dirty. They called me "dog eater" which made me feel so ashamed. I never admitted to them that I had eaten a dog during the Khmer Rouge time, when I was starving. I felt so lonely, awkward, and sad. There was no war and I had food, but I wasn't sure if this was better than living under the Khmer Rouge.

When I was about to enter sixth grade we moved to a Mexican neighborhood. Our house was surrounded by three bars, and someone smashed my brother's car in broad daylight when it was parked in front of our house.

I was home alone one night when a man came to the door and said he owed my brother money and wanted to give it to me. When I opened the door he put on a ski mask and shoved me into a closet. He proceeded to trash the house and took our radio and VCR. I ran out the back door and through the snow in my bare feet and pajamas to the neighbor's house where I called the police. When the police came they just hassled me for being home alone, and when my brother came home, he beat me up.

Sixth grade was a good year because I liked my teacher and I finally had a friend. His name was James. The following year I went to a middle school which had many Asian refugees but it was too slow for me, and I got in fights with the other kids. We moved again, this time to a middle-class black neighborhood. We got along with the people there, and I began to realize that economics and living conditions had more to do with people's frustration and anger than race. I also learned that the poor blacks and Mexicans resented Asians because they believed Asians took away their jobs.

I didn't like living with my brother, so in ninth grade I moved to Lafayette, Colorado to live with relatives. My new school was all white and I didn't have any friends. I felt isolated, lonely, and suicidal. I had to baby-sit for my "Aunt's" kids and my "Uncle" had a band which was so loud I couldn't do my homework. I started hanging out with the Mormon missionaries who came to our door. They wanted me to be their translator. I was baptized in the Mormon religion, but I soon became disillusioned with that church because many religious people seemed to be stuck-up and into their own religious world.

Next, I moved in with James, my friend from sixth grade. His family was born-again Christian and when I went to his church, we held hands and yelled Hallelujah! We watched movies about the world coming to an end and all the people who needed to be saved. When my Mormon friends phoned me, James' mom became very upset and said it was sin to associate with them. "I don't deserve this," I thought to myself. "What am I doing here?" I just wanted my mother. I wanted to leave. I wanted to die. I phoned my Mormon friends and asked them to come by, and when they arrived, I had my suitcase packed.

At that point, I moved back in with my brother because there was no place else to go. It was awful because when my sister-in-law was mad at my brother, she took it out on me. My brother had a band that practiced on the weekends, so I couldn't think or sleep. I went to a black middle-class high school where I was disrespectful, rebellious, and got in trouble. I truly hated myself, and I hated being Cambodian. I didn't trust anyone and felt pessimistic. I didn't think any good would come out of the world, and believed people would just keep fighting each other.

My luck finally turned when my history teacher recommended me for a special international studies program at Denver West High School, and I was accepted. I made friends, and my teachers encouraged me. We learned about the world and had United Nations debates. I met people who worked in international fields, and I traveled to Europe and Israel. I started thinking about human rights and women's rights, and I learned to see things from different perspectives. When I turned eighteen, I became a US citizen and changed my name to Chath pier Sath because I wanted to create my own identity. Chath means roots and I liked that concept.

After finishing high school, I attended World College West in Petaluma, California, where I majored in international service and development. It was a very caring environment, but I got burned out from studying about oppression, human rights abuses, environmental crises, and racism. I was overwhelmed by all the injustices in the world and felt small and vulnerable. I cried a lot and was frustrated. Then I became active in student organizations and helped organize an annual hunger banquet, sold crafts from Mexico, and volunteered for the

Homeless Independence Project. I began to discover who I was and my purpose in life.

I started reconnecting with my heritage through the Cambodian community in San Francisco. I learned Cambodian dance from a woman who used to perform at the royal palace in Phnom Penh, before the Khmer Rouge came to power. One summer, I lived in the Buddhist temple and did chores for the monks. The old nun at the temple was like my grandmother, and I knew I would always have a home there.

The next two summers I lived in Stockton, California, which has a large Cambodian-American population, and was a translator for Baha'i missionaries. The Baha'i believe all religions are one and they teach about world peace and unity through diversity. I discovered that Cambodian Buddhists are accepting of other religions and believe that as long as you're not hurting someone you are OK. Their practice is a process of internal cleansing. I believe religion is a personal journey.

I was excited when I met a woman in Stockton who knew my mother. I also met a man who told me he was going blind because the Khmer Rouge beat him. Most of the Cambodian people didn't want to talk about the past. Old ladies shoved money in my pocket and told me to live in the present and be happy.

During college, I traveled to the Soviet Union and saw human suffering on a different level. The system was hard and people suffered on the inside, not being able to say or do what they wanted and not having choices in their lives. They were depersonalized and their dignity and human worth were taken away. People were kind to me, and I connected with them on a soul level. Going there gave me deeper insights and made me realize that our world is in a state of chaos and humanity has a long way to progress. We are still in a learning process.

After graduating from college, I got a job with the Southeast Asian Refugee Resettlement Project in San Francisco doing AIDS education and distributing condoms. In 1994, I decided to go back to Cambodia, fifteen years after I left. I was sponsored by CANDO, which is like a Peace Corps for Cambodian-Americans, and I was given an assignment to work with Human Rights Vigilance, a Cambodian organization.

I traveled back to Cambodia in a group of fifteen Cambodian-Americans. It was the first time I was with Cambodians who were my age and cared about the same things I did. That was important to me. I got on the plane in Bangkok and as I flew over Cambodia, I felt a sense of joy. I was surprised when I heard the flight attendant speak Khmer.

When we arrived in Phnom Penh, I felt overwhelmed and was completely speechless. The city was alive with vendors selling food on the street, the same as I remembered. I stared at the people who had dark skin like me, and it hit me that I really was in Cambodia. When I walked into a Buddhist temple for the first time, smelled the incense, and heard the monks chant, all my memories of Cambodia poured into my mind like water. Even if I didn't know people in Cambodia, I felt connected with them, in contrast to the United States, which seemed to me very cold in mind and heart.

I had an emotional reunion with my family. My sister Sarin came with her four children, and I met my uncle who seemed like a father to me. My brother Tee didn't recognize me, but we hugged. When my youngest sister Chantha saw me she fainted and her jaw became very tight. She has a weak heart and can't think about sad things. Little by little they told me about their lives, about how they were robbed and beaten, and how they struggled to survive. They wanted me to know everthing that had happened since I left.

My sister Chantha runs a business in which people order products from Thailand through her, and she travels to the city of Poipet to pick up the goods. She told me about the conflicts and misunderstandings between our family here and in America. I have learned to not take sides, but to just listen to their stories because I don't want family division. We need to learn how to help each other, to be family, because we don't have parents, we just have each other. My three brothers are married and support their families, so I feel responsible for my sisters.

When I first met my brother Thai, he and my cousin took me to a bar. It was a trippy experience for me. The room was full of smoke, men were dancing with men, and there were prostitutes. My brother ordered a bar girl for me. I didn't expect that. She sat with me and explained that she was Kampuchea Krom, ethnic Cambodian from south Vietnam. When I walked into the bathroom I saw a man who was waiting to massage your back while you pee. I jumped when he touched me and said no. There were slow dances, Khmer circle dances, and rock-and-roll in Chinese, Thai, and English. When we were getting ready to leave, my brother handed me the bill, and I had to pay for everything. My relatives think I'm rich because I am from America.

I visited my old home village of Namit. The elephant statue at the entrance was all that was left. The rest was destroyed, overgrown, and full of landmines. My sister Sarin lives near there. Some people in her village said they knew me as a kid, but I didn't remember them. I met one of my childhood playmates, who now has a wife and two children. His face brought back old memories.

My sister Sarin arranged a ceremony for our dead mother and for her husband, who was shot by thieves in 1992. We went to the field, dug up her husband's bones, and then the monks chanted. My sister Chantha, the sensitive one, screamed and fainted. We washed the bones, piled them up, and burned them. We took the ashes to the temple and put them in a stupa (Buddhist shrine), along with a picture of my mother. My nieces and nephews cried, and I felt remorse. I saw death as something that was in the past, and I didn't think it was necessary to do all that stuff with the bones, because it just brought the sadness back. I figured I must have lived in America too long.

Recently I met my older sister Hieng from Kompong Cham Province. She lived with my grandmother when we were growing up because my mother had too many children to care for, so I didn't really know her. I still feel responsible for her and bought her a sewing machine. Now she comes to me for money, but I don't always have it to give to her.

During my first few weeks in Cambodia, I couldn't speak Khmer very well which made my brother and uncle laugh at me. People on the street stared at me. They saw that I walked with confidence and noticed that my clothes and my speech were a little different. They thought I was Thai or Indian, but not Cambodian, which hurt a little. Now I teach English to the neighborhood children, and the little kids love me.

The poverty in Cambodia is shocking to me, and I feel pity and compassion for the poor. Cambodians like to give to poor people because they believe it helps them earn merit for their next life. I don't think it helps the beggars in the long run, but my educational background in international development made me conscious of not imposing my own view.

When people ask me about America, I try not to paint too glorious a picture, and explain that there are hardship and pain there, too. I describe what I experienced and explain that many Cambodians in America are uneducated and on welfare. I tell them how Cambodian-Americans struggle with their identities because they are disconnected from their birthplace and their roots, and I explain that many Cambodian children get involved in crime. But people in Cambodia don't understand those problems.

One day, I went to Toul Sleng Museum, the former Khmer Rouge torture center, only because a friend wanted to go. The blood stains were still on the floor. I looked at the photos and could picture the whole scene in my mind — the torturer, the victim, and where the photographer stood with his lens. I imagined how each person must have felt and I pretended I could hear their voices. Did the photographer feel forced, or did he like it, I wondered?

The weapons were there, pincers to pull out finger nails and the electrical shock apparatus. Even children were killed here. Is it possible? Is it part of us? I walked past the photos and wondered whose daughter, son, husband, wife they were. Their eyes stared in rage and haunted me. I tried to imagine being chained in a tiny cell. There were lots of statues of Pol Pot. Someone had put an X on his face and written swear words in Khmer.

I thought about the madness of the Khmer Rouge. It was like they were possessed, and killed without emotion or compassion. Every one of us has darkness within, but we learn through experience and education to control our anger. I think people without good experiences in life suddenly had the power to do anything and darkness overcame them. There are countless mass graves in the world, not just in Cambodia. We gather the skulls to remember. In the United States we built a holocaust museum because we have to remind ourselves.

I am learning more about the subtleties of Cambodian culture, like the belief in magic. The jaw of an animal, such as a wild boar, is supposed to protect a person from bullets, and special Buddhas are used to keep away danger. Many Cambodians take it very seriously, but I don't rely on magic. I believe there is a supernatural force that we don't understand, but I think it's more magical when we start living and facing our own problems, because when we resolve them we feel triumphant.

I love the religion in Cambodia. People are devoted to Buddhism and it makes them gentle. There is a big contrast between brutality and gentleness in Cambodia, from one extreme to the other. I like the fact that people feel compassion and are willing to help others. Cambodians give me a lot of love and laughter and make me feel special.

Buddhism is more a tradition than a religion in Cambodia. It has become integrated into the culture, with ceremonies relating to life and death. Sometimes I feel frustrated and think Cambodians' religious tradition keeps them stagnant and not wanting to change. They blame everything on karma and become sorrowful, and as a result there's very little progress.

I am Baha'i and believe in universal peace, the equality of women and men, and the oneness of God. Baha'i gives me perspective and guidance in my life. All religions teach us the same principles, to be good human beings. My religion encompasses my life goals: to be helpful and not harmful; to serve other people; and to be at peace and not vengeful with rage, anger, or hatred. I still have intense rage and anger, but I want to eliminate them and I deal with them by writing or taking breaks and listening to music.

At Human Rights Vigilance I write grant proposals, work as an interpreter, and talk to funders. Human Rights Vigilance helps educate the police because Cambodian police are not well-trained. The government pays police only ten dollars per month, not enough to feed their families, which is why there is corruption.

The police often ask us if human rights protect thieves. We tell them we just want fair treatment for the prisoner, to not beat him, and to grant him a fair trial. Human Rights Vigilance has a good reputation with the police because we discuss what's relevant, such as their role in relation to Cambodia's new constitution. We teach about current laws, like the one that outlaws the Khmer Rouge, and the new immigration act. We help the police understand how they can bring about a more civil, peaceful, and democratic society.

Human Rights Vigilance asked me to speak before a group of army generals. I told the generals that we have human rights cases in the United States, and some are racially oriented, like the Rodney King case in Los Angeles. I was talking with my hands and they started laughing, which made me feel really stupid.

During the national elections in 1993, there were numerous reports of human rights abuses, shooting, and beatings. Women were found chopped up and men were castrated. People here are full of anger and there's a lot of cruelty. I try to be careful. If someone is offended, even by something trivial, he might pull a gun. The police hang out in bars, get drunk, and start shooting.

Politics in Cambodia lacks ideology and unity, and there's a need for good leadership and better skills. After the election, the political parties left their signs up and kept the divisions going. When newspaper editors curse politicians, they end up assassinated. Cambodia has a long way to go in the field of human rights.

I believe artists could help create awareness about human rights. Artists play an important role in society, but they aren't cultivated or appreciated in Cambodia. Everyone enjoys entertainment. Karaoke is everywhere, but there are very few plays. Cambodian music is always slow and songs are just about love. The artists here should try some new ideas.

The movies here are really bad, because the producers don't know how to edit. There's not much action and there are long speeches, which makes it very boring. Thai culture is infiltrating Cambodia through TV. Cambodia needs a non-profit organization to support the arts. Rather than encourage the arts and human progress, the Khmer Rouge killed the educated people who could have helped them build an equal and just society. Their actions contradicted their vision for society.

The Khmer Rouge took away my childhood and made me live in constant fear, hunger, and desperation. Subconsciously I am still affected, because whenever I hear a loud noise, I jump and have flashbacks to images of war. I see and feel the deprivation I went through.

I wish my life had been different, that my family was still together and that I could have attended Phnom Penh University. But my experiences strengthened me and helped me understand the human condition, so now I can connect with other people in the world who are struggling and dying, hoping and surviving. We have more in common than we think. When I see other holocausts around the world it makes me wonder what we are doing. The Khmer Rouge experience made me feel like I must do something, because I don't want it to happen again.

Chath, a full-time volunteer for Human Rights Vigilance, discusses the grant proposal he is writing to secure funds for police training. Looking down on the meeting is a portrait of King Norodom Sihanouk, surrounded by silk flowers and colored lights. Although the king has very little official power, he is still revered by the Cambodian people as the head of state.

Chath is concerned about human rights in Cambodia. Inside this prison in Kompong Thom Province, inmates wait for their families to bring them food. Church World Service has been working to improve prison conditions and helped establish a prison garden, so inmates can raise vegetables. Prison officials have not yet agreed to remove the iron rings on the floor used to shackle prisoners.

When he comes home from work, Chath usually teaches English to the neighborhood children, but today he is helping them make kites. They are standing in front of a typical house in Phnom Penh which is well secured against the high incidence of theft. Hundreds of thousands of unemployed poor people have poured into to Phnom Penh during the past thirty years after being displaced by the civil war and the Khmer Rouge.

Halimas has lived near big rivers all of her life. Here she navigates a fishing boat on the great Tonle Sap River, remembering the days when she struggled alone to support her four children as a fisherwoman. In the background, a similar long wooden fishing boat is tied along the shore of the Cham village where Halimas lives.

Halimas ❧ Cham Fisherwoman

Halimas is Cham, a Moslem sect in a Buddhist country. Her ancient ancestors lived in the Kingdom of Champa which flourished across Cambodia and South Vietnam from the second to the fifteenth centuries. Currently a small minority group, the Cham people were targets of cruelty and murder during the Khmer Rouge regime. Halimas was thirty-seven years old when the Khmer Rouge assumed power in 1975. She barely survived the brutal labor camps and lack of food and medicine. Since 1979, Halimas has lived in dire poverty with her widowed daughter and three grandchildren. Her life improved a little in 1994 when she received a small loan from a women's association, which allowed her to buy goods to sell at her roadside stand and earn a little income.

The Cham village where Halimas lives is north of Phnom Penh, on the banks of the Tonle Sap River. As we drove through the village, the white-washed mosque with its onion-domed roof stood out as the most significant building in the community. Like the Buddhist temples, most of the Cham mosques were destroyed by the Khmer Rouge, and only about 20 out of 113 have been rebuilt. I noticed that most of the women on the street had their heads covered with a *kramar* (scarf) because they are Muslim. We stopped at the office of the Cambodian Women's Development Association and a staff member took us to meet Halimas.

Halimas graciously welcomed us into her home, a one-room shack on stilts. We sat down on a colorful grass mat and she handed me a simple yet beautifully woven palm fan to blow away the mosquitoes. Shy at first, Halimas willingly told her life story. She paused often, weak and out of breath, overwhelmed by the sadness of the memories. We didn't stay long, because soon she was exhausted and so was I.

As we prepared to leave, her precious three-year-old granddaughter came in and infused us with a little hope and joy. Halimas' three grandchildren had just returned from a walk through the village where the two older boys sold sweets from trays they carried on their heads. The little girl grabbed on to her mother's skirt, and with wide eyes told us about the big dog she had seen.

The next time I visited Halimas I learned how her religious practice helped sustain her through the worst times. When she was starving during the Khmer Rouge regime she prayed that she would feel full after eating her tiny ration of food, and she did. I noticed how thin and frail she still was, worn from a difficult life. Yet amazingly able to transcend her own poverty, warm-hearted Halimas often reaches out to help relieve the suffering of others.

Halimas:

Working on the water was an adventure because the river was never quiet, and we didn't always catch fish. Once a storm came up suddenly and the wind was so strong and the waves so big that we couldn't get back to shore. I was exhausted and afraid and started crying as we were tossed about until the storm finally passed.

I started fishing when I was fifteen. I left my parents' rice farm and married a fisherman. My husband and I worked very hard, fishing the Tonle Sap River from a boat with a long net. When we caught fish in the evening, we kept them alive overnight and sold fresh fish in the morning. The rest of the fish we sold smoked or salted.

My husband and I made just enough money to feed our six children, one daughter and five sons. I was heartbroken when my four-year-old son died from an illness. Later, another son died when he was six. We lived with my in-laws for ten years before moving into our own house in Kompong Tralach Village.

We are Cham. Cham people have lived in Cambodia for a long time and we are Muslim. Our beliefs are similar to Buddhists in some ways, but we have different customs. The most important part of being Cham is praying five times a day. Men usually go to the mosque to pray with the priest, while the women pray at home. I cover my head with a *kramar* when I walk more than seven steps from my house. Cham people say a special prayer before killing an animal, and we only eat meat that has been blessed in this manner, otherwise it is considered a sin. We don't eat pork at all.

In 1965, my husband was struck by the plague. I took him to a hospital and they gave him medicine, but he died within a week. I grieved the loss of my husband as I continued to fish alone. People felt sorry for me because fishing is a man's job. Women usually just help. It was very difficult for me to feed my young children, and we just barely survived.

About half the other fishermen on the Tonle Sap River were Vietnamese who lived in their own villages. We spoke different languages, so we couldn't understand each other, but in general, we got along well. Of course, it depended on the person. Once my net got caught on a Vietnamese fisherman's net and he became angry. He raised his paddle in the air and cursed me. In 1970, the Vietnamese were sent back to Vietnam by the Lon Nol government and then my life was quiet and peaceful. But the peace only lasted a few months, until the Khmer Rouge went to war against the Cambodian government.

One day, I went to catch fish, but instead I caught a dead soldier. I didn't tell the children, because I didn't want to scare them. I tried to release the corpse, but when I untied my paddle to push away the body, my paddle fell in the river. I jumped in the water to get the paddle and to my horror, I accidentally touched the dead body. It was impossible to wash off that terrible smell, even with soap.

The next time we were affected by the war was about two years later, when Lon Nol soldiers came down the river in a boat and the Khmer Rouge attacked them from shore. I grabbed the children, ran from the shooting, and hid at a neighbor's house until it quieted down and I felt safe enough to go back home.

When the Khmer Rouge took over in 1975, they ordered me and my four children to move to the center of Kompong Chhnang Province, about thirty kilometers from our home. When we arrived, we built a tiny hut from bamboo and thatch. The Khmer Rouge distributed one can of rice a day for every ten people, which was not nearly enough to fill our stomachs. We made a watery rice soup and added any edible vegetable matter we could find, which made the food resemble the cooked mush that is fed to pigs.

A few weeks later, the Khmer Rouge took away my children to live in work groups. I only saw them every month or two and I worried about them daily. I had no choice but to keep working, gathering firewood and carrying it on my head to the communal kitchen. The strenuous work exhausted me, and I started coughing up blood. When I sat down to rest, I was very shaky. "You are pretending to shake. It is better to kill you," the Khmer Rouge threatened. They scolded me for resting, so I got up and started working again. I sobbed as I did my best, and they criticized me for crying. Then I collapsed.

Every day I became weaker and weaker. I had swelling in my legs, and my knees were larger than my head. My legs became so badly infected that I couldn't walk and could only scoot along on my bottom. But even when the Khmer Rouge saw the terrible sores on my legs, they still accused me of pretending to be sick. I was sure I would be killed. I was surprised when they let me work at home and brought me palm leaves, which I sewed into roofing. The Khmer Rouge treated me with traditional medicine, and when I recovered, they forced me to work harder than ever, transplanting rice.

One day, I heard the terrible news that my family had been accused of being former Lon Nol soldiers. The accusers were a Cham couple who knew my family before the Khmer Rouge came to power. Our family used to fish in the same area as that couple, and years ago there was a small argument between our families, which was never resolved. That couple held the anger inside, and now they used this opportunity to take revenge on us. Within twenty-four hours, the Khmer Rouge killed my sister, three brothers, and their families.

My sister had always been terrified of the Khmer Rouge and had done everything they ordered, but that didn't save her. The soldiers came and bound her hands, her husband's hands, and her children's hands. Then they tied the family all together with a single rope and led them away, walking in a line. I didn't dare watch for fear of my own life. Instead, I hid in the forest and cried in anguish.

Months later, the vengeful couple was killed by the Khmer Rouge in the same manner as my sister and brothers when it was revealed that they were former Lon Nol soldiers. I wasn't surprised, because I believe that if someone tells a lie, it will catch up with them.

We were forbidden to speak Cham. The Khmer Rouge spied on us and tried to catch us speaking our language so they would have reason to kill us. "I am not afraid of dying," I told them. "My husband and two of my children have already died, so I don't care if I die. It takes time to get used to speaking Khmer. Like a young ox in training, it takes time to learn. If you compare yourselves to me then maybe you feel jealous because I understand a little Chinese, Khmer, and Vietnamese. Perhaps you are afraid we will criticize you when we speak Cham, but I can tell you that it just takes time to get in the habit of speaking Khmer." The Khmer Rouge soldiers laughed at me.

Before the rainy season came, the Khmer Rouge ordered us to cut down trees, plow the land, and prepare a new field for planting corn. This was a very painful period for me, because I was starving and had no strength to work. I nearly crawled home after work each day. I knew of hungry people who were caught stealing food and taken off to be killed. I prayed not to feel hungry, and instead, to feel full all the time so that I wouldn't have to steal. From then on even a small amount of rice made me feel full, and I was able to keep myself from stealing food.

One day, the cook made a soup with pork, which I am forbidden to eat because I am Muslim. Even if they threatened to kill me, I would not eat pork. I asked for salt to put on my rice instead of the pork soup and they said, "We made a nice soup for you, why do you need salt?" That day I ate bland rice and swallowed it with water.

In 1978, the Khmer Rouge told me that they were taking my eighteen-year-old son Ry to be trained as medical staff, but later I found out that they took him to be a soldier. He died in a battle with the Vietnamese at Lung Vek. My nieces discussed whether or not they should tell me, and decided that I might try to go see him if they told me he was only injured, so they broke the terrible news to me during lunch. I fainted and remained unconscious for a day and a night.

Full of sorrow and pain, I went to get my son's body, because I wanted to have a funeral at home. On the way I met some Khmer Rouge soldiers who told me that they had just come back from burying my son. I fainted again. The soldiers gave me a massage and rubbed my skin with the edge of a coin, but they couldn't revive me. They asked my nieces to care for me, and the young women carried me home in a hammock and stayed with me until I woke up the next day.

The Khmer Rouge held a big Buddhist funeral that lasted three days and three nights for all of the dead soldiers. The Khmer Rouge asked me to come to the ceremony and put soil on the grave. I told them it would be a sin if I joined a Buddhist funeral and asked permission to have a Cham funeral at home.

I felt a little better when the Khmer Rouge agreed to let me hold a Cham funeral and gave me extra rice and a chicken so I could prepare food for the ceremony. First, I made special noodles and chicken soup, and then I invited a Cham priest and three Cham elders who had studied Islam to come to my house to chant. The priest prayed for my son and I served food to everyone. I followed all the steps of a Cham funeral ceremony but I could not invite many people because I didn't have much food. I believed my son would be reincarnated.

I was harvesting rice on the day the Vietnamese came. I watched the Khmer Rouge run away but I didn't think I needed to escape, so I kept working. A Vietnamese soldier came and handed me a paper with writing and a picture of the new leader. I couldn't read, so I asked the soldier to read it to me. He summarized it by saying that I should go back to my native home and not follow the Khmer Rouge. He asked if I knew where the Khmer Rouge were hiding and I said, "I haven't seen any of them. I am a just a working person." The Vietnamese soldier told me to continue harvesting and then he left. I looked around and saw that I was alone, so I took a basket of rice and walked directly to my native village of Kompong Tralach, without going back to my Khmer Rouge hut. I never wanted to go back.

When I reached Kompong Tralach, I discovered that my three children had not returned. I realized that the Khmer Rouge must have taken my children with them when they fled to the mountains. Crying in despair, I told the Vietnamese soldiers that my children had been captured. I loved my children and couldn't bear the thought of losing them. The Vietnamese soldiers told me not to worry because they were pursuing the Khmer Rouge in a truck and would bring the children back. The soldiers instructed me to stay at the main road and watch for my children. I begged them to let me go with them, but they said I didn't need to come. For several days I slept along the road and waited.

Many people came back, but I didn't see my three children. One night there was shelling nearby, and I prayed to Allah for protection. When I awoke the next morning I saw a lot of dead and injured people. I waited at the main road until people stopped coming back, and then I went to another road to watch for my children. When they finally arrived I didn't recognize them because they were so thin. My son called to me, and I fainted. The children massaged me until I woke up. I was overjoyed to see them. My oldest son Mat was eighteen, my daughter Noar was fifteen, and my youngest son Man was thirteen.

We slept near the road that night, and the next morning we started walking back to Kompong Tralach Village. On the way home we were shelled by the Khmer Rouge and ran from the explosions. When the Vietnamese drove down the road a few minutes later, we told them about the shelling, and the Vietnamese soldiers got off the truck to search the area for the Khmer Rouge. We saw them capture and shoot the Khmer Rouge soldiers. To reward us for helping, a Vietnamese soldier drove us the rest of the way to Kompong Tralach and gave me permission to take rice from the storage building. I filled two ox carts with rice and shared it with my one surviving brother.

My three children and I were so happy to be together, but we struggled to support ourselves. We built a very small hut to live in and planted rice. About a year later my niece came and invited us to come live near my brother in Chrang Chamres Village, about ten kilometers north of Phnom Penh. I asked permission from the head of Kompong Tralach Village to move to Chrang Chamres. When he agreed I left in a small boat, escorted by a Vietnamese soldier, while my children walked to Chrang Chamres, pushing a bicycle with all of our goods on it. It took them two days to arrive.

Not long after, I bought a load of bananas for my daughter Noar to take back to Kompong Tralach to trade for rice. Noar traded one bunch of bananas for three cans of rice and ended up with two hundred kilos of rice, which was enough to feed us for about four months. But the officials wouldn't let her take the rice out of their village. I had to go there and beg them to let us pass, explaining that I didn't intend to sell the rice and that I needed it for my family. I begged and cried and prayed for three days. Finally, they let me take the rice, and I brought it back by boat.

I made fishing nets for people in Chrang Chamres and was paid with rice, which I traded for whatever I needed, including lumber for a house. Later, when money came into circulation, I was paid 10,000 riels ($4) for two to three weeks of work. I was grateful when my brother and other villagers helped me clear trees next to National Highway Number 5 and build a little house and a stand to sell things.

My daughter Noar stayed home and helped me sell ice, firewood, fruit, and soft drinks at our stand, while my youngest son Man went to school. The government school was free, but Man had to give money to the teacher to buy supplies, like chalk.

One of our family's happiest occasions was Noar's wedding, in 1981. I arranged her marriage with her husband's relatives. It is our custom to not allow the couple to meet each other before marriage. The groom gave me 750,000 riels ($300) for the wedding, and I spent another 500,000 riels ($200), which was all of our savings. In preparation for the wedding we killed a cow and cooked lots of food, including curry and wedding cake. I was worried that I wouldn't have enough to feed all the guests during the three-day ceremony.

On the first day, close to 100 friends, relatives, and neighbors went to the special tent that was pitched outside the groom's house. The priest blessed the bed of the groom, then the groom got in bed and was blessed. After lunch, everyone except the groom came to our house and the priest blessed the bride's bed and the bride. The next day the couple sat on the bed together and were blessed. After the guests were fed on the third day, the wedding ended.

In 1984, Noar's husband became a government soldier. He had been depressed and angry because the Khmer Rouge had killed his entire family and he wanted to fight back. He came home regularly to see my daughter and their two sons until 1989 when only a letter came home. It said that he was killed by Khmer Rouge in Kompong Chhnang Province and instructed us to go to the local government office for more information. I was so upset that I ran out of my house and down the road toward the office. Some people saw me running and put me on a motorbike and took me there.

We were all devastated by the news of Noar's husband's death. My son Man stopped going to school. He had completed five grades and said he did not want to continue studying because he was needed to help support the family. But it was difficult for him to earn money. First, he sold snacks in the village and worked for fishermen for 5000 riels ($2) per month. Then he got a job on a motor-taxi cart that went to Kompong Som Province, collecting the fare from passengers, loading and unloading goods. During that time, he came down with malaria, and now he gets sick quite often and sometimes vomits blood.

My daughter Noar remarried but soon became upset when she discovered that her second husband drank all the time and had another woman. He left my daughter when she was six months pregnant, and took all their money and valuables. I had hoped her life would improve when she remarried, but it got worse.

My daughter doesn't want to marry again, so she lives with me and we try to support her three children. Noar started attending the literacy class offered by the Cambodian Women's Development Association, but she dropped out after a few weeks. The class was at lunchtime, and it was too difficult for me to watch the children, prepare lunch, and sell things at our stand, all by myself.

My son Man married and had two children, but his wife was mean. When he became sick and couldn't work she became angry and threw him out. I wanted to help, and asked the village elders to talk my son into going back to his wife. My son refused, so I let him decide his future. My children have problems, as I do. I think it is my sin from my last life that causes me to meet so much misfortune in this life.

My oldest son Mat married in 1983, and now he has three daughters. In 1992, he was worried because he couldn't earn enough money to support his family, so he went to live with my brother in Kompot Province, and work in the lobster fishing business. Later, his wife and children joined him in Kompot.

After the Khmer Rouge regime ended, I wanted to start a small business to earn an income, but no one would give me a loan. Finally, in 1984, I borrowed 100,000 riels ($40) from a Chinese man at very high interest. It took me almost four years to pay it back.

In 1994, I borrowed 50,000 riels ($20) from the Cambodian Women's Development Association and used the money to repair my roof and to buy things to sell at my stand, such as soft drinks, ice, bananas, and oranges. I am one of a group of five women who took out loans, and each of us contributes 300 riels per day to create an emergency fund. I pray that my family won't get sick, but if someone does, then I know I can borrow money to pay for medicine.

Before the national election in 1993, the Hun Sen political party had a meeting in the mosque and gave a *sarong* (skirt) to every woman. There were many political parties and I didn't know much about any of them, but I decided to vote for FUNCINPEC because it was the royalist party. I felt happier during Prince Sihanouk's reign because we had peace, and I never heard the sound of shooting or shelling. The Hun Sen government collected young men for the army, and I always worried about my sons.

I hope that in the future I can earn more money from my hard work. I wish the angels would help me, but first I need to help myself. I need more capital to purchase materials to make hammocks to sell. I buy second-hand sweaters, unravel the yarn, roll it into balls, and tie it into hammocks. Even though I am careful to spend my money wisely, I often worry about how we are going to survive. Sometimes we don't have enough food.

November and December are good months for us because people from the countryside come to our village to buy fish, and while they are here, they buy fruit, ice, and soft drinks from my shop. My daughter Noar and I also work cleaning fish. We earn about 2500 riels ($1) for cleaning a basket of fish, which takes a couple hours. We keep the fish heads and make fish paste to sell.

Today, each fisherman catches less fish because there are more fishermen. Some use electric shock, which kills all the fish, even the small ones. The Vietnamese sell the small fish and are very good at making money. I am afraid that in a few years all the fish will be gone because so many Vietnamese have come to Cambodia.

I am glad that I live in Chrang Chamres because it is a Cham village, and my son and grandsons had the opportunity to learn to read Arabic in the mosque. During the Khmer Rouge regime, the Cham women became accustomed to not wearing *kramars* on their heads when they left their houses, and now some women don't wear them.

Each year I look forward to celebrating the Cham holidays. We have a holy month around March, called *Khe Bours* (Ramadan), and during this time we eat only before dawn and after sunset. Three months after *Khe Bours* ends we have a three-day holiday, called *Bours*, when we take food to the priest and pray. I pray for my ancestors' well-being, for better living conditions in my next life, and for happiness and no divorce in my family.

The word "Cham" in Khmer means "remember" and I believe Cham means to remember everything Allah said. I believe in Allah, even if I don't know whether He has helped me. I never do anything bad, like stealing, because when I am good, I feel peaceful. I try to help others. When someone dies, I help wash the body and prepare the funeral ceremony. Maybe my kindness to others has helped me. I am poor, but there are some who are poorer than me, and I give them money or rice. If I have something, I will give it, and when someone is in trouble, I try to help.

Halimas and her daughter sit on a grass mat in their small thatch hut and create colorful hammocks with yarn from unraveled second-hand sweaters. The two widows and three children work, eat, and sleep in this room. The white mosquito net hanging on the wall next to the pictures of popular celebrities will be tied over them when it is time for bed.

Halimas watches with pleasure as her two grandchildren enjoy a Cambodian-style slurpee at her roadside stand. The hand-cranked ice shaving machine on the table was bought with a small loan from the Cambodian Women's Development Association.

Millions of women and children were driven from their homes during the past three decades of war and violence. The government gave this displaced homeless family a small lot near the city of Siem Reap to build a house on, but no land to farm or other means of earning a living.

SOUL SURVIVORS

Daravuth joyfully holds his baby son. He and his wife, who is also an orphan, built their house on orphanage property. Over 500 friends attended Daravuth's wedding; about half were his "brothers and sisters" from the orphanage. Almost everyone in Cambodia has recreated family after losing parents, brothers, and sisters during the Khmer Rouge period.

Daravuth ❦ Orphan

Daravuth was one of the 250,000 children left orphaned after the four-year genocidal rule of the Khmer Rouge. Like most Cambodian orphans, he doesn't know his actual age or birth date, but he thinks he was about twelve years old in 1975, when Pol Pot seized control. Daravuth cannot remember much about his childhood, which is not surprising because memory loss is common among trauma victims. After the Khmer Rouge period, Daravuth grew up in a government orphanage. He was kind and well-liked and often acted as a mediator between the children and orphanage administrators. Daravuth was a bright, enterprising, and hard-working young man who found ways to earn money, get ahead, and avoid military conscription. He learned English, and now he has a good job with a foreign organization.

I stepped over garbage and mud puddles as I crossed the orphanage compound on my way to visit Daravuth. The former Catholic girls' school was in disrepair, and when I peeked into the old chapel, I saw beds strategically placed to avoid drips from the leaking roof. I found Daravuth's simple house tucked between a dormitory and the school.

Daravuth was talking with a friend, while his shy wife, also an orphan, held their cute gurgling baby boy. We sat chatting beside the Ping-Pong table, which Daravuth shares with all the orphans. I learned that Daravuth helps out when there are problems or someone is in need. When children miss dinner at the orphanage because they were out studying, they come to Daravuth's house where they know they will be welcomed and fed. Daravuth is everyone's big brother.

I asked Daravuth why he built his house on the orphanage property. "Why should I leave the orphanage? This is where my friends are," he answered. It is difficult for the orphans to move away, even when they are grown up, because most do not have relatives to live with or enough income to pay rent.

Not remembering his past has been frustrating for Daravuth. There is a widowed woman who believes she may be his mother, but Daravuth does not recognize her. The woman, who also expressed some doubts about whether Daravuth was her son, took him in after the Khmer

Rouge fled but then left him at the orphanage a few months later because she was too poor to feed him or put him through school. "How could she do that to me if she was my real mother?" Daravuth asks.

In spite of his difficult childhood, Daravuth is a friendly, jovial person who enjoys life. I was impressed by his generosity and noticed how the sweetness of the human spirit shines through him.

Daravuth:

I can't remember much about my life before Pol Pot. I don't remember my parents or how many brothers and sisters I had. I suppose I must have been in school. When the Khmer Rouge came, I do remember walking out of Phnom Penh with my family, carrying two bottles of water. We crossed the Monivong Bridge at the south end of the city and walked a few more kilometers to Kien Svay Village where the Khmer Rouge fed us. That part stands out in my mind because I didn't like the food and couldn't eat it because it was mostly pork fat.

From Kien Svay, we took a boat to Kompong Cham Province. Two of my uncles were put in jail, and the rest of my family was sent to a forest village named Tapum in Chras District, Kratie Province. I was separated from my family and put in the youth group.

The main thing I remember about the Khmer Rouge period is that we didn't have enough food. I ate banana leaves. I found crabs, snakes, and worms and cooked them in a condensed milk can. I made traps out of saplings and caught small animals. It was a very hard time and I was so hungry that food became the only thing that was important. I didn't think about anything else, even my mother was not important. I never heard any information about my family, although later I learned that not many people were killed in that province.

In 1978, the Vietnamese took over Kratie Province. I walked down the road with everyone else, not knowing where we were going. I heard a woman call out, "Sonny." She came up to me and said I was her son. I didn't recognize her, but I went along with her anyway and lived with her and her seven children. I called them "brother" and "sister" even though I couldn't remember them as being my real brothers and sisters. I came to think of them as my foster family.

I found an earring with a gem in it and gave it to my foster mother who traded it so we could move out of the forest and live closer to the main road. A month later, we moved to the town of Kratie, taking with us the four cows we claimed when the Khmer Rouge left.

My brothers and I built ox carts to trade for food. I watched a man repair bicycles and learned how to do that. One day, I saw a woman walking down the road with her daughter and old mother. She was carrying all that she owned, a heavy load of rice and some cooking pots. I gave her one of the bicycles I had repaired. The woman started crying and said, "Nobody was watching over me, only you. Bless you."

We didn't have enough to eat, so I searched for food in the forest. My mother was Buddhist and told me not to kill animals. "They want to live like we do," she said. "Don't even take chicken eggs. You should know that. You're not like my son, because you love to kill, but you look like him."

My foster mother sold our four cows to get enough money for us to take a boat to Phnom Penh. Once we arrived I didn't recognize anything because the trees had grown and the houses had broken down. When I was young the roads looked big, but now they looked small. We didn't have money or rice, so I fished in the city sewage canal. I picked through garbage and looked along the road for plastic bags or aluminum cans to sell to the Vietnamese.

After about six months, my foster mother took me to Orphanage Number Two, where her brother worked, and left me there. A year later she brought another son to live at the orphanage, and the following year, a third son. She said she was poor and didn't have enough money to support her children or keep them in school.

We had been separated for four years during the Khmer Rouge regime. How could she do that to me if she was my real mother? The problem is I can't recall anything. Someday I will go back to Kratie Province and ask the local people if they remember me and can tell me about my mother and my family.

I don't remember my real name, but my nickname before the Khmer Rouge was Poch, which refers to the youngest child. Daravuth is the name of the son my foster mother lost. My last name was different from some of my brothers and sisters. Sometimes I feel like she is my real mom and other times I feel like an orphan.

At first there wasn't enough food at the orphanage. The government gave us corn and a little rice to eat, and we had Cambodian soup made from watergrass and small fish. The orphanage was like a prison, controlled by the orphanage staff, and we were forbidden to leave. When my friend Hang went out and was caught, they tied him up and beat him. I secretly slipped out to buy food, but never got caught. We played volleyball, Ping-Pong, basketball and soccer. I learned to play the *roneat*, which is like a marimba, made from wood and bamboo. We studied traditional folk dances, such as the coconut dance, and in 1983 I traveled to Vietnam with the orphanage dance troupe on a ten-day tour. I attended school at the orphanage and learned very fast. In one year I passed three grades and the next year I passed two grades. I liked school and loved to study. When we had to memorize, I turned it into a song to help me remember. I was the best student in mathematics, and I borrowed the instructor's book so I could teach myself. In 1984, Orphanage Number Two closed, and we were moved to Orphanage Number One.

I worked very hard and earned money by cutting hair, washing cars, butchering pigs, and climbing trees to pick coconuts. I made fish hooks from motorbike spokes and went fishing. I did construction work, poured cement and built walls. I learned how to do everything, even repair the electrical system at the orphanage. When I had money, I bought fish and invited the other orphans to eat with me. They grew to like me.

The director saw that I was good at working with the other children, so in 1985 he had a meeting and asked them if they wanted me to be chief of orphans. They all agreed, and after that I coordinated all the children. When the orphanage needed to haul wood, load rice from a warehouse, pick up fish, or dig up the grass around the buildings, I would get a group of ten or twenty orphans together to do the work. When the director gave us money, I divided it up, giving some to each kid while keeping a portion to buy extra food. They liked me because I was fair. My room was always full of orphans, and I was like a brother to them.

The orphans and the staff didn't always understand each other. When the girls got angry because they had only gotten one new dress in a whole year and said something strong, I said it nicely to the staff. If guests came, I gathered all the orphans together and the girls performed classical dance, while the boys played traditional music. I usually played the drum.

In 1984, I started worrying about being taken away to be a soldier. Every year there was a meeting at the orphanage where they tried to persuade us to join the military. The recruiter talked about the communist way and said, "If you don't want to serve the government as a soldier, then get out of the government orphanage." Then he instructed the girls to tell their boyfriends, "If you want my love, you have to be a soldier first."

We didn't want to join the military because we feared we would be killed or wounded. Disabled soldiers become beggars in the market because the government doesn't take care of them. We understood that very well. Would joining the military bring peace to Cambodia? No. The military recruiter took between 50 and 100 of my friends at the orphanage, but only about a third wanted to go. The recruiter said to my friend Yoeun, "Your shoulders are big enough to wear an officer's rank." Later, Yoeun was shot by the Khmer Rouge at Tonle Sap.

A boy with mental problems named Mach was taken to the hospital. They said he was fine and put him in the military, and he died in 1990. Among my other best friends in the military, one died, one lost his leg when he stepped on a landmine, one was shot, and one broke his neck. I heard someone say that orphans shouldn't be put in the military because we are "only one life," which means we are the last person alive in our family.

I hoped my student ID would protect me, but I had to be careful because sometimes the military just took a young man off the street and tore up his student ID, unless he was an official's son. When they asked me to join I said, "Yes, I want to be a soldier, but I want to finish my education first." I told them that we will have a better military than the Khmer Rouge if our soldiers are more educated.

Most orphans changed their age, and so did I. I can't remember my birthday, but I think I was born in 1963. Whenever the officials asked my age, I lowered it because I was afraid I wouldn't be able to stay in the orphanage and I wouldn't be able to finish school if they knew I was older. First I changed my birth date to 1969, and later to 1971.

The director of the orphanage, Nop Poung, was like a father to us. He treated us very well, let us watch TV, and promised us a good future. He walked around the orphanage and told the group leaders to look after us. The vice-president of Cambodia, Pen Sovann, came to visit the orphanage every week. He cried when he saw the orphans. "Why do you cry?" the young children would ask him, but he didn't answer. Phnom Penh Mayor Keo Chenda gave the orphanage a car and a van.

If foreigner visitors made a donation, the Ministry of Social Action expected the orphanage to hand over some of the money to the Ministry, but Nop Poung didn't give it to them because he wanted all the money to go to the orphans, to help the children until they grew up and found jobs.

In 1987, the Department of Social Affairs decided to get rid of Nop Poung. One hundred orphans marched over to Mayor Keo Chenda's house to protest. The guard wouldn't let us in, so we split into two groups and one group pounded on the fence at the side of the house while the other group walked in the front gate. Mayor Keo Chenda was nice to us, gave us Coke and cake, and asked why we came. We said we didn't want the director of our orphanage to leave. "Don't worry about that," he said. But afterward they took some of the orphans to live at the detention center for thieves and prostitutes for one month because they wanted to separate and scare us. The director we loved had to leave in 1988.

In 1990, a man from America named Daniel came to the orphanage and asked me to work for him. He was helping young orphans get adopted. I was glad to have an opportunity to practice speaking English because, until then, I had only copied English from a book. I worked as Daniel's assistant, driving, translating, and looking after people who stayed with him. I helped him select orphans to sponsor in driving school. I lived at his house for two years, and when he went back to America, I returned to the orphanage.

I had bad luck after I finished high school. I didn't know what I wanted to do; I really didn't want to be anything. I applied to Phnom Penh University in language in 1992, but I failed the exam. I had studied hard and wondered why I didn't pass. The only students who passed were children of high-ranking officials and children whose parents paid a bribe. Poor children didn't pass, but I still blamed myself and thought I wasn't smart enough.

I drove cyclos and motorcycle taxis to earn money until late in 1992, when I got a good job with a foreign organization. I work with nice people and feel happy there, which makes me hope that I can keep my job for a long time. I help support my foster mother because I would feel bad if I found out she was my real mother and I had never helped her. I visit her every week, and she is kind to me.

I met my wife Somanak in 1984, when I moved to Orphanage Number One. Her mother and father had been killed by the Khmer Rouge, and she came to the orphanage with her five brothers and sisters. Her brother was one of my best friends. I took an interest in Somanak and watched her but didn't talk to her for two years. After high school, Somanak was trained as a midwife.

We were married on August 8, 1993, and our wedding party lasted all day. We served lunch and dinner to our 500 guests. All 230 orphans came to our wedding, along with my friends from work. We had a Buddhist ceremony with monks chanting. As is customary, Somanak rented ten dresses to wear during different parts of the ceremony and party. The guests gave us gifts of money which more than paid for the wedding, which cost $2000. People had so much fun eating and drinking that they said, "Why don't you have another wedding?"

Daniel gave us round trip tickets to Hawaii and California as a wedding gift. I enjoyed Hawaii. The food was good, the weather was pleasant, people were friendly, and it was nice to walk around, but it was expensive. I didn't like California because of the air pollution and nobody spoke to each other. America is safer than Cambodia because there are laws that protect people. In Cambodia, police order people around and take them to jail without reason. Traffic cops often shoot their guns in the air.

When we returned home, Somanak and I built our house on the orphanage property. I couldn't afford to buy land to build on and besides, I like living at the orphanage. The orphans are my friends and it's easy for them to come over and visit me. We love each other like brothers and sisters.

I don't want to leave, but I know that some day we will have to move out. The administration has been talking about selling the orphanage, because the land is valuable. They have proposed giving each orphan $200. Where would we live? I called a meeting with the other orphans and said, "This is your problem too. We won't let them separate us or make us fight each other. We are brothers and sisters." We collected money to hire legal help and file a petition.

The orphanage staff don't care if the children have enough food, or water to bathe, or a good place to sleep. I spent $150 to build a well for the orphans to use to wash their clothes and bathe because the water tank was often empty, and the staff didn't care. They just come to work, sit in the office, and don't check to see if the children are in school or if they are studying. We don't have a dance troupe any more, because when foreigners donated money to the orphanage after a performance, the dancers never got any, so they quit.

I like to go to bars with my friends. We drink and dance disco or traditional Khmer dance. I don't allow my wife to go because it's not proper for a Cambodian girl to go to a bar. There are bar girls to dance with.

I work out in the gym every day, and I have weights and a bench press at home that the orphans use. I like to share what I have. I enjoy talking with the other orphans about what happened in their day. When I find out about job openings I tell the orphans to apply and I recommend them. Sometimes I buy medicine for the orphans when they are sick or take them to the hospital. When they have problems, like getting in a fight or a traffic accident, they come to me.

Being nice just comes from my heart. I didn't learn it from anyone. I feel like all Cambodians and all the people in the world are brothers and sisters. We have the same hands, legs, eyes, faces, and we are all alike. Just our skin color and language are different. If we are cut, we all bleed. I believe that when we get angry we should only stay that way for five or ten minutes, and then let it go. It is best to just walk away and try to forget the bad thing. Then it's gone.

I always feel happy. I don't worry or think about problems. When something comes up, then I deal with it. Why worry if I can't do anything about it? I am content with my life. I have a good job and lots of friends. My son was born in 1994. His name is Darapiset and I love him very much.

When he was a child, fishing was one of Daravuth's favorite pastimes. Children who were born in the 1960s and 1970s missed the simple pleasures of childhood as they struggled to survive during and after the Khmer Rouge period.

These boys were conscripted into the Cambodian army at a young age. The military recruiter comes to the orphanage frequently and many of Daravuth's friends became soldiers and were killed or wounded in the ongoing war with the Khmer Rouge.

Lieng stands pensively at the gate of her parents' former house, next to the post where she wrote a message to her family in 1979 telling them that she survived and had come looking for them. No one in her family read the message because everyone was dead by the end of the Khmer Rouge's cold-blooded reign.

Lieng ❧ Medical Doctor

Lieng and her husband were twenty-nine years old and in their final year of medical school when Pol Pot took over. Lieng's husband, parents, and every family member living in Cambodia died under the Khmer Rouge, leaving her alone in 1979 to raise and support her two children. Only fifty doctors survived the Khmer Rouge's massacre of Cambodia's educated citizens. Therefore, Lieng was quickly appointed director of the emergency room of a major hospital in Phnom Penh. She worked to the point of complete exhaustion, and when she collapsed on the floor, her supervisor sent her to Russia on a month-long holiday. Even though Lieng is close to retirement age, which is fifty in Cambodia, she chose to go back to school for a postgraduate degree in anesthesiology so she can teach at Phnom Penh University, because in 1995 there was only one trained anesthesiologist in all of Cambodia.

I met Lieng when she was doing AIDS education as a volunteer for a women's organization. She reminded me of my favorite aunt, calm, gentle, and strong, with the biggest heart imaginable. Like the old-fashioned family doctor, her presence alone has a healing effect.

I was a little surprised when Lieng asked if we could meet at my place for the interviews. She said her roof leaked when it rained, which made me curious to see where she lived. One morning, after a big thunderstorm had turned Phnom Penh's streets into rivers full of happy splashing children, I went to visit Lieng. When I reached her house, I stood in amazement as I gazed at her simple bamboo and thatch hut. My admiration for her grew as I realized her personal struggle with poverty, as well as her commitment to simplicity and her sacrifice to humanity.

Like most Cambodians, Lieng has not fully recovered from the losses during the Khmer Rouge regime, but her grief is barely noticeable as she tirelessly devotes herself to her work and responsibilities at home. Only when she goes to bed at night does this brave woman give in to the tears she holds inside.

Over the months of my interviews with Lieng, I observed the construction of her private clinic, a tiny two-room structure being built in front of her house. Lieng's private practice serves as her primary source of income, since her position in the public hospital pays only $20 per month.

It was a Sunday afternoon when I went to say good-bye to Lieng. This time the streets were dry and dusty because the rainy season had ended abruptly. I found Lieng's daughter tending the small pharmacy in the new clinic's front room while Lieng cared for a patient in the back. I wasn't sure when I would return, but I knew I would never forget this amazing woman doctor whose humility, selfless dedication, and healing services to wounded Cambodia practically earn her the status of a saint.

Lieng:

April 17, 1975 is stamped on my mind because our lives were changed forever after that date. I could have left Cambodia before 1975, but I didn't consider it because I had no idea the Khmer Rouge would be so cruel. My father used to say that even if Cambodia became communist, it would be OK because communists believe in equality.

I was in my fifth year of medical school at the time. My father was a surgeon and he wanted one of his children to become a doctor. I agreed, because practicing medicine is a service. We call the income *trachak*, friendly money. I could have gone to school in France where three of my six brothers and sisters lived, but my father thought it would be better if I studied medicine in Cambodia where the education was more practical. There were about fifty students in my class, and I was one of five women. My husband, Toek, was also in medical school. We had a five-year-old daughter, Chhada, and our son Noravin was two.

The war came to Phnom Penh shortly after the coup in 1970. The Khmer Rouge aimed their artillery at military centers in Phnom Penh, but the rockets missed. I felt sad when many civilians died from the shelling.

At first we were very happy when the Khmer Rouge took over Cambodia because we thought the war was over. They marched into Phnom Penh like a parade, and we congratulated them, clapping our hands and yelling "Bravo! We want peace." We were shocked when the soldiers turned and pointed their guns at us and ordered us to leave our homes. They said it would only be for three days, but if we didn't cooperate, we would be shot.

My husband became very anxious when he saw the Khmer Rouge shoot a Lon Nol soldier on the street. He urged us to hurry up and leave. I nervously held my two young children as my father, still dressed in his white doctor's uniform, packed a small box of medical instruments and my mother gathered jewelry, gold, and clothes to take with us. During the war we lived at my father's medical clinic on

Monivong Boulevard, so we wouldn't have to risk getting hit by artillery while traveling back and forth to our house.

The Khmer Rouge came to the door and forced us to leave immediately, so we couldn't go upstairs to get the rest of our things. My family had three cars, and we wanted to take one for my pregnant sister, but we couldn't because there were 100,000 people in the street, so we walked. We watched in horror as the Khmer Rouge killed people, former Lon Nol soldiers and civilians who didn't follow orders. Blood filled the streets.

We planned to meet up with my in-laws and travel with them, so when we reached their street, my parents, daughter, and three sisters stepped off the main road. Instantly, a soldier pointed his gun at them and ordered them to lie down on the ground. The crowd pushed me, my husband, and our son forward and, to my alarm, our family became separated. I cried a lot, but knew we had no choice. We could have died if we tried to follow them. Only an angel could have helped us then.

We walked southeast, by way of Highway 1. The Khmer Rouge didn't allow us to stop and rest until dark. We had left home with practically nothing and had to share the few clothes my youngest sister had packed for us. I bought pork for dinner. I didn't realize it would be the last time I would spend money in four years.

We traveled for a week, forced ahead by the Khmer Rouge, until we were near the Vietnamese border in Kandal Province. The air was full of smoke from a burning temple, and I saw the swollen rotting bodies of dead Lon Nol soldiers. I heard a husband and wife quarreling, and when the fact that he was a former Lon Nol soldier slipped out, the Khmer Rouge came over, took him away, and shot him.

We were ordered to move in with a farming couple, into their wooden stilt house. They didn't trust us "new people." Every two or three days the Khmer Rouge gave each person a small can of rice and a little salt. It wasn't enough, so we ate fish and clams that we caught in the river. Then the Khmer Rouge took away my small radio, which distressed me because I lost touch with the outside world.

We stayed in Kandal Province for two months. Every day I watched and waited for my parents and my daughter as I worked, caring for young children while my husband labored in rice fields. One day, the Khmer Rouge announced that we could move to our native villages. My husband decided we should go to Kompot Province in hope of finding my parents and daughter.

The Khmer Rouge took us south, by boat. The first night we slept in a temple, and then our group of 100 traveling people walked across Takeo Province. It took us all day to cross a stretch of land where nothing was growing, not even grass. We needed fuel to cook our rice, so my husband broke up the wooden shoes that were given to him when he was cutting thorn trees.

The journey to Kompot Province took two months. It was exhausting and on the way my husband became very sick with malaria. First, I traded gold for medicine. Then the local people told me that *sdav* tree leaves would bring down his fever, so I prepared a medicinal tea which proved to be effective.

After crossing the Neareay Mountains, we finally arrived at our native village of Trapeng Thom. We were disappointed to learn that my parents and daughter were not there, but we were glad to find my husband's parents and my cousin Sophine. We asked the Khmer Rouge leader if we could live with my in-laws. He allowed us to stay only two days and then sent us to live in Trapeng Cheutiel Village about eight kilometers away. We became very sad when we learned that the Khmer Rouge had killed my newly married brother-in-law, just because he wore glasses. The Khmer Rouge thought people with glasses were educated and should be purged from Cambodian society.

For four years I lived like a slave. At first I told the truth about being a doctor, but people warned me to hide my identity, lest I be killed, so then I said I was a hospital worker. Many of the local farmers, the "old people," scorned me because I didn't know how to winnow rice. I couldn't work very hard, being still weak from the miscarriage I had shortly before we were evacuated from Phnom Penh. I also had a bad knee and couldn't walk very well. I was grateful to an older woman who treated me with sour herbs and stopped my knee pain. At first, my job was to dig out tree stumps, which was very difficult work. Later I was assigned the miserable task of making compost from human feces.

One day, my husband and three young men were discussing education while they worked in a field, unaware that Khmer Rouge spies were hiding nearby and listening to them. The next day the three young men were taken to "study" at Stung Keo, and we never saw them again.

A few months later, my husband was sent far away to do heavy work, while I worked close to home, watching children and planting rice. The water in the rice paddy was chest-high and full of scaly green leeches. I hated the leeches, which were as big as three fingers, and I tied the bottom of my pants in several places to try to keep them out.

Not long after my husband left, the Khmer Rouge ordered me to live near the weaving center, which was the central meeting place. When I asked why, they told me that they wanted to observe me because I was one of the "educated people." I had to be very careful about what I said. They watched everything I did, even boiling water. I hid two syringes and a little gold in a coconut tree near my new house, but I was afraid the Khmer Rouge would find them, so I put them in the hem of my blouse. Then they watched me bathe, so I buried my valuables. One day the Khmer Rouge told me to move back to Trapeng Cheutiel Village, and I was disappointed when I couldn't retrieve the gold and the syringes.

In 1976 the Khmer Rouge forced us to "vote" for Ta Mok to be our regional leader. We weren't given a choice, only a marked ballot which we were told to put in the election box. The Khmer Rouge promoted their "new society" by showing us a film which had scenes of laborers carrying dirt and told how they were improving Cambodia.

When I heard that Khieu Samphan, one of the top Khmer Rouge leaders, was coming to our district, I went to meet him. He was a neighbor of my father's in both Paris and Phnom Penh; and I wanted to ask him if he would help me find my father. I waited, but never saw him. I remember hearing that when Khieu Samphan's mother tried to arrange his marriage, he refused to marry any rich girls. He wasn't a talkative person, but he was kind and not corrupt. I was surprised to learn that he was part of the Khmer Rouge. Their actions were so cruel, and I didn't think an educated person would behave that way.

One time, when my work crew was out harvesting thatch, we found a snake that was more than twenty-five feet long and over a foot thick. The Khmer Rouge made a woman catch it with a rope, and then twenty people carried it back four kilometers. The Khmer Rouge said it could be traded to the Chinese for a tractor if we kept it alive, but it died along the way. The Khmer Rouge leaders divided the snake's fat among themselves, because it is good for healing wounds.

In 1976 there were twenty families living in my village. One by one they were killed. I had just delivered the baby of a former Lon Nol soldier, when the Khmer Rouge took the whole family away to be killed. One day, when I was harvesting rice, the Khmer Rouge came and I watched them tie the hands of two women behind their backs and march them away to be executed. Next, an ethnic Vietnamese woman and her entire family were murdered. I felt sick when I saw the legs and hands of a dead ethnic Chinese girl sticking out of the ground after a dog dug up her grave. By 1977, only four families in our village were left. Terrified that we would be the next to die, we focused solely on our work and never spoke to each other.

Later that year, all of us were sent to build a dam between two mountains at Malich, along with people from five other villages. I had to be careful, because I was watched all the time, even when I slept. So when I saw my father's driver there, I pretended not to know him because I didn't want anything to happen to him. The Khmer Rouge ordered us to run up the mountain, carrying dirt and rocks. They tried to make us compete for a reward.

In February of 1977, I visited my sister-in-law in the district hospital while my husband and four-year-old son stayed in the village. The week after I returned home, the Khmer Rouge took my husband away, I don't know why. He had been building a dike, and the small shovel he was using had broken. Maybe that was the reason.

The Khmer Rouge tied his hands behind his back and made him walk in front of them. He passed by the field where I was harvesting rice and I ran toward him. "Do you want to die," the old people called after me. I remembered my son, and I knew I had to turn back. My spirit was not in my body, but I felt responsible for my young child. I felt helpless and very sad because I had already lost my parents and my daughter. Now my husband was gone. I walked around unconsciously, on automatic, feeling like I was living without my soul.

After my husband was taken away, I was afraid the Khmer Rouge would come for me. No one wanted to be seen speaking to me. For a while, I wore two pairs of pants and two shirts, on the chance I met my husband and could give him an extra set of clothes. It was during harvest time, and we were not allowed to leave our huts at night. At about eight in the evening someone came and asked me to help deliver a baby. I thought it might be a trick, so they could accuse me of being out at night, so I didn't go. The next day, when I went to work, I noticed that my group leader was very surprised to see me. Perhaps he thought I had come back from the dead.

I survived the Khmer Rouge by working hard, keeping my identity a secret, and not talking too much. When I helped deliver a baby, the family usually gave me some food. I think being nice to my neighbors, being flexible, and not arguing also helped, which was easy for me, because I have a gentle nature. A man asked me to marry him after my husband was taken away, but I refused and said I was too old. The local people said, "No, you are like guava fruit, better with age," but I still declined.

The Khmer Rouge ordered me to move near the mountain, where my sister-in-law lived. I had to build my own house from bamboo and thatch. I worked in very cold, chest-deep water, pulling out rice seedlings for replanting, until nine or ten at night. The weather was cold and I didn't have a blanket for sleeping, but fortunately it was harvest time and our soup was thick with rice. Usually, the Khmer Rouge gave ten people only one small can of rice each day.

When I got my rice ration, I ate some, then put the rest in a coconut shell and took it back to my young son. One afternoon, a woman told me that the Khmer Rouge had seen me do that. I didn't care because I wanted my son to survive, and I was worried about his nutrition. He was hungry and often ate tree bark and tiny frogs. I planted sweet potatoes for the Khmer Rouge, but I didn't have the right to eat them, and instead I ate banana tree trunks and papaya tree roots.

During the dry season I used a mosquito net to catch small fish, and during the rainy season I gathered dead fish, salted them, stored them in the roof thatch, and later made them into fish paste for my son. One day, I saw a hole in the stream bed. I was afraid there might be a snake in it, but I put my hand into it anyway, felt something soft, and pulled out an eel. My son was so happy to eat eel.

I became worried when my son turned very pale and anemic. The treatment for anemia was to put a nail in sour palm juice and drink the iron-rich potion. So I went to the place where they made sugar and asked for palm juice and, since I was there, a little sugar. I was astonished when they gave me both. It was the only time in four years that I ate sugar. I was lucky during those years because I never got sick, although I also never menstruated.

I took my sick little boy to the "hospital," which was in a former school. I had to go there because the Khmer Rouge wouldn't let me care for him at home and miss work. When we arrived, they assigned my son a bed and the "nurse," a twelve-year-old girl wearing black Khmer Rouge clothes, came over and asked what illness he had. She just inquired, but then gave the same medicine for everything. The Khmer Rouge used traditional medicine, tablets of different colors. They also had serum for injections, sweet and salty water stored in soft drink bottles covered with plastic bags. That water frightened me as did their injections of coconut milk. Fortunately, my son improved and three weeks later, we returned home.

The old people taught me how to make traditional medicine from herbs, and when my son had worms, I pounded *sang ke* tree leaves and made a cake for him to eat. When he had diarrhea I used guava leaves, and for dysentery I used kakas leaves and bark.

My cousin Sophine became sick, so I took her to the district hospital where they had better medicine. The hospital was in a temple, and as we arrived I saw seriously ill patients being carried there in hammocks since the Khmer Rouge would not allow ox carts to be used for transporting sick people. The Khmer Rouge never used anesthetics for small operations, so the screams of patients filled the building. I didn't watch because I feared I might be accused of being too inquisitive. I recognized a man working there who was a trained medical assistant. Later I heard that he was killed by the Khmer Rouge.

In January 1979, we were relieved to hear that the Vietnamese had taken over Phnom Penh. If I had a husband or man to direct my life then maybe I could have escaped from the Khmer Rouge at that time, but I was passive and was forced to go with them through the forests of Kompong Speu and Pursat Provinces as they fled from the Vietnamese. My five-year-old son and my cousin Sophine were with me. We saw many Vietnamese soldiers and tanks, and at one point, we had just crossed a dry canal when artillery exploded directly behind us.

I didn't trust the Khmer Rouge leader, because he killed people, so we slept under a storage building where it would have been difficult to murder us. The weather was extreme, too hot to travel during the mid-day, and cold and damp at night. I became sick with a high fever. My head was burning, and I thought I might die. A woman and her family gave me a very bitter tea made from the *nim* tree and took care of me until I recovered.

We had to cross Sam Sep Chuan (Mountain of Thirty Levels). Small children, old people, horses, cows, and anyone who couldn't climb the steep mountain were left behind to die. We started before sunrise and walked for forty-two hours without food or water. On the second day, I cut a vine to get some liquid for my son. We arrived at midnight, totally exhausted, at a place with murky water that we used to cook rice. The next day, we walked past Oral Mountain where the smell from dead soldiers was horrendous.

We lived in Pursat Province with the Khmer Rouge for one miserable month. They let us bathe only once a week. One day, the Khmer Rouge ordered the people of Bak Kan Seng Village to dig a pond. When they finished, the Khmer Rouge massacred them and pushed them into the hole they had dug. So when the Khmer Rouge told us to dig a small pond, I felt weak from terror because I knew we would be killed the next day.

By a stroke of luck we were saved the next morning when some people passed by and invited us to escape with them. It was March of 1979, and I walked home with my son and my cousin Sophine, through Kompong Chanang Province toward Phnom Penh. It was a difficult journey. At one point we ran across a stream to escape being killed by the Khmer Rouge.

As soon as I arrived in Phnom Penh, I went directly to my old house hoping to find my relatives, but no one was there. I walked through the empty house and saw that most things were just as we left them, four years ago. Our books on Buddhism were still on the shelf along with my husband's class notes and my father's dissertation. A Vietnamese soldier came in and told me that no one was permitted to live in that area. As I was leaving, I stopped and wrote a message to my family on the front gate saying that I had come looking for them. Then I walked over to the medical clinic my parents had struggled to build and saw that the new government had taken over the building.

A couple of days, later I ran into Sovan, my cousin and friend from high school and she invited us to come live with her. Every morning I went out begging for food. When some kind people gave me two or three cans of rice, I pounded it into a powder and fried it with banana to make *chek chean*, which I then traded for more rice.

I wandered around the city, alone and barefoot, collecting basic household items, like an iron. There were plenty of goods available, and if I had been more ambitious I could have become rich, but I didn't want to take more than I needed. I saw appliances stored in buildings;

whole rooms of lamps, radios, and televisions. Later, I heard that they were taken to Vietnam.

I gradually found out what happened to my family. A man who escaped from the Khmer Rouge at the end of 1978 told me that my husband had been put in prison, in a cave in Chrous Mlou mountain, and when the Vietnamese came, the Khmer Rouge threw hand-grenades into the prison and killed everyone.

I learned from a cousin that my mother became sick and died along Highway 1 only three months after she left Phnom Penh. My sixty-year-old father worked in Kompot Province, tending cows and making rope until 1977, when he became sick and was taken to a hospital. They gave him an injection that killed him, and he was thrown into a mass grave with other corpses. I heard that my daughter was dead.

My three sisters who left Phnom Penh with my parents all died. Uthiucharey was pregnant and gave birth along Highway 1. The baby died shortly after delivery and then Uthiucharey died. Her husband, a university history professor, was in Australia at that time. Pol Pot invited the intellectuals who were living abroad to return and then killed them. Uthiucharey's husband came back to Cambodia in 1977, and we assume he was murdered because no one has ever heard from him.

My second sister, Kola Watano, was so upset after her husband was killed by the Khmer Rouge that she went insane for a while, and later she and her daughter died. My youngest sister Panha Theariny was taken away by the Khmer Rouge and murdered for no reason. I was the only surviving member of my family in Cambodia in 1979.

Not long after I arrived in Phnom Penh I met Dr. Khun Nget, one of my father's former students. He asked me to work in a clinic next to Tek Tla temple. For the first time in four years, my son and I had enough rice to eat. Later, a friend from medical school advised me to apply for a job with the Ministry of Health. I was assigned to work at April 17 Hospital. I don't know why they chose that name for a hospital, because it is so full of pain. It is the day the murderous Khmer Rouge regime began.

The hospital was filthy, and the first thing I did was clean it thoroughly, with help from the other medical staff. We didn't have enough medical supplies, equipment, medicine, or staff, but we did what we could. I went out and bought plaster for making casts, and we collected medical supplies from other hospitals. I worked on the third floor in general medicine, with only one other doctor, mainly caring for malnourished patients who were very skinny and had big swollen bellies. There were only two doctors in the hospital who had expertise, and they came over from Vietnam.

After the Khmer Rouge regime there were only forty doctors left in the country. Nearly all the older doctors had died, so we had no specialists or experts. There wasn't a single psychiatrist in Cambodia. Only eighteen out of the fifty medical students in my class survived, and I was the only woman. I still had two of the seven years of medical school left, but the last year is practice. I went back to medical school and graduated in nine months because Cambodia desperately needed doctors.

After receiving my medical degree, I became director of a hospital's emergency and recovery rooms. Some of my colleagues worked in Cambodia a while and then went to live abroad because the conditions here were so terrible. Hang Nor was one of the survivors from my medical class. He worked in a refugee camp in Thailand, and later was the lead actor in the film *The Killing Fields*.

At the end of 1979, I asked a French TV reporter who was visiting the hospital if he could help me find my relatives in France, so he took a picture of me and sent it to France. I was overjoyed when my relatives wrote me. When the hospital director found out what I had done, he sent me away to study communist policy and eat corn for a month with sixty other people at a re-education center in Phnom Penh run by the Vietnamese. After that experience, I was careful about speaking to foreigners.

In 1980, a relative bicycled 150 kilometers to bring my daughter Chhada to me from Kompot Province. I could hardly believe it was Chhada. I thought she had died. I didn't recognize her until I studied her face and saw that it resembled her father's. I felt sorry for her, but I held back my tears because I thought I needed to be brave.

I wanted to have a normal mother-daughter relationship with Chhada, but we were not close like mothers and daughters who stayed together. I felt a barrier between us that blocked her love for me. When Chhada was young I knew she was very intelligent, but after the Khmer Rouge regime she never did well in school and didn't want to continue her education after completing high school. The Khmer Rouge made her carry heavy loads on her head, and I saw the scars on her scalp. She was very different from her brother, who lived with me during the Khmer Rouge regime.

I saw a picture of Pol Pot for the first time when I hosted a French delegation at the hospital and accompanied them to Toul Sleng museum, the former Khmer Rouge interrogation and torture center. I stood there in disbelief when I realized that Pol Pot had been my French teacher in 1961 at Chareoun Vichea High School, when his name was Saloth Sar. I was shocked! I imagined how terrible his mother must have felt to have had such a child.

I just don't understand why Pol Pot ordered Cambodians to kill their own people. I didn't know him well, but I remember he was a very serious person. Later, I discovered that the wife of Ieng Sary was my Khmer literature teacher at Norodom High School. Pol Pot, Ieng Sary, and Khieu Samphan were the three top leaders of the Khmer Rouge in 1975, and still were twenty years later, and I knew all of them.

At the beginning of 1981, I was elected leader of the Hospital Trade Union, organized under the authority of the Communist Party. Besides working at the hospital, I also taught physiology at the University of Phnom Penh Medical School. In 1982, I went to Hanoi to study emergency room procedures, because at that time Vietnam was the only place we could get a scholarship. In 1983, East German doctors came to work with us, and we watched, slightly amused, as they quarreled with the Vietnamese doctors over technical points.

In 1984, I was awarded a scholarship to study in East Germany, but decided not to go because I didn't want to leave my daughter Chhada, who was fourteen years old. A couple of years later, when I applied to study abroad, the Ministry of Health refused to let me go because I admitted I had relatives in France.

Under socialism we were trained to work hard and set a good example for the next generation. I worked at the public hospital six days a week, seven hours a day. The government paid doctors only $20 per month, so I needed to have a private practice at home, to earn extra income. In 1984, I was so exhausted I collapsed on the floor with *bak kamlang* (broken strength). I was sent on a month-long holiday in Russia on the Black Sea with twenty other people, but it wasn't very relaxing because I was one of the leaders.

If I compare 1980 with 1990, I can see that our living conditions improved under the new communist government, but there were also problems. Some Vietnamese came to cooperate, but others wanted to dominate us and control our thinking. Cambodia was only open to the USSR and other communist countries. No one was permitted to study French or English, only Vietnamese was allowed. The high school curriculum didn't include history, because they didn't want anyone to know about other cultures or think of improvements. When the Khmer Rouge regime ended, everyone was equal, barefoot and bare-handed, but now many high-ranking government leaders own several houses.

Up until 1985 the government had a plan which called for cutting down trees at the Thai border and making roads to carry guns and equipment for the war with the Khmer Rouge. Cambodia didn't have many men left after the Khmer Rouge regime, and now we have even fewer because more died from stepping on landmines near the Thai border. Poor men were taken away to work at the border, but rich men just paid a bribe and stayed in the city to run their businesses and get richer. I wished we would have stopped fighting the Khmer Rouge and tried to negotiate. I also think we need to investigate why the Khmer Rouge killed so many people.

I see many problems in Cambodia today. Government corruption makes the average person worse off. The education system is not good. Students can attend school only half a day because there is a lack of teachers, so they don't learn a full curriculum. Videos are a bad influence on young people, in my opinion. There are a lot of Vietnamese people coming to Cambodia, and I am afraid our country could be taken over by Vietnam.

In 1992, I passed the entrance exam to get a postgraduate degree in anesthesiology, and went through a three-year program with nine other doctors, studying under a visiting French expert at the University of Phnom Penh. It was more difficult to remember the lessons because I am older. I finished school at age fifty, which is retirement age, but I agreed to work and teach in the medical school for six years.

I had good parents and I appreciate how they supported me and encouraged me to go to the university. When I started medical school I just wanted to get a degree, and afterward I planned to stay home and take care of my children. Now I'm glad I have a degree because I see that widows who didn't have careers prior to 1975 met more difficulty than I did, as they tried to earn money to support their children.

Since the Khmer Rouge regime, I've seen a lot of insane women on the streets of Phnom Penh. My aunt used to be a fine person, but she lost her sanity after the Khmer Rouge killed her husband and children; now she doesn't make sense when she speaks. I thank God I am still sane.

Nearly half of the older women in Cambodia have health problems related to the Khmer Rouge period, and as a medical doctor I see a lot of nervous disorders and circulation problems in women. When something triggers a woman's memory, like seeing a person's face who reminds her of her dead husband, it is common for her to have a seizure, during which her feet and hands become cold, she becomes pale, her eyes shut, it is difficult for her to breathe, and sometimes she faints.

When I reflect on my life, I see that it has not been a happy one. As a widow, I have to make all the decisions, and I don't have anyone to discuss them with. I miss feeling my husband's love for me. I used to worry about my children and was afraid I could not provide a good future for them. But I tried to be a good mother, to teach my children about Cambodian culture and how to be good citizens.

I don't worry as much as I used to. I feel satisfied knowing that I chose a good husband for my daughter Chhada. He is kind and likes his work as a doctor. Chhada sells medicine at my home clinic and cares for her little boy. My son Noravin is studying at the Institute of Agriculture, and he will get a job when he graduates. I just continue to work hard and am patient, because to be human is to always have problems, big or small. People see that I am strong and solid, like a stone, but my heart is very soft.

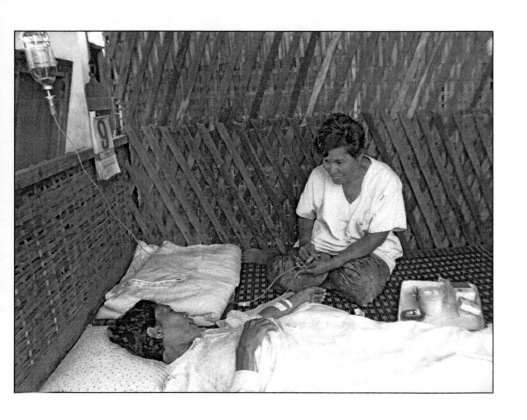

*Dr. Lieng administers an IV of vitamin C to a patient at her private clin-
ic. Technologically impressive western medicine is usually preferred over
traditional herbal medicine. Dr. Lieng maintains a private practice to
supplement her low income of $20 per month from her position at the pub-
lic hospital. Only half of Cambodia's women and children have access to
even the most rudimentary health services and there is only one doctor for
every 6,300 people. One third of all deaths in children could be prevented
with vaccines.*

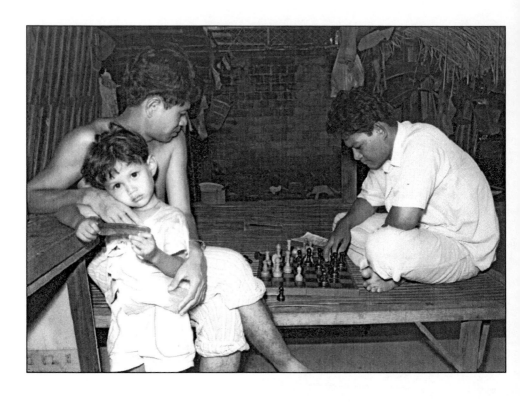

Sitting on the bed Lieng's son, who is a university student studying agriculture, carefully plans his next move in the game of chess he is playing with his brother-in-law. Lieng's young grandson finds chess rather boring.

Dr. Lieng administers anesthetic to a patient in an operating room in Phnom Penh. She is studying under a French doctor from Medicine Sans Frontieres so she can teach anesthesiology at Phnom Penh University Medical School. In 1995 Cambodia had a population of ten million and only one trained anesthesiologist.

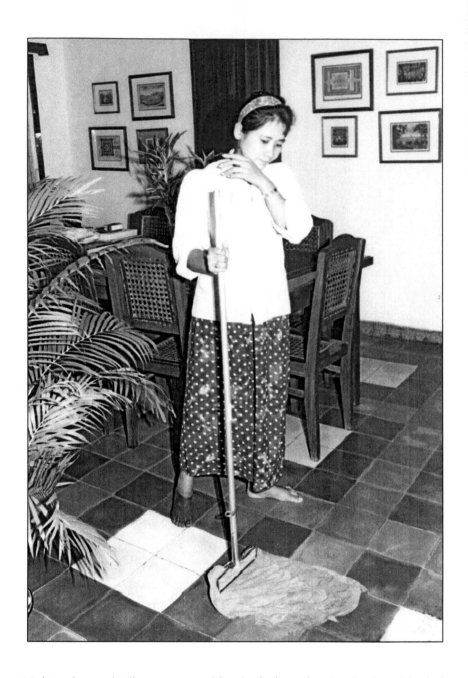

Maline cleans the floors as one of her daily housekeeping duties. She feels fortunate to have a good job since there are over 30,000 landmine victims like herself living in Phnom Penh and most are unemployed.

Maline ✤ Landmine Victim and Housekeeper

Maline was a country school girl when she stepped on a landmine in 1991 and became a victim of the civil war between the Khmer Rouge and the Cambodian government. Maline's story leading up to this catastrophe begins in 1975 when her father, a Red Cross worker, was killed by the Khmer Rouge. After the Pol Pot period her mother struggled to support three children by growing sugar cane. Maline helped her mother earn money by selling vegetables from village to village, which is how she stepped on the mine. When Maline regained consciousness and realized that her leg had been amputated, she wished she were dead. Landmines do more than just destroy a limb—they shatter the psyche. It was through a prosthetics project run by the American Friends Service Committee that Maline was fitted for an artificial leg. She learned sewing as a vocational skill at Maryknoll, a foreign aid organization that helps amputees. Maline gradually recovered her self-esteem and rebuilt her life, and now she has a good job as a housekeeper.

At first I didn't realize that Maline had an artificial leg. All I noticed was her sweet disposition and how she kept herself busy cleaning my friend Linda's house, washing clothes by hand and carefully ironing them, changing beds, and mopping floors. I was stunned one day when I walked into the kitchen and saw Maline's artificial leg leaning against the wall in the corner. I couldn't imagine the pain she must have experienced. Later, I learned that Linda had gone to Maryknoll to hire a housekeeper because she felt compassion for landmine victims.

I had the pleasure of living in Linda's house during part of my stay in Cambodia and became friends with Maline. I noticed her love of art, and appreciated the way she filled the house with beautiful tropical flowers, cut from the yard. Maline's clothes were attractive, and I was impressed when I found out that she had designed and sewn many of them herself.

As I interviewed Maline, I discovered her dry sense of humor and enjoyed her descriptions of Cambodian foods, holidays, and traditions in the context of rural life. Highlights of her year come when she returns home to see her mother and friends and celebrates special holidays like the New Year or Ancestors Remembrance Day. As is typical in Cambodia, Maline devotes herself to supporting her family, and now, instead of being a financial burden, she actually is the major breadwinner (or perhaps in Cambodia it is "rice-winner"). Maline's life has taken a turn for the better and she even has a suitor.

Maline:

My mother put me in a basket and carried me to our relatives' house in Kompong Cham Province the day the Vietnamese drove out the Khmer Rouge in 1979. I don't remember much because I was only six years old. My mother balanced a pole on her shoulder with baskets hung from each end. One basket was filled with everything we owned, mostly clothes, and a pot for cooking rice, and my brother and I took turns riding in the other basket.

My father had been killed by the Khmer Rouge when a villager reported him to the authorities saying he didn't know how to plow. It was true, my father didn't know anything about farming because he used to work for the Red Cross and was raised in a wealthy family. My grandfather was a customs official, and the Khmer Rouge killed him too.

My mother worried about how she could support us. First, we lived with my father's relatives in Kompong Cham Province, but my mother could not find a way to earn a living. After a few months, we moved to Rokakaong Village along the Mekong River, where my mother's relatives live, about thirty-two kilometers from Phnom Penh in Kandal Province. We lived with my grandmother in a simple house on stilts. My mother told me that my grandmother's old house was the most beautiful in the area, before the Khmer Rouge destroyed it. I had to use my imagination because all that was left was the staircase. My grandmother still owned the land and was able to give my mother a sugar cane field to farm and earn an income.

My cousin Vandith came to live with us in 1979 since he had no family or home. The Khmer Rouge had killed his parents because his father was a doctor and his mother was a teacher. A few years later, another cousin, Seun, moved in with us so he could attend Prek Anhchanh High School. His father was killed by the Khmer Rouge because he was a teacher.

In 1983, I started school for the first time, at age ten. I liked school, especially literature, but I wasn't very good at math. Sometimes the teachers hit the students. My mother and my teacher were friends and my mother told her with a smile, "Look after Maline, and do anything you want to her, but leave the eye and the bone for me." But I was never beaten.

Our family was poor, and I worked very hard helping my mother. Some days I felt sorry for myself because most of my classmates didn't have to work as much as I did. I got up before dawn and cooked breakfast, usually rice and fried fish, which my mother took with her when she left at sunrise to work in her sugar cane field. After breakfast, I washed clothes and prepared food for our pig while my cousin Vandith hauled water from the river and filled the big earthen storage jar. If I didn't get up early, I would be late for school because I had so much work to do.

When school ended around mid-day, I came home and prepared lunch for my mother and her two helpers and carried it to the sugar cane field. I liked to make sour soup with rice and sometimes I took them sliced cucumber, eggplant, and *prahok* (fermented fish).

After delivering lunch to my mother, I went back to work around the house and looked after the chickens, ducks, pig, and cows. Ducks are good layers, and I gathered the eggs. My mother usually sold the animals we raised, but sometimes she hired a man to butcher one for us to eat. No one in my family wanted to kill our animals, not even my brother. We had seen them walking, so how could we kill them?

In the afternoon I wove *kramars*, the cotton scarves we use to protect our heads from the sun and dust. My grandmother taught me to weave, so I could earn a little income. I enjoyed weaving so much that my mother promised to send me to study silk weaving after I finished high school.

At sunset, I prepared dinner for our family. Usually, I took the leftovers from lunch and added some fried fish or pickled radish with lemon and sugar. If I didn't have dinner prepared, my mother would scold me because she was tired from working all day and didn't want to cook. In the evening, I wound thread onto the weaving shuttle while listening to the news and my favorite songs on the radio. I did my homework by fish oil lamp or candlelight because we don't have electricity in the countryside.

I liked Sundays because my friends came to visit me. I prepared food for them while we talked. After eating, we walked in the fields behind my house and they climbed the fruit trees and picked sapodilla, guava, and oranges. We would make beautiful bouquets with the sunflowers, jasmine, and spider flowers that I planted in front of our house.

My family always went to the Buddhist temple for big celebrations, such as *Pachum Ben*, Ancestors Remembrance Day, and *Chaul Chhnam*, the Cambodian New Year. Twice a year we bought clothes and took them to the nuns and poor people who live at the temple.

My mother told me that when I was a baby I wasn't able to cry, so she took me to the temple and found the monk who makes *kratas*, a special necklace for spiritual healing and protection. He wrote a prayer and blessing on pieces of flat soft metal, rolled them around a piece of string, and tied the necklace around my neck. I think it worked, because my mother told me that by the time I was a year old I could cry loudly.

My mother became sick and couldn't work. I wanted to earn some money to help support our family, so I started selling food in nearby villages on the weekends. I usually sold bananas, coconuts, onions, sugar, or monosodium glutamate. I used a bicycle that my uncle in Battambang Province bought for me when I was young. At first I had to ride it standing up because I couldn't reach the pedals if I sat on the seat.

"I don't want you to quit school," my mother told me. I continued to study until 1991, when I was nineteen years old and in ninth grade. Then I stepped on a landmine.

It was Sunday morning and I rode my bicycle to Toul, a neighboring village, to sell coconuts and sour cabbage. On the way home I had to cross a big lake by boat because the bridge had been destroyed years ago by the Khmer Rouge. I walked my bicycle down an ox cart road between rice fields, which was the border between Kandal and Kompong Cham Provinces. There had been fighting in that area between government troops and the Khmer Rouge four years earlier, in 1987. I had never been on that road before, but everyone said it was safe. There were people walking in front of me and behind me, but I was the one who stepped on the mine.

"Mother! Help! I stepped on a mine," I screamed, and then I passed out. The market women who were walking near me ran to the main road and asked the government soldiers for help. The soldiers said they couldn't go to the site of the accident because they might be attacked by Khmer Rouge soldiers, since the government only controlled the main road. They told the women to bring me to the main road.

Then the women made a hammock by tying a blanket to a pole, and brought me to the road. From there, the soldiers carried me ten kilometers to the clinic in Batheay Village. There was no medicine in the clinic, but the medical staff gave me an IV. I was still unconscious and my face was black, like a dead person's. No one thought I would live.

I was about twenty kilometers away from home when I stepped on the mine, so it took a few hours for my mother to arrive at the clinic. The next day, my mother hired a motorcycle cart to take me to a hospital in Phnom Penh. The driver said he would charge 15,000 riels (about $6) to take me to the hospital, but if I died on the way he would leave my body beside the road because it is bad luck if people die while you are transporting them. My mother offered the driver 20,000 riels if he would bring my body back if I died, but he insisted on 60,000 riels.

The first hospital we stopped at in Phnom Penh refused to take me because my case was too serious, so my mother took me to Loaksang Hospital and pleaded with them until they agreed to admit me. My blood pressure was very low, and they couldn't find a vein in my arm to give me a blood transfusion, so they used one in my neck. They put me in a room for the nearly dead and covered me with a white sheet. I spent one week in that room, while my mother cried and cried.

My mother went to get my uncle who lived in Phnom Penh. He had a doctor friend who operated on me and helped us a lot. I didn't wake up until two weeks after my accident.

At first, I didn't know that my leg had been amputated because I was covered with a sheet and there was a pillow under it that looked like my leg and my foot. I wondered why everyone who came to visit me cried, so I asked if my leg was cut off. They lied and said no, only the bone was broken. They didn't want to tell me the truth because they thought I was too weak to take the shock of bad news. When the doctor came to remove the stitches in my leg, he lied and said he would take off the brace, and if I could not walk on that leg, then it would have to be amputated. At that point I realized my leg had already been cut off, and I passed out.

When I woke up several hours later, I didn't want to live anymore. I felt ashamed and believed I must have done something bad in my past life that caused me to step on the mine. Now I was a burden to my family. I should have listened to my mother when she warned me not to go near the village of Toul because the soldiers there took away beautiful young girls.

A Frenchman who worked in the hospital saw me crying all the time and wanted to help me, so he took me to visit Wat Than. He told me that after I healed, I could live at Wat Than. There I would get an artificial leg, and I could learn typing, sewing, or carpentry. When he showed me an artificial leg, I felt faint and could not speak. The leg was made from leather and was ugly. It was not the same as having my own leg. He told me I should learn to walk on it, and then go to Thailand to get a better-looking one.

The hospital put patients next to me who had stepped on land-mines, and it made me extremely sad, so I left after one month, even though the doctor wanted me to stay longer. I lived at home for five months and felt depressed knowing I would have to rely on other people to help me for the rest of my life. My teacher tried hard to persuade me to come back to school and offered to give me a ride, but I couldn't go back. I was too embarrassed about what had happened to me, and I didn't think I could concentrate.

During the rainy season it became almost impossible for me to get around because the ground was muddy and slippery, so my mother took me to live at Wat Than and learn to sew in their six-month training program. They made an artificial leg for me, but I had a lot of difficulty learning to walk on it. Maybe walking would have been easier if my leg had been amputated below my knee instead of above. My stump was raw and swollen and bled every day.

I believed I would never be able to do anything with my life. I was full of despair and felt extremely depressed and angry at myself. I decided to kill myself and sent a cyclo driver to buy sleeping pills. That night, when I went to bed, I took thirty-five of them.

The next morning, the nurse came to give me an anti-infection injection. She became worried when I didn't wake up, and she ran to get my uncle who lived near Wat Than. When my uncle opened the mosquito net surrounding my bed he discovered that I had taken the sleeping pills. They rushed me to the hospital, and one of the Wat Than staff went to get my mother.

When I woke up, I realized I wasn't dead and wondered why. I became angry at my mother. "Why did you bring me to the hospital? I wanted to die," I told her. My mother cried and begged me not to kill myself. She said she could earn enough money to support me. I felt sorry for her and decided I should stop talking about suicide. Later, friends of my family told me that if I had died, my mother might have gone insane.

The sleeping pills made me nearly blind for two weeks. While I was in the hospital, my friend the Frenchman gave me medicine for my eyes and said he wanted to take me to a park to cheer me up. I refused to go. I didn't think it would make me happy, since I couldn't walk. I spent one week in the hospital, and then I went home with my mother. She brought my artificial leg, but I never used it because it was heavy and unsightly. I hated it.

I blame the war for what happened to me. That's why I stepped on the mine. We have had a lot of war in our country and everyone tries to win. I think it's because we don't understand each other.

After living at home for many months, I returned to Wat Than to finish my training program because I enjoyed sewing and did very well. They made me a better-looking leg, and I learned to walk on it without the use of crutches. When the program ended the school selected two of the best students to stay on to work, and I was one of them. Then one day an American woman named Linda came and asked if I wanted to be her housekeeper. At first I wasn't sure, but she came back and asked me again. I considered Linda's face and sensed that she was a kind person, so I decided to take the job because I could hide from the world.

Today I am happy and calm like Linda. She is like a sister to me, and when she went back to visit America, I missed her very much. I looked at her photograph every day and wished she was home. I don't know English very well, and when Linda returned I felt frustrated because I could not express how much I missed her and how happy I was to see her again.

My mother doesn't worry about me because she knows that I have a kind employer. I am able to save money and support my brother who is studying to be an electrician at the technical college in Phnom Penh. He lives with my uncle and pedals a cyclo to earn money. I live with my cousin Vibol, who takes me to work on his motor bike and brings me home each day. Vibol distributes medicine to prisoners for Licado, a human rights organization.

On the weekend, I enjoy sewing clothes for myself. It is less expensive to make my own clothes, and it is fun to choose the color and the fabric and create my favorite designs. I notice other people's clothes, and consider whether the color suits their skin tone. My dream is to be a seamstress.

Sometimes I still feel discouraged. When I compare myself to others, I see they are stronger. If someone pushes me a little, like in a crowd during a big ceremony at the temple, it is easy for me to fall down. Once, when I went to the market I heard a woman say, "It's a pity that a girl with a beautiful face lost her leg. If it had been me, I would rather be dead than alive." I still have pain in my eyes from taking the sleeping pills. My eyes water, my hands shake, and I often get a fever.

Right now I feel sorry for my mother because a flood destroyed her sugar cane field, and she only earned 30,000 riels ($12) for the crop this year. I am glad I can help support her because she was very kind to me when I was growing up. I liked it when she made me special snacks for a treat.

I worry about what will happen when Linda goes back to America and my job ends. My grandmother is getting old, and she needs expensive medicine for her high blood pressure. I became hopeful when I started working for Linda, but I wonder who will help me survive when I am old.

My favorite holiday is *Chaul Chhnam*, the three-day New Year celebration in mid-April, and this year I took a week-long vacation. Two days before *Chaul Chhnam* I cleaned the house and helped my mother prepare special foods. I cut banana leaves for her to make ansom, which is a roll of sticky rice with pork and mung bean paste in the middle, wrapped in banana leaf and boiled. I helped make *treap bay*, a sweet dessert of sticky rice and sugar, and I picked papaya, pomello, sapodilla, and guava from the fruit trees behind our house.

I created a beautiful altar in front of our house. I covered a table with a pretty green cloth and set out fruit, flowers, two glasses of water, soft drinks, a bowl for incense sticks, two candles, and a centerpiece, which was a section of banana trunk that had five candles and five sticks of incense in it. The candles and incense are lit the moment the new Buddha comes and the new year begins. The time is different each year, so we listen to the radio to find out when it is. This year it was in the middle of the night, and my mother got up to light the candles and incense, but I kept on sleeping.

The day before *Chaul Chhnam*, all my relatives, about ten of them, came over to visit. My older cousins gave presents, such as money, cloth, or special foods, to their parents. Later, my girlfriends stopped by and we talked, laughed, and teased each other. We discussed whether we wanted go to the temple at eight or eleven the next morning, and we decided what clothes we would wear because we liked to dress in similar colors and styles. Since I lost my leg, I only wear long skirts that cover my artificial leg, so now my friends wear long skirts too.

We go to a different temple on each of the three days that we celebrate *Chaul Chhnam*, to offer food to the monks and to pray for our ancestors. Offering food to the monks is a good deed, which helps our ancestors, and then our ancestors help us. I pray for a good future and to do a good job at work. I listen to the monks pray, but I don't understand them because they chant in Pali.

After we leave the temple, we stop to watch the young people playing games outside. I prefer to watch because the games can be rough. I was knocked down once, even before I lost my leg. Many of the games have a team of girls against a team of boys, such as *pruat*, tug of war. *Angkounh* is a game where three *angkounh* fruit are set on the ground and the players try to hit them by throwing another piece of fruit. The winner gets to knock everyone on the knee. In *dandeam slek cheur*, a tree branch is placed in the middle of the field, and when a number is called out, a player from each team comes running up and tries to grab the branch and carry it back to her team. When it gets dark, we get a big lamp and keep playing late into the night.

A couple of days after *Chaul Chhnam*, while I was cooking rice, my cousin Seun asked me to marry him. I was not surprised because he has asked me many times, even before I lost my leg. This time he tried to persuade me, and said he will look after me for my whole life and won't leave me, because my mother looked after him while he was in high school. He said that if I let my mother arrange a marriage with someone I don't know, I might be unhappy, but with him I already know the true feelings of his heart.

Seun is twenty-seven years old and works for the Department of Agriculture. My mother wants me to marry him, but I haven't agreed. I love him like a brother, and besides, I couldn't bear to be his wife and hear someone say to my husband, "Why did you marry a girl without a leg?"

When I went home in October this year for *Pachum Ben*, Seun asked me again. This time I didn't refuse, just told him that I need to repay my debts and save some money. My mother sold our cows and most of our valuables to pay my medical bills, and I still owe Linda $80 from the $200 I borrowed for my cousin Vandith's wedding. A wedding costs about $500, and Seun's salary is only 40,000 riels ($16) per month. My mother announced, "The decision is up to me, and I have decided you two will marry in December."

My life is getting better and I have more hope.

Like this man on a bicycle, Maline used to ride from village to village and sell food to help support her widowed mother. One day on her way home, she was walking her bicycle down a dirt road, following the people in front of her, when she stepped on a landmine.

Happy to see her old sewing teacher at Wat Than, Maline gives her a big hug. The vocational training program run by Maryknoll and the prosthetics project run by the American Friends Service Committee helped Maline rebuild her life after she stepped on a landmine and lost her leg at age nineteen.

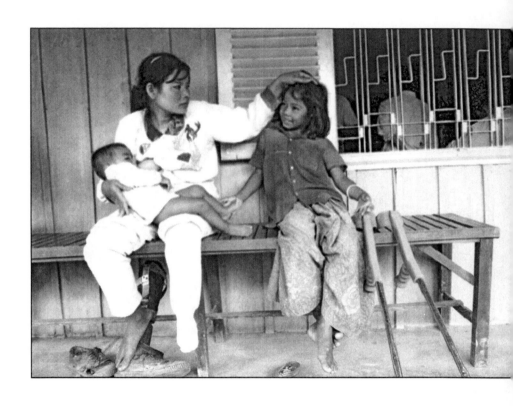

Most landmine victims are civilians. Here a mother nurses her baby and tenderly touches her daughter as she waits to have her artificial leg refitted at a Vietnam Veterans of America Foundation prosthetics facility.

SOUL SURVIVORS

Aun and her cousin meditate in the ornate Buddhist temple which is primarily used for special celebrations. Through Vipassana meditation, Aun calms her mind and aligns herself with the spiritual teachings of the Buddha which help her transcend suffering.

Aun ❦ Buddhist Nun

Buddhism has been the central focus of Aun's life, starting in childhood when it was the only comfort she found for her severe arthritis. Aun enjoyed studying and practicing Buddhism so much that she became a nun when she was in her mid twenties, even though she was married. Cambodia has various levels of Buddhist nuns. An independent woman, Aun would often leave her husband and daughter and go to the mountains to meditate for weeks at a time. Aun's health has always been poor, and she was in the hospital with high blood pressure at age forty-nine when the Khmer Rouge evacuated Phnom Penh in April 1975. Aun refused to renounce her religion under the Khmer Rouge, and wouldn't stop shaving her head or wearing the nun's white clothes, which could have cost her life. Instead, miraculously, she ended up teaching Buddhism to Khmer Rouge leaders. Like many women, Aun was widowed during the brutal Khmer Rouge regime. Afterward, she and her daughter lived at a Buddhist temple near Phnom Penh.

I walked beneath the shady palm trees, past the golden temple with its ornate tile roof, on my way to the nuns' huts, miniature one-room thatched cottages lined up in a row. I imagined it must be pleasant to live a simple contemplative life in a such a peaceful setting and supportive community. It felt like a place of dignity and honor for older women.

As soon as I met Aun, I noticed her spunk and her inner strength. As we sat talking on her tiny front porch in the quiet ambiance of the temple compound, one of her neighbors walked past carrying coconut shells to burn for cooking fuel, and paused to say good morning. Aun started telling me her courageous story, and a little while later, her cute five-year-old grandson came over for a visit. She gave him a piece of fruit. Her cousin, also a Buddhist nun, sat with us and listened as she prepared her betel nut chew, carefully cutting the nut, and wrapping it in a green leaf that she first coated with a pink chalky paste. Most older women in Cambodia have dark-stained teeth from chewing this mild stimulant.

One of the highlights of my stay in Cambodia was when Aun took me to the mountain where she goes on retreat to meditate. I hired a taxi, and Aun loaded the car with gifts of food for the monks and nuns who live there. The "mountain" was actually a tall hill, with a few trees on it, rising out of flat rice fields. We drove to the top, where a new temple replaced the old one that had been destroyed by the Khmer Rouge. First, we lit sticks of incense and set them in the bowl before the huge statue of Buddha that was decorated with blinking colored lights. Then we sat in quiet meditation, surrounded by painted murals of Buddha's life. Aun showed me the cave entrance where she likes to sit and meditate. As we drove home, I felt thankful that I had the pleasure to get to know Aun, a woman of high integrity and spiritual devotion.

Aun:

I have always loved Buddhism. As a child, I went to the temple with my parents and brother and listened to the monks chant, while my mother lit incense, prayed, and gave food to monks. We visited the temple on holy days, which fell on the first and fifteenth day of each lunar month. I liked seeing my mother dressed in a beautiful silk skirt, with a scarf tied diagonally across her white blouse.

When I was fourteen, I started having terrible rheumatism in my knees. It was so painful that I cried often. My parents gave me all kinds of traditional Khmer and Chinese medicines, but nothing helped, and when I was eighteen, a doctor told me that my rheumatism was caused by a weak heart, possibly from rheumatic fever, and there was no cure. I was tired of living. The only comfort I found was from studying Buddhism. I liked to read books about the teachings of the Buddha, and I practiced Buddhism by following the first five precepts: do not kill, steal, have sex, lie, or drink alcohol. On holy days, I followed three more Buddhist precepts: do not eat dinner, sing or dance, or go to entertainment.

My family lived in Phnom Penh, and my father worked for the government. He encouraged me to go into business because government salaries were too low. I studied French, Chinese, and Vietnamese, and opened a stall in the central market where I sold clothes. I wasn't happy, and I told my parents that I wanted to live in a temple and study Buddhism. My parents left the decision up to me, but they gave me advice, "You should marry, so that in the future you can rely on your children. If you don't, your life will be difficult when you are old."

I followed my parents' advice, and consented to an arranged marriage when I was twenty-six years old. I had the first glimpse of my future husband on the day before our wedding. My parents chose him because he was a good person, he liked Buddhism, as I did, and he was financially secure. He owned a hair salon business.

Our wedding followed traditional Khmer custom, starting in the morning when the guests walked with the groom from his house to mine. When he arrived, I came out and together we carried unopened betel nut blossoms into the house and offered them to our parents. Then rice porridge, cake, and fruit were brought out in pairs, such as two plates of cake or two trays of oranges, and served to our guests. Next, the groom's feet were symbolically washed with perfume. The ceremony continued all day and night, and I was glad when it ended because I was nervous and didn't feel well. Afterward, we lived with my parents for a month, as is customary.

I helped my new husband in his hair salon, and learned how to cut and perm hair. Not long after we were married, I became pregnant and my health declined further. The doctor was afraid that I might die during labor because of my weak heart, so I had a Cesarean. My condition following childbirth was very serious, and I was unconscious for a long time. My twin sons died a couple of weeks after they were born, and I never even saw them.

It took me a long time to recover, and I grieved the loss of my babies. When women are pregnant, they usually dream that they are given something valuable, and I dreamed someone gave me diamond earrings. I was told in the dream that I didn't need to clean the earrings, but I didn't listen and wanted them to look better, so I brushed one, and the diamond came off. After my sons died, I realized that my dream had predicted their deaths.

The following year, I decided to follow my deepest desire, and I left home to live at a temple and study Buddhism, not because I disliked my husband, but because I loved Buddhism. I didn't think earning a lot of money in my husband's business would be beneficial for my next life. Only good deeds, like helping people, would help me to have a better life next time. My husband didn't forbid me to go because that would have been considered a sin. Instead, he escorted me to the temple. I shaved my head, wore white clothes, vowed to obey the precepts, and in doing so, became a Buddhist nun.

I asked my husband to divorce me and marry another woman, but he refused and begged me to come back to him. "You're clever," he said. "Now you are free to study Buddhism, and you want to tie me down in another marriage." He promised that after we saved enough money we would buy a house, rent it out, and support ourselves with the earnings, so we could both travel and study Buddhism. I liked his plan.

I traveled a lot in my Buddhist practice. I went to mountains and forests to meditate for weeks at a time, to train my heart. Sometimes I meditated with other nuns, but often I went alone. I took some rice and dried fish and lived in a cave or empty hut. If there wasn't a place to stay, I hired a man to build a small thatched shelter for me.

When I was meditating on a mountain, I felt very happy. Sometimes I didn't see anyone for a whole month, but I was never lonely. I became like a wild monkey, afraid of people. When my environment was peaceful, I felt peaceful. I liked to listen to the wind in the leaves more than a song, because it is more melodious. Local people warned me about tigers, wolves, and snakes in the forest, but I wasn't afraid. I never saw any because honest people who follow the Buddhist precepts don't see wild animals. I only saw big trees.

During my meditation I wanted to steady my heart, mind, and body, so I concentrated on one word or phrase from the Buddhist teachings, such as "impermanence" or *put-to*, which means "supported by the Buddha." I also learned a higher level of meditation, called *vipas-sana*, where we reflect on how and why we were born. The Buddha tells us that when we have a body, we have sorrow, and the sorrow comes from many sources. I knew people who sought money or a husband, and I saw how it created sorrow for them.

During the following eight years, I traveled to nearly every province in Cambodia and stayed at over forty sacred mountains, sometimes near cities and sometimes in remote forests. I enjoyed meditating on the mountains so much that I always found it difficult to leave, but each month I went to meet my husband in Phnom Penh, and we divided the rental income from the house we had bought. Occasionally, we lived together for a short time before separating to go to different mountains or temples to meditate and study Buddhism.

My husband and I didn't want to have more children, but when I was thirty-six years old I dreamed someone gave me a gold ring, and later I gave birth to a girl. When my daughter Chay Yien was two and a half, I left her with my mother and went back to the mountains to meditate. I loved my daughter, and returned home often to spend time with her and my mother. My husband and I took turns caring for my mother and our daughter. When I went away to practice Buddhism, he looked after them and was very kind to them, and when I came home, he left to practice Buddhism.

My husband and I sold our hair salon in 1972. We wanted to do something charitable with the money, so we built a *wat* (Buddhist temple) in Phnom Penh, and named it Wat Vipassanoram. We wanted to support the people who practice Buddhism, and we knew that this good deed would help us in our next life. Someone else donated the land, and we paid for the construction of a nice tile-roofed house for the monks to live in, many small huts for the nuns, and a pavilion for chanting, prayer, and meditation. I chose honest monks to live at Wat Vipassanoram and tried to screen out the corrupt ones who kept the money that people gave them. I lived there with my daughter and mother, and when I was away, my husband stayed there. My mother liked living at the temple and practicing Buddhism, so she became a nun, too.

In 1973, my mother traveled with me to a temple near the city of Battambang to practice Buddhism for three months, and one morning she peacefully passed away in her hut at age sixty-seven. I was very sad. We put her body in a simple coffin and set it in a decorated one that belongs to the temple, and then we took it to the hall where we chant prayers. Normally, the ceremony lasts one to three days, but we preserved the corpse and continued chanting for seven days, while we waited for my brother to come from Phnom Penh. He had a hard time getting a plane ticket, due to the war between the Khmer Rouge and General Lon Nol. We recorded the chanting and played it over and over on a loud speaker, all day and all night, and when he finally arrived, we cremated my mother's body.

After that, I traveled to a mountain in Battambang Province to meditate, but the area was occupied by Khmer Rouge soldiers, so I flew back to Phnom Penh. I placed my mother's ashes in a stupa at our temple, and we held a funeral ceremony 100 days after her death, and another ceremony one year after her death, according to tradition. Each time the monks came to chant and pray that our good deeds would be passed on to her spirit. We also held a *pakchay buan*, a ceremony at which we give a monk everything a person needs to live, such as a pillow, tea kettle, and dishes, and he prays that they be sent to my mother's spirit.

In 1974, my husband and I built a Buddhist temple near the ocean. I chose the city of Kompong Som because it was quiet and a good place to meditate. I bought land not far from the city center and hired someone to construct the buildings. I loved living in that peaceful setting, but my health problems forced me to return to Phnom Penh.

I was in the hospital with high blood pressure when the Khmer Rouge took over and evacuated Phnom Penh. The soldiers ordered us to leave the hospital. I was so dizzy, I could only walk about 100 meters, holding on to my thirteen-year-old daughter, and then I needed to stop and rest. I was sweating profusely and wanted to go rest at my temple in Phnom Penh, but the Khmer Rouge wouldn't allow us to go anywhere except out of the city. When night fell, we had no choice but to sleep in the street.

The Khmer Rouge told everyone to return to their native province, and since I was born in Phnom Penh, I decided to take my daughter to

Takeo, my husband's native province. I was so surprised and happy when, in all the crowds of traveling people, I ran into my husband. He was pleased to see us too, and we went together to his native village of Prey Lvea. Unfortunately, his parents weren't there, so we walked on to the next village and met his cousin, who let us stay with him.

The Khmer Rouge questioned us about our background, and I told them that I used to be self-employed. Of course, I could not hide the fact that I was a nun, because my head was shaved and my clothes were white. When the Khmer Rouge told me that nuns were stupid because they worshipped concrete, I told them they misunderstood, that we respect the Buddha, not the concrete.

Eight months later, the Khmer Rouge sent us to live in Battambang Province. They put us on a very crowded train, where we had to squat on the floor with our knees up, packed together for many hours. When it was time to get off the train, I couldn't straighten my legs or stand up; my rheumatism had gotten so bad that I couldn't walk. My husband struggled to help me, and sometimes we fell down together. We asked a young man to carry me on his shoulder. My knees were very swollen, and I had a high fever. I drank twenty-eight pots of medicinal tea, which didn't help much, but eventually my temperature came down and the swelling reduced.

The Khmer Rouge moved us three times during the first year, and we ended up living in Kok Lun Village in Preah Net District. My daughter had to work making fertilizer, my husband made baskets for carrying soil, and my job was to scare away birds during the rice harvest. I sat next to the rice field, and when I opened a big umbrella and shouted, the birds flew over to the next rice field. I still couldn't straighten my legs and had to waddle around in a squatting position. Since I couldn't get to the communal dining area, my daughter brought me my small ration of rice.

Everyone became very skinny due to lack of food, and it was difficult to survive. We dug up the roots of banana and papaya trees, boiled and ate them just to fill our stomachs. We picked leaves and ate them; in fact, we ate everything that wasn't poisonous. When some people were caught trying to take a few potatoes, the Khmer Rouge killed them right there in the potato field.

My husband became very sick and had severe swelling, first in his legs and face, and then in his whole body. There was no medicine to treat him, so I traded a gold locket for some vitamins, which made him feel stronger for a day, but there were no more vitamins to buy. He used two sticks to steady himself, and tried to walk to get his food ration twice a day. He was afraid that if he wasn't able to walk to the dining area, the Khmer Rouge wouldn't allow him to eat. But he often fell to the ground, and the neighbors had to help him home.

I felt sorry for my husband, and shared my tiny ration with him. And when my daughter was sick, I shared my ration three ways. My husband got malaria, and I felt terribly frustrated because there was nothing I could do to help him. I was full of sorrow when he died in 1978. My daughter followed the funeral procession and reported back to me that there was no coffin, but they put him nicely into a grave and didn't just throw him in a hole.

I could have died during the Khmer Rouge regime, as so many people did, but I think I survived because of my *bon* (good deeds). To my amazement, the Khmer Rouge didn't take me to be killed. Instead, they fed me and let me stay home. Perhaps there was a spirit looking after me.

The Khmer Rouge forbade the practice of religion, so I could only practice Buddhism secretly and pray silently. I never stopped being a nun, and continued to shave my head and eyebrows and wear white, even when everyone else wore black. The Khmer Rouge ordered the monks to stop wearing their orange robes and to work like everyone else. If the monks refused, they were killed. The Khmer Rouge always told me to wear black. "But I like white clothes better," I replied. Then they asked me where I got the soap to wash my clothes, since they never gave us any soap, and I told them that I made it from ashes.

I was annoyed when two Khmer Rouge leaders woke me in the middle of the night to interrogate me. The young women asked me a lot of questions about my background and accused me of being the mother of a general. "You just talk because you have a mouth," I told them. "That's not true. I was self-employed as a seller. Why don't you ask me these questions in the morning?" I was not worried because I had done nothing wrong, and in my heart I was not afraid. If they wanted to kill me, I would sit quietly and pray. I would ask them to kill me with the first blow and not beat me to death. I was glad when they left and didn't hurt me.

One evening, a local woman came to me and asked if I would teach her to read and write. The only book I had was the *Kehe Piska*, a small book about Buddhism that I secretly kept hidden under my pillow. Because she wanted to read, she also learned about Buddhism from that book. One day she said she was afraid of being caught and killed, so I told her we should stop for a while.

I, myself, was not afraid of punishment because the Khmer Rouge had begun teaching people to read during the last months of 1978. I went to Nguen, the Khmer Rouge leader who had interrogated me at night, and told her that this woman wanted to learn to read, and the only book I had was about Buddhism.

Nguen asked me about Buddhism, and when I started explaining, she became interested. I told her that Buddhism was practiced in other countries in the world, not just Cambodia, and that it is based on the advice of the Buddha. There are three parts: discipline, the rule of sin and good deeds, and education of the heart. I told her about the eight precepts and how karma works: when we do good we receive good, and when we do bad we receive bad. I explained that Buddhists try to help others, observe holy days, meditate, and study the teachings of Buddha.

I told her that Buddhists have ten rules of right and wrong. Three are about the body: don't steal property, kill animals, or commit adultery. Four are about speaking: don't curse, lie, encourage arguments, or gossip. The last three are about the heart: don't be greedy, hold a grudge, or confuse right and wrong.

Nguen kept coming back to learn more about Buddhism, and she brought other Khmer Rouge leaders with her. I told them the story of the Buddha's life, how they could visit the place where the Buddha lived in India, and why people like the Buddha. When I explained the meaning of the Buddhist teachings they started to understand. "We all live together, so be generous. Just think about the present, not the past or the future. If you follow the first five precepts then no one will hate you," I advised.

"Why has Buddhism come to an end now, when it was supposed to last 5000 years?" they asked. "It will continue," I said. They argued with me and said all the temples had been demolished and the books on Buddhism were burned. "If the Khmer Rouge leaders try to destroy our culture, they will fail," I said. "Go and ask other Khmer Rouge, in a whisper, if everything was destroyed." After three days, they returned and said I was right, not all the Buddhist writings were destroyed, some were kept in the fine arts school in Phnom Penh. "Buddhism has ended for bad people, but it is still alive in good people," I told them.

At first, Nguen didn't believe in Buddhism. Then one morning, when we were talking, she saw a spirit behind me that looked like a monk; maybe that experience changed her mind. She and her comrades continued to come to my house every day for several months. At first, Nguen called me "old aunt," but later she called me "mother," and she secretly brought me eggplant and other vegetables.

During the Khmer Rouge period, I had a dream that occurred several times. A French five-star general and his Vietnamese wife came to visit me, and I invited them into my home. He liked my young daughter and carried her around. Before he left, he opened a briefcase and gave me money. Following this dream, I experienced good luck, and people gave me food, like fish or a snack. Food was the most valuable thing during the Khmer Rouge regime, more valuable than gold.

One day I heard gunfire in the distance, and someone told me that Vietnamese soldiers in a big truck had come to help us. The Khmer Rouge disappeared and the Vietnamese told us we could return home. It was difficult for me and my daughter to get back to Phnom Penh, because I couldn't walk, I could only waddle in a squatting position. I was thankful when, occasionally, the Vietnamese soldiers drove us a short distance in their truck.

Eventually, we arrived at Kilometer Nine, north of Phnom Penh, where we stayed for ten months. Vietnamese soldiers lived across the road, and I helped them as an interpreter. They gave me food and vitamins and soon I was able to walk with two canes, and then one cane. I continued to get better until I could walk without a cane. My daughter sold spices and earned three to four small cans of rice a day.

In December of 1979, I visited Wat Utara Watey, a temple that was a few kilometers down the road, and met the monks and old people who lived there. The Khmer Rouge had destroyed the statues of the Buddha, but not the temple. I obtained permission to live at Wat Utara Watey, and used the last of my gold to hire a man to build me a small hut. At first, I worked there, serving food to the monks, eating the leftovers, washing dishes, and digging up the grass in the courtyard. But later I stopped working because I was too old.

I am good friends with the other nuns at Wat Utara Watey and we help each other. Kind people give us clothes once or twice a year. People invite us into their homes to perform special ceremonies and this is how I earn the money I need for food and medicine. We chant and pray that their good deeds will go to their ancestors. Good deeds are never lost; if they don't reach the ancestors, then they come back to us; we don't need to worry about that.

My body is weak and I never feel well. I am cold, tired, and I sweat a lot. My eyes are bad, so I can't see well. I am only sixty-nine, but people ask me if I am eighty because I am often sick. Our body does not belong to us; if it did, we could stop it from becoming sick. We can be well today and sick tomorrow. This is the nature of impermanence that the Buddha spoke about.

Each day is the same—I get up early, before dawn, to pray, and sometimes I boil water and make tea. I don't study Buddhism any more, because the knowledge is in my mind. When I wake up at night and can't sleep, I just lie there and think about what I did right and wrong that day. If I remember a mistake, like gossiping, I will try to correct it in the future. When someone makes me angry, I try not to argue with them, and instead, train my heart to be more patient.

Every afternoon at five o'clock, I chant for an hour with the other nuns and monks, and then I come back to my hut to meditate and pray. First, I pray for the spirits of my father, my mother and all the relatives who have helped me, and then I pray for everyone else. I pray for peace in Cambodia and all the nations in the world, that there will be no more war.

If everyone practiced Buddhism, we would have peace, but not everyone does, so it is difficult to attain peace. War is caused by greedy people who want power or land. I feel sorry for those who were killed by the Khmer Rouge, because they died for no reason.

I feel very lucky to have my daughter living nearby and cooking for me. Her husband works in the wine factory, and she earns money by selling snacks to school children. When she runs out of money, I give her mine. I have three wonderful grandchildren who bring me a lot of joy. My mind is peaceful, because I know that if I follow Buddhism, my good deeds will go with me to my next life.

Lunch at Aun's peaceful hut consists of rice, soup with fish and vegetables, and bananas. Food has become sacred to Cambodians because most nearly starved to death during the Khmer Rouge's ruthless reign. These nuns live simple contemplative lives and are supported by donations from the community. There is a Khmer custom for old women to become nuns and spend their last years living at a Buddhist temple as they prepare for death. They serve the monks by washing clothes, cleaning, and preparing meals in order to earn merit and bring good fortune in their next life.

Aun and another Buddhist nun pay their respects at a memorial site for victims of the Khmer Rouge. Bones found in a mass grave fill the vault, and the iron bars that once pinned down prisoners at a nearby torture center now rest on the decorative lotus blossoms surrounding the crypt. Aun's husband died during the Khmer Rouge's bloody rule, along with nearly two million other Cambodians.

The Khmer Rouge destroyed hundreds of the Buddhist temples in 1975, but most have been rebuilt in the traditional Cambodian architectural style, with distinctive ornate roofs. Stupas surrounding this temple are filled with urns containing the ashes of the dead. Each year, Cambodians make a pilgrimage to the temples bringing food and incense on Ancestors Remembrance Day and the Cambodian New Year.

Serey Phal sits in quiet reflection wearing a heart-shaped locket with a photo of her deceased parents. Her personal altar consists of a bowl of incense sticks, a candle, a Buddha figure, and a fork and spoon. The silverware is most treasured because it is the only keepsake from her parents that survived Pol Pot's reign of terror.

Serey Phal

Women's Organization President

As a child, Serey Phal dreamed of becoming an ambassador when she grew up, but her hopes were destroyed in 1975 when the Khmer Rouge marched into Phnom Penh. Serey Phal was separated from her family, and sent to a labor camp at age fifteen. Her father, a teacher, was killed by the Khmer Rouge, and the following year her mother became sick and died. After the Vietnamese ousted the Khmer Rouge, Serey Phal searched for her younger brother. When she found him she vowed to support him and fund his education, as her parents would have. She found a job as a housekeeper at the Cambodia Women's Development Association, and through her hard work, intelligence, and unwavering determination over the next fourteen years, she worked her way up to president of the association. Today, Serey Phal helps poor women help themselves, through loans and skill training, and she often travels abroad to speak on behalf of Cambodian women.

I met Serey Phal at a conference on Cambodia in Washington, DC in 1993. At first glance, she appeared soft-spoken and frail, but I soon learned that she is astute and powerful. I was impressed when I saw her step out of Cambodia's cultural mold for women, a role of silence and timidity, and speak out clearly and directly about the issues facing women in Cambodia, including prostitution. Serey Phal's strength seems to come from her unwavering dedication to improving the lives of Cambodian women.

Back in Cambodia, I saw Serey Phal in action. Her life revolved around her demanding work directing the Cambodian Women's Development Association, which is one of the largest women's organizations in Cambodia. Serey Phal is a private person, and I never visited her home, but I realized that she doesn't spend much time there. She works long hours and often sleeps at the office, which she prefers because it is quieter. Although she is under a lot of pressure and must feel the stress, Serey Phal appears pleasant and calm.

Serey Phal lovingly remembers her deceased parents and feels their spiritual presence and protection. She honors her mother and father by emulating their values of compassion, service, and commitment to education.

After getting to know Serey Phal through interviews and by visiting her organization's projects, I gained so much respect for her that I asked her to administer the Cambodian Women's Scholarship Program. Serey Phal's life is testimony to the human spirit's ability to rise above tremendous difficulties and make a valuable contribution to society.

Serey Phal:

I was the oldest child, and I always had more responsibilities than my siblings. Before the Khmer Rouge came, I lived in Phnom Penh with my parents, two sisters, and brother. My mother worked as a secretary in the Ministry of Foreign Affairs, and my father was a high school math teacher in the city of Svay Rieng, which is 124 kilometers from Phnom Penh. He lived in Svay Rieng during the week, and I always looked forward to Friday night, when he came home for the weekend. I remember cooking when I was about twelve years old, because my father preferred a meal prepared by a family member, instead of our hired help.

My family was well off. I didn't know any poor families, but my parents taught me not to feel superior toward poor people and instead to feel sympathy for them and to help them. "We are all human and we all want to live in happiness," they told me, adding, "there are many reasons why people are poor." My father helped poor students in Svay Rieng by tutoring them during lunch, because when they went home after school they had to work for their parents and didn't have time to study. When the students graduated, he helped them find jobs, and if the poor students wanted to go to the University of Phnom Penh, he let them live with us and helped them buy their textbooks.

My mother was equally compassionate. One day, when I was eight years old, I saw our domestic helper Sopheah pick a fruit from our *kra khop* tree. I wanted that piece of fruit, but she didn't want to give it to me, so I started crying. When my mother came out and asked what was wrong, I told her that Sopheah hit me. My mother went back inside, called me to her and said, "Tell me the truth."

When I admitted that I wanted the fruit, my mother said that I should have asked for the fruit, and if Sopheah refused to give it to me, then I should go play with my many toys and dolls. She told me that Sopheah's parents were very poor and could not support her, and that's why she had come to work for us. "How do you think it feels to have to live with another family?" she asked me. "Put yourself in Sopheah's place." Then my mother spoke to Sopheah, who was sixteen-years-old, and told her that she was old enough to share.

The war started in 1970, when the Khmer Rouge joined forces with the Viet Cong against the Lon Nol government, and we often heard the sound of gunfire. The war impacted everyone, and my mother complained because goods had become more expensive. People from rural areas came to Phnom Penh to escape the violence, and I saw them living on the street and begging.

The schools in Svay Rieng closed in 1970, when the Americans started bombing, so my father came to work at the national insurance company in Phnom Penh. My parents were very worried, because they remembered the wars with the French and the Japanese. There was no discipline in the Lon Nol troops, so people didn't trust them and were afraid of them. My parents carefully watched over us, especially me, because bad people kidnapped girls and sold them to brothels. They drove me to Beung Trabek High School every morning, and came back to pick me up after school. I went to Beung Trabek, because it was the only high school that taught English.

As the Khmer Rouge closed in on Phnom Penh, the situation became more serious, and I heard rocket attacks almost every day. Many people were killed. School was often canceled, so my parents hired a teacher to instruct me at home. The Lon Nol government was not in control, and corruption was widespread. The university students demonstrated against the government.

The Khmer Rouge marched down our street on the morning of April 17, 1975. I was surprised when I saw the Khmer Rouge soldiers dressed in black; I had imagined they wore red clothes, as their name implied. Each soldier carried a gun, and had a hammock tied to his waist or thrown over his shoulder. I was amazed at how young the soldiers were; some weren't big enough to carry a gun. In the street, the Khmer Rouge announced that everyone needed to leave the city for three days, to "protect" us from American bombing, while the new government "rearranged" things in Phnom Penh.

My family hid in our house and dared not open the door. At noon we heard the bell at our front gate. Our house guard opened the gate and a group of seven soldiers came in and asked for lunch. As I prepared the food, they spoke to my parents calling them "father" and "mother." "Angka wants you to leave," they said. "Take only the things you need for three days and don't go far, because after three days you will return home." My father doubted them and asked, "Is it true that it will only be three days?" "I am your son. It is true," the soldier answered.

My father didn't believe them and said we should take as much as possible. My mother packed rice, dried fish, canned fish, cooking and eating utensils, gold, and jewelry, while I gathered my clothes and tied them up in a piece of cloth that I wanted to make into a dress. At about five in the afternoon another group of soldiers came to our house and ordered us to leave. We got in the car with all our things and drove out the front gate, but we didn't drive far because there were hundreds of people in the street. Our car moved at the speed of a slow walk. We slept in the street that night, on our way north to National Road Number 5.

We abandoned our car the next day because the Khmer Rouge had eliminated money, and we couldn't buy gasoline. The soldiers kept pushing us on, so we took a small boat across the Tonle Sap River. "You cannot stop here," they said when we reached the other side. "Where is our destination?" we asked. "Angka is over there," they answered, pointing down the road. I was looking everywhere for Angka and expected to see someone named Angka sitting on a hill surrounded by people. My father explained that Angka was the name of the new Khmer Rouge government.

We walked until the Khmer Rouge finally allowed us to stay in a village, and we set to work building a shelter out of small trees and thatch. Early the next morning, young people with guns came and forced those of us who came from Phnom Penh to do hard work in the rice fields. In the evening, Khmer Rouge spies hid near our huts. If they heard anyone talk about missing their "old life" or about being hungry, they reported them to Angka. We were totally controlled, and if we said something wrong, we became the enemy.

The Khmer Rouge ordered me to cut my hair, which was down to my waist. I liked it long, so I told them I could still work with long hair, but they said, "If you want to help us build the country, you must cut your hair. Women with long hair protect their husbands. Women with short hair defend our nation." I really did not understand, but I knew we weren't allowed to oppose anything. I cried when my mother cut my hair, and her tears came too.

Every night we had to attend a meeting and listen to the Khmer Rouge instruct us on how to change our way of thinking and speaking. They taught us about criticism and self-criticism, and made us report each day on what we achieved, as well as our shortcomings. Our vocabulary changed, even the word for eating. My family was educated and spoke to each other with respect. We used the word *pisar* to invite parents and guests to eat, and we used the word *nham* to call children to eat. The Khmer Rouge eliminated the politeness from our language and told us to use the word *hope* to call everyone to eat.

Three months later the Khmer Rouge moved us to Pursat Province. We walked to the river and the Khmer Rouge transported us first by boat and then by truck. Riding in the truck made me sick, and I fainted. My mother treated me by massaging my back and chest with aromatic oil, and then she rubbed my skin with the edge of a coin to release the *khyol*. The driver allowed me to sit with him in the cab of the truck. He was kind and gave me some fruit. He told me that if I didn't want to be separated from my parents, I should tell the Khmer Rouge I was a widow. "If you tell them you are single then you will be put in the youth group, and you will live far away from your parents," he warned. Later I told my parents what the driver had said.

We were taken to a rural area in Pursat Province, close to a mountain, near Kam Peng Village in Krakor District. We built another shelter, and a couple days later the Khmer Rouge came and asked us about our background, "What did you do in Phnom Penh? What is your position in your family?" I told them that my husband was a teacher, and that we had become separated when he left for school in the morning.

The Khmer Rouge didn't believe me because I was only fifteen and city girls look young, so they placed me in the youth group, separated from my parents. I felt cold, like a baby bird without feathers, but I couldn't cry because we weren't allowed to show our feelings. My sisters and brother were placed in the children's group. "All children belong to Angka," they told us.

I brought a photo album of my family and friends, and when the Khmer Rouge official found it he said, "Only capitalists have photographs. Peasants never have them. If you have them, then you are a capitalist and you cannot live in this society." I was very upset when he took away my photo album because it was very important to me, but I couldn't say a word, I could only watch.

My group had to work very hard, making fertilizer, planting rice, building a dam, and digging a canal. My father plowed rice fields, cut down the forest on the mountain, and climbed palm trees to get juice for making sugar. My family lived in the same district, so we occasionally saw each other. My mother gave each of her children a fork and a spoon to eat with. She also gave us jewelry to trade for food, but we still didn't have enough to eat, so I cooked and ate cockroaches, crickets, black scorpions, centipedes, crabs, snails, and wild grasses.

At night, I slept next to my friends in a long shelter, without mosquito netting. One night, a boy from security came and touched my leg. I woke up with a start. "What's wrong?" I asked. He said I had to come to a meeting at the commune center. "Only me?" I asked anxiously.

It was a full moon, and when we arrived I could see the people who worked for Angka, including the chief of security, standing in front of the house that served as the commune center. There were "new people," city people, sitting there. The boy who brought me reported to the chief of security, but I couldn't hear what they said because they whispered. The chief looked at me and said "No, not this one. I want Miss Phim. Take her back and get Miss Phim." Phim was one of my friends. I didn't know where she was from, but I knew her father had been killed.

I was surprised when I was allowed to return, and believed that the spirits of my parents must have followed me and taken care of me. As I got back in bed, I thought about how tired I was, and how I would have to get up early, so I went back to sleep. I never saw Phim again because all the people taken that night were killed. I don't know why. I didn't see the murders myself, but sometimes I would see a leg or an arm in the woods, left by an animal that had eaten part of a corpse.

Late in 1975, my mother told me that the Khmer Rouge had accused my father of being a general and killed him. I started to cry. I had seen relatives die, but only now did I know how much pain other people felt when they lost someone they deeply loved. I stayed with my mother for only one night because I had to report back to work the next day.

In 1976, the Khmer Rouge sent one of my sisters to Tonle Sap to catch fish, and my other sister and brother were taken to Battambang Province. My mother was moved to another district in Pursat, and I was sent to Sna Ansa Village near the city of Krakor. I felt despair because we could no longer contact each other or visit.

I didn't hear any news about my family until 1978, when a Khmer Rouge officer came and told me that my mother had gotten sick and died. At first a voice in my head said, "No, I don't believe it. My mother couldn't have died." Then I thought about how she must have been very depressed and worried because her husband was dead and she was separated from her children. I believed that caused her to become sick and die. I asked my supervisor if I could visit her grave. "Angka will take care, don't worry," he told me. "You are Angka's child, not your mother's child." I felt like an orphan and wondered when it would be my turn to die.

My thoughts turned to the future, and I worried about what would happen to my sisters and brother. I was the oldest and felt I was responsible. I considered what my mother did for my brother and sisters, and I wondered what I could do for them. When I pictured their faces, I saw the eyes of children who are longing for something, which made me weep with sadness.

Every night I prayed, "Please free us from Angka," and in 1979 the Khmer Rouge were driven out by the Vietnamese. A Cambodian soldier said to us, "We have come to help our people, and we are cooperating with the Vietnamese. You can go home now." I considered what I should do. I knew my parents were dead, but I hoped my brother and sisters were still alive and could find their way home, so I went back to Phnom Penh.

When I arrived, I tried to go to my old house, but I wasn't allowed to enter that neighborhood because it was occupied by Vietnamese troops. I happened to meet my high school math teacher, and she invited me to live with her since I had no place to go. Most of her family had been killed too. The only food we had was a ration of corn that had been donated by the Soviet Union. We didn't care for corn because in Cambodia we eat rice, but we were grateful to have food.

I waited in Phnom Penh for a few weeks and then decided to travel back to Pursat Province to search for my younger brother. I found him, but I didn't recognize him at first because he had grown. We looked at each other for a few moments, and then he asked me, "Are you Bong Thom?" "Yes," I said. Bong Thom was the nickname he used to call me by because I was his eldest sister. We hugged each other and couldn't say anything. I cried very hard because we had missed each other for a long time.

My brother was ten-years-old, too young to know where to go when the Khmer Rouge left. A family had invited him to stay with them because they didn't have enough labor, so he was tending cows and was not in school when I found him. I asked the old woman if I could take him back with me to Phnom Penh and she kindly agreed. I found a school for my brother and left him to live with my teacher while I went back to Pursat Province to look for my sisters. I asked everywhere, but I couldn't find them, so I returned to Phnom Penh with sadness.

My teacher and I looked everywhere for employment. For several months I did odd jobs in exchange for rice. I cared for a neighbor's children, washed dishes, and went to the countryside to work in the fields. When we couldn't find work, we didn't eat. Every night I worried, "How will I survive? How can I take care of my brother? I know my parents would want him to go to school." I needed steady work.

One day, when I was working in a village, I met two employees of the Women's Association. They were gathering information about how many women didn't have rice or needed clothes, so they could appeal to international humanitarian organizations for aid. The villagers told them, "This girl works really hard. She is very active and has helped everybody. Can you give her a job? We think she is educated."

The Women's Association hired me as a housekeeper for their office, and I cleaned floors, washed windows, and boiled drinking water. I felt very grateful to have regular employment. Step by step they trained me, and when I learned to type, I became a part-time secretary and cut back my housekeeping duties.

The staff of the Women's Association were former housewives, and I felt my ability was equal to theirs. "Why can't I write the documents

I am typing?" I asked myself, and decided to study them so one day I could write them. I asked questions and the staff taught me. In the meantime, I was promoted to full-time secretary. On the days when I didn't have work to do in the Women's Association office, I asked if I could accompany the staff to the villages. I learned how the Women's Association helped widows whose living conditions were very low.

In 1982, the First Women's Association Congress was held, and to my delight, I was elected to the Women's Committee as a permanent member, responsible for research. I gathered data from villages, wrote reports, and produced educational materials. Two years later, I was appointed editor-in-chief of the Women's Association magazine and had the opportunity to study journalism for four months in Phnom Penh and for three months in East Germany. The Women's Association was part of the Cambodian government, and it received support from other communist countries.

One Sunday in 1986, a woman I knew came to my house and asked what my name used to be. "It hasn't changed," I answered. Then she asked if I used to have a nickname. "My mother called me Serey Thom (big girl) because I was the oldest," I told her. "How many sisters did you have?" she inquired. "Two, but I think they died," I replied. "What are their names?" she asked. "Milley and Tevy," I answered.

Then she gave me a letter. My hand was shaking and tears came to my eyes as I read it, because I recognized the letter. It was from my sisters. They listed the names of all our family members and said they lived in Bowell Village in Battambang Province. They had heard their older sister was still alive, but they couldn't find her in Phnom Penh, so if anyone knew her, could they please give her this letter.

My sisters had a friend in Phnom Penh who felt sorry that our family had been separated for so many years. She wanted to help, and if she couldn't find someone who knew me, she was going to publish that letter in the newspaper.

With great joy I immediately left for Bowell to see my sisters. They told me that when the Khmer Rouge regime ended, a family had taken care of them. Then they both married and had children. Tevy was now divorced, so I brought her and her two daughters to live with me and our brother in Phnom Penh. I bought her a stall in the market so she could work selling groceries in the day, and go to school at night. Tevy finished her studies in 1990 and married a man who worked at the plastics factory.

Milley decided to remain in Bowell, near her husband's family, even though the security was very bad. The Khmer Rouge shelled the city, and school was often closed, so she sent two of her sons to live with me in Phnom Penh and attend school here. My brother continued his education, all the way through medical school.

The fork and spoon my mother gave me when we were separated by the Khmer Rouge are all I have left from my parents. They are worth so much to me; I wouldn't sell them for $5,000. I keep them in a special place, next to my Buddha statue on my altar at home. Every night I light the candle and incense and pray to my parents to express thanks to them and ask them to look after our family. When I travel abroad, I take the fork and spoon with me. My parents are with me all the time. They are the real Jesus or Buddha who looks after me.

My brother and sisters lost their spoons and forks. "I really do not understand why you could not keep them," I said to them. My brother replied with a smile, "My dear sister, don't you know that everyone uses a spoon to put food in their mouths and the mother uses a spoon to feed her children? You are the eldest sister in our family, and when we lost our parents you become the second parent. The souls of our parents wanted you to keep the spoon because you represent the parent who feeds the children. If all of us still had spoons, who would be the parent? That's your responsibility and you needed to know that."

In 1988, at the Second Women's Association Congress, I was elected vice-president and became responsible for the Women and Development Program. I set up programs in villages, such as income generation projects, health education, literacy, and child care. I also contacted international organizations to request financial support.

After the national election in May 1993, we reorganized the Women's Association as a non-governmental organization and named it the Cambodian Women's Development Association. I was elected president. Our goal is to empower women by building self-reliance and self-sufficiency. We have vocational training and credit programs, we help high school graduates find jobs, and we have an HIV/AIDS education program that is directed to people in villages and brothels. We are funded by the United Nations and foreign organizations, and we currently have 16 staff members, plus 374 volunteers in the villages.

I often think about how to improve the status of Cambodian women. Women's issues are not recognized since we don't have women represented in our government. Men do not clearly comprehend women's problems because they are not in the same situation as we are. If we want to help women participate more in government and decision making, we need to think about women's education as part of the long-term plan because at the university level only ten percent of the students are women.

Education alone is not empowering because Cambodian women feel scared and hesitant, so we must encourage them and build their self-confidence. Cambodian men should learn to value and respect women, and the school curriculum ought to be changed to convey these concepts. We also must address the underlying difficulties that keep girls from attending school, such as poverty.

When I travel to other countries for meetings, I am often asked about the Khmer Rouge. I tell people that the Khmer Rouge are still the Khmer Rouge. If they were in control they would kill our people again because they have not changed their way of thinking. You cannot make a dog's tail straight. All the people in Cambodia lost relatives, and I think the Khmer Rouge should be punished. My father died, and I know who killed him. I want to know what happened in the minds of the Khmer Rouge that made them murder people. Hitler was crazy, but Pol Pot was worse. He destroyed Cambodian society and made us live like animals. It was hell.

While living under the Khmer Rouge, I thought to myself, "We won't stay in this situation forever. Cambodia is just one country and people in the rest of the world will do something to help us." I wanted to survive to see that change, to see what the future would look like, and to see what would happen to the Cambodian people. Cambodians were always gentle, soft, and faithful, but the opposite qualities appeared during the Khmer Rouge period. I expected the situation would get better, and that hope made me struggle to survive.

Now I am thirty-five years old, and I haven't married yet. In the future I may, but right now I don't have time. After work, I still work. Men in Cambodia are changing, but most want their wives to have time to comfort them. Even if their wives don't cook, they want them to arrange the food and sit with them at dinner. If I married a man who didn't have the same values and goals as I do, how could we stay together? I find that women support each other, and the women in our projects give me strength to work.

My life is similar to the lives of women around the world. I face the same problems as women in other developing countries. Cambodians have many difficulties because our country is one of the poorest. I have decided to work hard and sacrifice, so that the next generation can have a better life. When I talk to women of different nationalities, they all say, "We want to live in peace. We want our children to live in happiness." This is the common wish of women all over the world.

When I was a child, people used to ask me what I wanted to do when I grew up. "I want to be an ambassador," I answered. But the Khmer Rouge shattered my dream, and I had to start my life over in 1979. Now, my work includes explaining the problems of Cambodian women to women in other parts of the world, and I bring back to Cambodia the experiences of women from other countries. I have become an ambassador of women.

It is bath time at this day care center established for the children of mothers who are enrolled in vocational training courses. Serey Phal would like to help more Cambodian women learn income-producing skills so they can improve their living conditions. There are very few day care centers in urban areas and even fewer in Cambodia's rural areas. Working mothers must depend on older children and extended family to provide child care.

Serey Phal's organization provides credit to poor women which helps lift them out of poverty with dignity and provide better lives for their children. This mother received a $20 loan which she used to open a small food stand. With her meager income she is now able to improve her children's nutrition, send them to school, and buy medicine when necessary. UNICEF recently provided low-interest loans which averaged $50 to over 10,000 women. The women successfully used the funds to start income-generation projects, and overall repayment was ninety-six percent.

This ethnic Cham student enthusiastically writes her lessons in beautiful Khmer script. Literacy classes for women are offered by Serey Phal's Cambodian Women's Development Association because approximately half of the women in Cambodia are illiterate. Only ten to twenty percent of the students in higher education at the university and technical schools are women.

A child prostitute stands in the doorway of a bedroom at the brothel. An empty chair is reflected in the mirror. What would her life have been like if poverty hadn't forced her into this humiliating, soul-killing work?

Bopha ❧ Prostitute

Bopha* was only six years old when the Khmer Rouge took over Cambodia, but she was still put to work. One day, as she was tending cows, she peered through the bamboo trees and witnessed the Khmer Rouge's secret bloody killings. After the Khmer Rouge regime ended, Bopha helped around the house because her farming family was too poor to send her to school. As a young adult she wanted to start earning money, but it was not easy to find work. Bopha accepted a job as a housekeeper in Phnom Penh, but when she arrived she was deceived, raped, and abandoned. Poverty, desperation, and despair forced Bopha to turn to prostitution for employment.

Early one sunny morning I was traveling to a rural village with Indra Devi, a women's organization, to observe their AIDS education program. I asked if they ever work with prostitutes. They said they do and offered to take me to a sex-industry-based village where they had given educational programs.

We drove to the center of the village where market women were selling vegetables and fish. I was surprised to see how roughly people treated each other. After we explained to the mayor that I wanted to interview a sex worker, he took us to a hair salon where we met the owner and several of her "girls." As we entered, one of the young women grabbed the mayor's crotch and they both laughed. Everyone was polite toward us, and one of the girls agreed to an interview.

When we returned for the appointment a few days later, we were told that the young woman had changed her mind. The mayor, trying to be helpful, took us to a restaurant/brothel along the river where several young women and a man wearing lipstick were hanging out. The mayor asked if anyone was willing to be interviewed, but no one volunteered. I thought we would have to give up, but then my translator Kosal launched into an explanation as to how this interview would help people understand more about prostitution and help stop the exploitation of women. At that point, Bopha, a quiet, pretty girl stepped forward and said she was willing. She said she had been tricked into pros-

* Bopha asked that her identity be concealed, so her name has been changed and she is not shown in the photos.

151

titution and she wanted other women to know so they could avoid the same trap.

I grew fond of Bopha, a victim of violence and poverty who has maintained her goodwill. During our conversations I learned that she wanted to become a seamstress, so I offered to support her in a vocational training program. In the end, she chose not to pursue the opportunity. I respect her courage and willingness to share her life story, even though she was ashamed of it, because she hoped it would help others.

Bopha:

I was born in Kompong Cham Province, near the rubber plantation where my parents worked. In 1975, when I was six, the Khmer Rouge took me and my two older brothers away from our parents and put us in a children's work group. Old women looked after us, and I saw my parents only once or twice a month. I had to work all day, carrying cow manure or cutting leaves for fertilizer. At the end of the day, I slept with the other children and was bitten by lots of mosquitoes. Once I became very sick with a high fever, and I ran away from the nurse because I didn't want to get an injection.

I ate porridge that was very watery because there wasn't enough rice, and I became so skinny that my head was larger than my body. I searched for snails and crabs to eat. I asked the cook for salt, and when she didn't give it to me, I stole it. I had one friend, Thea, who was two years older than I, and we stole sweet potatoes together.

My brother Vuthy's job was to look after the chickens, and one day I stole some eggs, but I got caught. That night the Khmer Rouge officials took me and Vuthy to a big meeting and told everyone about our error. They said they were going to dig a hole just big enough for the two of us because they wanted to make an example of us.

My grandmother begged them not to kill us. "Your grandchildren were naughty," the Khmer Rouge leader said. "Take me instead," pleaded my grandmother. "This time I'll have mercy on you, but next time you must train them better," the leader said. The next day they didn't give us any food, so we ate tangerine seeds and a few bites of my grandmother's rice ration. Our parents brought us food at night, and after three days the Khmer Rouge started giving us half a ration of rice.

After I finished work one morning, I walked into the communal dining room and saw a big bowl of cooked rice sitting on a long table. I climbed up on the bench and served myself two plates of rice because one plate was not enough. I accidentally dropped one of the plates, and it made a noise when it hit the ground. The cook came out and saw me.

I ran away and hid at my grandmother's house, but the cook came there and asked where I was. My grandmother told her that I went to look after the cows and asked, "Is anything wrong?" The cook told her that I tried to steal some rice and said, "Are you pretending not to know?" The cook instructed my grandmother to send me to the food storage building at four that afternoon. I told my brother Vuthy what I had done. He scolded me and asked me why I took the rice. "Because I was very hungry," I said.

I decided I had better go meet the cook, and on my way I met a woman. I told her what had happened and begged her to help me. She came with me and asked the cook to have pity on me and to forgive my mistake one more time because I was young and my parents were far away.

"It would be better if the parents were here, so we could take the whole family to be killed," the cook replied. The woman asked the cook to not be so cruel. But the cook said, "What would you think if I recently stole eggs and soon after I stole some rice? Next time I might steal something bigger, from the food storage building. Maybe this girl will never learn her lesson." The woman said, "Last time her grandmother begged to let her go, and this time I do." The woman looked at me and instructed me not to steal anything again. I promised I wouldn't and told her that I had learned my lesson. The cook let me go home.

My father was on good terms with one of the Khmer Rouge leaders, which made our village leader jealous and he hated my father. My father worried that the village leader might make trouble for me and my brothers. He advised us to switch to the formal language the Khmer Rouge had instructed us to use and call him *oue*, which was the formal word for father, so we wouldn't be accused of disobeying orders.

One of my cousins missed his parents very much, and he went home without getting permission. The Khmer Rouge became angry with him, and at first they punished him by not giving him enough food. Later they took him away and killed him.

The Cham family who used to live next door to my family loved me and often gave me snacks. One day, when I was tending the cows, I looked through the bamboo trees and saw that family and five other Cham families with their hands tied behind their backs. I stood frozen and watched with horror as the Khmer Rouge soldiers took the children by their feet and smashed their heads against the side of the well. Then the Khmer Rouge hit the older people on the back of the head with a hoe and pushed them into a big hole. Some people weren't dead, but they were still pushed into the hole, and corpses were piled on top of them.

It was horrible to see all that blood flowing out of people's heads and down their bodies. I was afraid that the same thing would happen to me, and I became terrified of doing something wrong. When I told my parents what I had seen they said I must not tell anyone because it is dangerous when someone knows these things.

When I realized that one of the killers was the cook's husband, I became afraid of going to the communal dining area. I worried about being taken to be killed, so I would often escape, making sure that my group leader didn't know, and secretly eat with my father. My father climbed palm trees and made palm sugar about three kilometers from the village, near a forest. He lived there and cooked his own rice.

One night I stayed over and slept in the hut with my father and a guard. The next morning my father told me that a tiger had come at night, but it didn't get the cows because the dogs scared it off. He said it was too dangerous for me to spend the night there.

At the end of 1978, a new Khmer Rouge leader came from Battambang Province, and he started killing the Cham people. I saw a Cham family run and hide in the rice field in front of my house, and I watched as the Khmer Rouge came searching for them and arrested them. The Khmer Rouge tied the Cham family's arms behind their backs, took them to the communal kitchen and tried to make them eat pork. The Chams refused to eat pork because of their religion, and when the Khmer Rouge forced them to, they vomited. Then the Khmer Rouge took them away to be killed. I didn't dare follow, but the next day I saw a new grave near the bamboo trees.

The Khmer Rouge killed more and more people. My parents and I were walking past Phnom Bros Phnom Srey (Mountain of Men and Women), when the Khmer Rouge drove up with a truck full of people to be killed. I could see that a big hole for burying had already been dug. I wanted to watch, but my mother told me not to because I might have bad dreams, so I held her tightly and didn't look. I was already having nightmares of the bloody killings I witnessed. The awful scenes loomed before my eyes, even after I woke up.

Just before the Vietnamese came in 1979, the new Khmer Rouge leaders killed the old Khmer Rouge leader who was a friend of my father's. My father was afraid they would kill him, too, so he hid in a house until the Vietnamese came and the Khmer Rouge left.

We were free, so I walked home with my brother Vuthy. At first, the new government made my family grow rice in cooperation with our neighbors. A couple of years later they divided up the land and gave a plot to each family. The government determined how many members in the family were "first strength," adults and teenagers, and how many were "second strength," children and old people. The land was allocated according to the strength in each family. My family had only a small field, and we weren't able to grow enough rice to feed us the whole year, so my parents had to sell a little gold and buy rice when we ran out.

My brother Vuthy went to live with my grandparents because they were alone, while I stayed with my parents and helped farm. I planted rice and green beans, and I carried water on my shoulder from the well. I tended a neighbor's cows, and was given a new calf as payment. We were happiest at harvest time, when we had enough rice to eat and didn't need to borrow.

When I started attending school, I changed my age from ten to six years old, so I could begin in first grade. I went to school for four years, but my mind wasn't clear and I couldn't concentrate because I worried about my parents' situation at home. When I came home from school I cooked lunch, but sometimes, during the rainy season before the harvest was ready, we didn't have rice, and then I came home and cried. Our living conditions continued to worsen, and we didn't have enough money to keep me in school, which made my parents feel badly.

My family was at home one very dark night when we heard a man come to the door and ask for a can of rice. "Why do you come at night?" my father asked without opening the door. "Why are you so mean?" the man demanded. My mother cautioned my father not to open the door. The man said, "Open it or I will shoot." When my father opened the door a man whose face was hidden by a *kramar* (scarf) entered and pointed a gun at my parents. I quickly hid under the bed, and my parents called out for help. The man ordered them to be quiet, and then he took all our gold and everything valuable.

From that point on my family was extremely poor, and our life continued with a lot of difficulty. We had to borrow oxen to plow our land, and we paid in rice, so our harvest wasn't nearly enough to feed us for a year. We borrowed from others, and each year we owed more and more.

My brother Vuthy had become a fisherman in the Mekong River in Kratie Province, and he invited me to live with his family, so I went there to help. His wife became jealous and said Vuthy loved me more than her, so I had to go back to live with my parents. My parents were protective of me and didn't want me to work outside the home, even though I was twenty-three years old. But I wanted to earn money, so I sold sugar cane and fruit in the village.

In 1980, my father arranged a wedding for my older brother Sotha, but shortly after they were married, Sotha became angry with his wife and left her to join the army. Eight years later, he returned home, tired of being a soldier, and remarried. His new wife grew flowers for a living, and she had relatives in the United States who occasionally sent them money. Sotha earned money by smuggling goods to and from Vietnam. Half of what he brought in was legal, and he paid a bribe to bring in the rest. I went to live with him, and he taught me how to smuggle.

One morning I took the bus from Ratanakin Province to Vietnam with four cases of cigarettes, worth about $900. I hid the cigarettes under a plastic sheet on the bus. When we reached the border of Vietnam, an official boarded the bus and inspected everything. When he found my cigarettes, he confiscated them. I begged him to let me pass with the cigarettes, but he wouldn't agree, so I tried to give him $450, but he wouldn't take it. I had been smuggling for about two months, and the other border officials had always taken a bribe, but this was a new official. I went home and told Sotha what had happened. He became furious and told my father.

I went back home to live with my parents, but my father wouldn't speak to me because I lost all that money. He would not say one word to me which made me feel really bad. Then a lady, a distant relative, said she could help me. She said that since I was having a lot of problems, I could go live with her aunt who was a teacher in Phnom Penh and needed help with cooking and washing. I told her that I needed to think about it. She asked me many times and when I said I didn't have the money to get to the city, she offered to pay my way. I thought she was a person I could trust because she was educated, so I decided to go.

That night I prepared two outfits to take with me. It was still dark when I quietly slipped out of the house the next morning. I didn't tell my parents because I knew they wouldn't have agreed to let me go. I met the lady, and we walked three kilometers, reaching the main road as the sun came up. Then we took a motorbike cart to the next district where we waited three days for a truck heading toward Phnom Penh, but none ever came. We were afraid my parents would find us, so we took a cart a little further and we met a truck carrying bananas. The driver agreed to give us a ride to Phnom Penh.

While we were waiting for the truck to leave, a car pulled up. I thought the lady I was with knew the two men in the car because she went over and spoke to them, but I didn't hear what she said. We rode in the banana truck, and the car followed us to the ferry dock at Pray Kadam Village. Before we crossed the river, the men in the car offered to take us to Phnom Penh and the lady accepted. They asked me where I lived and how I dared travel alone. I told them I was on an adventure and hoped to get a job in the city. The men said they could help me get a job and asked what kind of work I wanted. Did I want to do construction? I told them I would take any job.

When we reached Chloy Changval bridge, on the north side of Phnom Penh, I was puzzled and disappointed when the lady said she couldn't remember how to get to her aunt's house. I said I had a cousin who lived in the city, and the men offered to take me there, but I didn't know the address. Then the men invited us to come with them to visit their aunt.

First, they took me to Tol Kok, where the brothels were, and that's when I became afraid of those men. After they got out of the car, I leaned over and whispered to the lady that I was worried that they might try to sell me to a brothel. She didn't answer, and instead went inside with the men to have a soft drink. I stayed in the car. The men called to me to join them, and then the shop owner called me. Even the policeman standing in front of the building asked me to come in.

I wanted to escape, but I wasn't sure how to open the car door. When I finally got it open, I walked down the street, away from the two men. I met an old woman and asked her if this was the place where they buy and sell girls. She answered by offering me a job as a prostitute, but she used slang, so I wasn't sure what she meant.

After the men finished their drinks, they called me back to the car and said, "Let's go to our aunt's." I asked them to take me to the central market area, so I could look for my cousin. We drove around, but I didn't see her, so we left to go to their aunt's, down Highway 1. Along the way, the men stopped at a market and bought soap and snacks. They said they would buy clothes for me tomorrow.

They took us to a restaurant on the river and bought us a lot to eat. I wondered why they were so generous. They told me that this restaurant was their aunt's house and there were two rooms for sleeping. They handed me the soap and suggested that I bathe before going to bed. They showed me the bedroom and said it wasn't necessary to lock the door.

After more eating and drinking, one of the men knocked on my door. I was afraid and didn't want to open it. He came in, and asked if I ever had a husband or a man sleep with me. I told him no. Then he asked me to be his wife. I refused, but he proceeded to lock the door and arrange the mosquito net over the bed. I told him I wanted to sleep outside, but he wouldn't let me leave.

Then he raped me.

I cried and he tried to console me, saying that he would support me, but I continued to cry. He left the room to drink more, and I heard him talking with his friend. He came back and told me to go to sleep and not to worry. He promised to support me and said he would take me to live in the city tomorrow.

I went to the toilet and stayed there and cried. I thought about how that man deceived me, the consequences of losing my virginity, and how I couldn't face my parents. I was full of regret because when I was living with my brother, a man had asked me to marry him, but I refused because he was richer than me, and I was afraid he would look down on me. Now I wished I had agreed.

The man found me in the toilet and called to me to come out. The lady, who was sleeping with the other man, came over and said, "Why are you hiding? Everyone is looking for you." "Don't worry about me," I told her, "I can get home." The man told me to come back into the bedroom. I went in, sat on the edge of the bed, and cried. He pretended to sleep, and then he tried to pull me to him, but I pulled away, still crying. He got up and said that he and his friend were going out for a while. "Look after my suitcase. I will be back soon," he told me. "Lock the door and get some sleep."

The men came back at about nine the next morning, and the lady asked them why they hadn't come back at night. They claimed they had a flat tire. They hurriedly picked up the suitcase and promised to come back at one in the afternoon to pick me up. When I inquired why I couldn't go with them right then, the man said I could come, but that he was going take me to live at a bar. I said no because I figured he wanted to sell me to a brothel.

The two men left, and I never saw them again. I didn't have any money, I didn't know the city, and I had no place to go. I learned that this house wasn't their aunt's, and they had just rented those rooms from the restaurant owner. I asked the owner of the restaurant for a job, and he put me to work washing dishes, doing laundry, and serving food. Sometimes a kind customer would leave me a tip. The lady who brought me there stayed for a few weeks and worked as a prostitute. One day she left without telling me. At the end of the month, I asked the owner for my salary, but he said he wasn't going to pay me because the tips were enough. I was upset, because I needed my salary to get home.

I left that awful place, walked down the road, and asked to work at another restaurant. Now I am a waitress and a prostitute because it is the only way I can support myself. I pay $10 per month for my room and each customer pays me about $8. I usually have one customer a week. I had saved about $300, but then I got malaria and had to spend $100 for a doctor's visit and medication.

I am afraid of becoming sick with a fever, or getting pregnant, or contracting a sexual disease. As a prostitute, I need an injection to prevent diseases, like syphilis. I have heard of AIDS, but I don't know much about it. What are the symptoms? One morning I woke up feeling nauseous and realized I was pregnant. I asked my friend, another prostitute, to accompany me to the clinic in Phnom Penh to have an abortion. I felt anxious when we went, but I was OK afterward.

I have been here two years and I haven't gone home yet. My parents don't know where I am. I worry about my family, but I am afraid of seeing them. What would I say? I am saving money for them, and if I save enough I will go home at New Year's and ask for their forgiveness for being a prostitute. I will tell them that I made a big mistake. Then I will help my parents farm rice, and I will get a job.

I want to live alone and don't intend to marry or have children. I am full of sorrow because I was deceived and violated by a man. I have a niece and nephew. Maybe they will help me when I am old, but I can't count on that.

I regret becoming a prostitute. I know it's not a good thing, but now I need to close my eyes, go back home, and start a new life. I'd like to be a seamstress, and I want to save enough money to start a business. When I see students walking to school, I regret not having an education and wish I could have stayed in school.

I have one friend here. She works as a prostitute. She came here with a broken heart when her parents wouldn't allow her to marry the man she loved. Many of the women who work here come from very poor living conditions and this is the only way they can earn money to feed their children. I am angry at the Khmer Rouge and the thief for making my family so poor, which is why I ended up here.

I don't like being a prostitute. No one loves this job. People look down on me and talk about me behind my back. I know this is a bad job, but I am locked into it because it's the only way I can earn money. I want to save enough to pay back the $900 I lost, so my father will speak to me. I heard that prostitution is illegal in Phnom Penh. If the police came here, I would disappear because I don't want to be on TV or radio. I don't want anyone to know what my job is, since I plan to go back home. I hope my story will help the younger generation learn about the tricks of men. It is difficult to be a woman in Cambodia.

Tending cows is a job frequently assigned to children. Today Bopha is plagued by nightmares of the Khmer Rouge's bloody killings she secretly witnessed over twenty-five years ago as she stood tending cows behind a grove of bamboo trees. Many Cambodians suffer from depression, recurring nightmares, anxieties, and fears resulting from their experiences under Pol Pot. Cambodian society as a whole suffers from post-traumatic stress disorder, and there are practically no resources available, such as counselors or clinics, to help people cope with the emotional scars from the past.

Most Cambodians live on the edge of poverty, and just one crisis, like a flood or theft, can push them into destitution, which is what happened to Bopha's family. Floods like this one destroy the rice crop, leaving farm families hungry and desperately seeking another means of survival. In a survey of 300 prostitutes who came to Phnom Penh from rural areas, most of the women said poverty forced them to leave their homes because they had no way to earn an income. Over half of the women did not come to be sex workers, but were tricked or sold to the brothel.

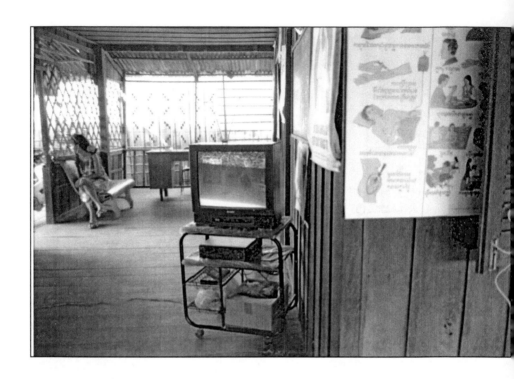

A prostitute sits in a health clinic near the brothels looking out to the street as she waits for nightfall. The TV video promotes AIDS prevention as do the posters on the walls. The UN mission brought 22,000 troops into Cambodia, primarily men, which resulted in the number of prostitutes rising from 6,000 to 30,000. In the year 2000 approximately forty-two percent of Cambodia's sex-workers were HIV positive. AIDS is spreading more rapidly in Cambodia than in any other Asian nation.

SOUL SURVIVORS

A woman peers into the empty shell of the Catholic church in Chanthan's village, as the drawing of a soldier looks over her shoulder. Over the last forty-five years many soldiers have come through this village to massacre the ethnic Vietnamese people living there. Since the decline of the Angkor Empire hundreds of years ago, the Khmer have resented the fact that Vietnam took over Cambodia's former territory (now South Vietnam) and fear further encroachment by Vietnam.

Chanthan ❧
Ethnic Vietnamese Farmer

Chanthan's* ethnic Vietnamese background has subjected her to violence throughout her life due to Cambodia's long-standing hatred of Vietnam. In 1954, she hid in her Catholic parish to avoid Khmer soldiers who were raping ethnic Vietnamese girls in her village. Afterward, she married a Khmer man for protection. Chanthan was one of the few members of her extended family to escape the massacre of ethnic Vietnamese by Lon Nol soldiers in 1970. Three years later, she survived the American bombing that destroyed her village. Chanthan was forty-one years old in 1973 when the Khmer Rouge took over. Her friendships with the local villagers protected her, but she suffered a great loss when her only child disappeared. Today, Chanthan has a loving husband and is financially secure, but she still lives in fear because Cambodians with Vietnamese ethnicity are still targets of violence.

We drove past beautiful pastoral scenery, rice fields, and children tending cows, on our way to visit Chanthan. As we pulled up to her attractive wooden house on stilts, I noticed bomb craters beyond her house. I kicked off my sandals and walked up the steep narrow plank into her home.

Chanthan greeted us, kindly offered us soft drinks bought for the occasion and showed us her simple house. The front room had several beds, and the back room was a kitchen. She took us into a storage room and pointed out her hidden altar, which had a picture of Jesus and a candle. Catholicism is a central part of Chanthan's life, but she is careful to conceal it, along with her Vietnamese ethnicity. Most Cambodians lived in terror for four years during the Khmer Rouge regime, but for Chanthan it has been a lifetime of terror.

Although many Cambodians acknowledge that they are grateful to the Vietnamese for ousting the Khmer Rouge, they also believe it was part of Vietnam's plan to control Cambodia. Today, Cambodians feel

---

* Since the ethnic Vietnamese are still harassed, I have protected Chanthan by changing her name and not including her photo.

their national sovereignty is threatened by Vietnam and this fear is translated into racism and violence toward all ethnic Vietnamese people.

My translator for this interview was a Vietnamese friend of Chanthan's, so Chanthan felt at ease and spoke openly with me about her life. I found her to be a hardy woman, with good business sense and a generous heart. As we sat on her porch, a Khmer neighbor came by and asked permission to use her driveway for his ox cart of vegetables. When Chanthan readily consented, he gave her a *kramar* full of cucumbers in appreciation. Kindness helps break down ethnic prejudices, and Chanthan's friendships have been key to her survival.

Chanthan:

My ancestors have lived in Cambodia for many generations. We speak Vietnamese and keep our traditions, like celebrating Tet, the Vietnamese New Year. My mother was born to Vietnamese-Chinese parents, along the Mekong River, and my father had Vietnamese-Khmer parents who fished the Tonle Sap River. My family owned six boats, and we earned a good income from fishing.

I became engaged to be married at age nineteen, but the Catholic priest at my parish didn't think it was a good match because I was born in the year of the monkey and my fiancé was born in the year of the tiger, so I broke our engagement. The next man who proposed to me was a Viet Minh soldier from Vietnam. He came to our village in 1951 and gave us propaganda about Vietnam's war of independence from the French. When he asked me to marry him, I refused. I didn't tell him that I sympathized with the French because they were Catholic. A month later, I heard he had been shot by the French.

The French and Khmer soldiers hated the ethnic Vietnamese who lived in Cambodia because they thought we supported the Viet Minh. One day they came to our village, raped girls, and arrested many people, including two of my brothers, and took them as prisoners to Mount Sam in south Vietnam. I was scared because if the French soldiers found out that I had spoken with a Viet Minh soldier, they would have shot me. My brother and I took refuge in our Catholic parish where the priest hid us for one week in a cramped, dark, secret room.

It wasn't safe to return home, so I hid in the home of a wealthy Chinese-Khmer family. My mother suggested that I marry the son in that family, even though he was sixteen years older than me, because having a Khmer husband would offer me some protection. He was a stern but kind person. I took my mother's advice and married him for my personal security. I quickly learned to speak Khmer, so I could talk with my new husband.

Shortly after we were married, we built our own house on land that we bought from the Catholic church. We lived in a village with about 200 Vietnamese Catholic families. I enjoyed going to mass every day and singing in the choir. My husband didn't like Catholicism, but he was very fond of my Catholic family and neighbors. We earned our living by selling firewood, vegetables, and pigs. We planted *um peal tuc* trees for firewood and we grew vegetables on our five acres, mostly corn and string beans.

I was very happy in 1960 when I discovered I was pregnant. I was twenty-eight years old and had dearly wanted children ever since I married. The midwife from a neighboring village and many of my relatives came to help when my son Seng was born. My husband lit incense and prayed for peace and good fortune. We were full of joy.

About that time, we started hearing people talk about the Khmer Rouge. The royal government issued a warning against supporting the Khmer Rouge and posted a photograph showing thirty captured Khmer Rouge being executed in Kompong Speu.

After the king was overthrown in 1970, General Lon Nol sided with the United States in the Vietnam War. One day, the Lon Nol soldiers came to our village and accused us of supporting the communist Viet Cong from North Vietnam. They arrested seventy-three ethnic Vietnamese people in our village, took them behind the church and shot them. We were horrified. I cried in anguish because they were my relatives, mostly nieces and nephews. We did not support the Viet Cong; we had never even seen them. They lived in the forest, far away from our village. As we were mourning and burying the dead, the Lon Nol soldiers murdered nine more people.

Our parish priest Father Thai asked the bishop in Phnom Penh for a truck to help the surviving people in our village flee to South Vietnam. Within two weeks almost everyone had left, including my eight brothers and sisters and their families. Before he moved to Vietnam, Father Thai buried the chalice and ten bottles of wine under the altar. He asked me to come to Vietnam, but I told him I would stay with my husband.

My niece and nephew urged me to change my Vietnamese name, so I took my Khmer grandfather's name. Each day I worried that the Lon Nol soldiers would notice that I looked Vietnamese or would hear my Vietnamese accent. Many government officials fled Cambodia with their Vietnamese wives, but General Lon Nol wanted them to come back to help the country, so he announced that Vietnamese who married Khmer before 1970 were allowed to stay. This policy included me, which made me feel a little better.

The Khmer have hated the Vietnamese for hundreds of years, and they call us *yun*, which is a bad name. They have always wanted to take back the southern provinces of Vietnam, that once belonged to Cambodia. The Lon Nol regime encouraged hatred of the Vietnamese by putting posters on street corners in Phnom Penh with a picture of a Vietnamese ruler setting his cooking pot on the heads of three Khmer he had buried alive.

My mother's health was not good, so she stayed with me in Cambodia. I grieved her death at the end of 1971. Our village did not have a priest because Father Thai had fled to Vietnam, so I went to Phnom Penh to ask the Catholic church for her last anointment and sacrament. I was grateful to a Buddhist monk who helped me take her coffin to the cemetery.

Early in 1973, there was fighting near our village, and the Khmer Rouge soldiers defeated the Lon Nol troops. March 19, 1973 was a day of horror because the Americans started bombing our village. We were terrified and ran for cover in ditches and forests as the explosions destroyed the temple, houses, and roads. The B-52 bombers, and another plane called Salap Kat, flew together in a formation of four over our village and each plane dropped four bombs. One bomb exploded right behind my house and another hit my mother's tomb.

The American bombing continued for two years, and the land became covered with bomb craters. The Americans wanted to kill the Viet Cong, but innocent people suffered, and many people I knew died. When I thought about Americans, I thought of death.

Shortly after the bombing started, the Khmer Rouge ordered us to come with them for three days, but it turned out to be nearly three years. All of the people in our village were relocated to the "liberated" zone at Kotom, close to the Vietnamese border. My husband, son, and I walked through the forest pulling a cart filled with our clothes, mosquito nets, cookware, and rice. I brought my rosary and our savings of 100,000 riels.

In Kotom, we bought a boat and lived on a lake near the Bassac River where we made *prahok* (fish paste) for a living. The poor people built huts to live in. The Khmer Rouge weren't very strict and life was fairly easy for us, except for the bombing. American B-52's dropped big bombs in the forest and small bombs along the road, and we often had to run for our lives.

The Khmer Rouge took over Phnom Penh in April 1975, and we thought it would be safe for us to return home to our village. We asked the local authorities for permission and were disappointed when they refused. In September, we quietly escaped because the Khmer Rouge had begun killing the ethnic Vietnamese and anyone else with light skin. We traveled at night, rowing our boat up the flooded backwaters of the Mekong.

When we reached our village, we found it overgrown and saw that everything had been destroyed, including homes and the Catholic church. I cried bitterly when I saw that my house had been dismantled. The people evacuated from Phnom Penh had used the materials to build huts or trade for rice. There was a family living on our house site, so we settled in behind them and made a shelter using the roof off our boat. The next week, a Khmer Rouge official borrowed our boat, and later he told us that he had lost it.

I worried about my relatives in Vietnam because the Khmer Rouge told us that the people there were very hungry and only had rice hulls to eat. I had no way of contacting my family and finding out how they were. I feared that they had starved to death.

The Khmer Rouge gave us a tiny ration of rice each day, and those of us who worked in the fields also received three spoonfuls of corn. We were forced to work hard, planting corn and potatoes. My husband had to carry human feces to the fields for fertilizer, and when he came home at night, I couldn't stand to be near to him because the odor was so bad. The road was covered with garbage and manure, and the whole village smelled terrible.

The Khmer Rouge investigated me thoroughly and asked the other villagers about my ethnic background. Everyone in the village knew me before the Khmer Rouge arrived, and they loved me, so they lied to protect me and told the Khmer Rouge authorities that I was half Chinese and half Khmer. I became even more frightened in 1976, when the Khmer Rouge started killing everyone with light skin.

My son Seng was sixteen years old when the Khmer Rouge took him to work with the other youth, several kilometers away, digging a rice field and crushing stone. He had almost nothing to eat, so he ate the toads and lizards he managed to find. When Seng's leg became badly infected, he came home to live with me. The Khmer Rouge gave him injections and black pills called *achtunsai*, which means rabbit pellets, and were used to treat everything.

His leg slowly healed, and one day a Khmer Rouge official came to take Seng back to his work group. I was afraid and worried, but I couldn't do anything to help my son. Before Seng left, he said, "Mother, we should jump in the river and drown ourselves because we suffer too much. I don't want to be separated from you." "No, son," I told him. "We have to believe in God. Maybe God will find a way to save us."

Every day a car would drive past, taking another family away to be killed. My husband saw the Khmer Rouge beat a pregnant woman to death because she had been caught eating a mango. Many of those killed had been turned in by other villagers. All the people who came from the city were murdered by the Khmer Rouge and only the country people survived. I prayed for protection. If I hadn't prayed, I would have been taken away and killed, as the other two ethnic Vietnamese families in my village had been.

In 1978, there was a shortage of rice, and we only had corn to eat. We were given a small ration at eleven in the morning and again at six in the evening. Half of our village starved to death, and I saw people die along the road, like dogs. I had very bad rheumatism and couldn't walk, so I stayed home and cared for the children who were too young to work.

Some people stole and ate the pigs' slop, and many of us secretly traded for food. Once, I bought a kilo of salt from the woman who cooked for the Khmer Rouge soldiers. I left her a gold ring worth $50, and she left me the salt. I nervously wrapped the salt in plastic, put it in a cloth bag, and hid it far behind my house.

Early in 1979, we heard about the Khmer Rouge's plan to take everyone, including old people and children, from all the villages in our area and kill them on January 7th, 8th, and 9th. According to the rumor, only a thousand beautiful Khmer girls would be kept alive. The Khmer Rouge were going to send the adults into the forest and feed them poisoned noodles, and they were going to make the children walk to a field about three kilometers away where a big hole had been dug to bury them.

On January 7th, the Vietnamese soldiers saved us. I was impressed with the accuracy of their artillery. When I saw the trucks and tanks coming down the road my heart sank because I was afraid they were Americans. After I realized they were Vietnamese, I still felt uneasy. But it turned out that they needed interpreters and asked me to work in exchange for rice.

I anxiously waited for my son to come home. I waited and waited, but he never came. I learned from his friend that the Khmer Rouge had taken Seng into the mountains with them when they fled from the Vietnamese soldiers. We knew the Khmer Rouge killed many people as they fled, so my husband and I wept with sorrow as we concluded that our son was probably dead. I felt very, very sad and wanted to die. Seng was my only son, my only child. Now I would have to live alone. Seng was very kind, never rough with other boys, and he was a good student. For a long time I couldn't let go of the small hope that he was still alive. I will always remember my son, although, after many years, his image has slowly faded in my mind.

After I realized that my son wasn't coming home, I went to Vietnam. I wanted to find my relatives, and I wanted to go to church because I hadn't been to confession in nine years. It was my first time in Vietnam. I was so happy to meet my family and friends and see that they had survived. Many people felt sorry for me because of what I had been through, and they gave me money. I found our former parish priest, Father Thai, and we cried together. I stayed for ten months and didn't want to leave, but my husband sent a letter asking me to return.

When I arrived back home in Cambodia, a local official told the family living on my property to move to the adjoining land so I could rebuild my house on its original site. My husband and I bought a pig that gave birth to twelve piglets, and we began raising pigs and selling firewood for our living.

I had become very fond of one of the children I cared for during the Khmer Rouge regime. I held Amara ever since she was a baby, and she loved me very much, so I adopted her as my daughter in 1980. I hoped that when she grew up she would continue living with me.

In 1983, my nephew's seven-year-old daughter Samura came to stay with us temporarily, when a flood destroyed her family's house. My husband asked her parents if we could keep Samura and raise her as our daughter, so she would care for me when she was older. Her parents agreed because they were very poor and knew that I didn't have my own children.

During the Khmer Rouge regime one of my neighbors was appointed village head. He had to report everything to the higher Khmer Rouge officials, which resulted in many people being killed. He protected my identity because we were old friends. We used to work together selling firewood and he would eat lunch at my house. After the Khmer Rouge left, he and his son began to drink heavily, and now he has gone mad and is always silent. Under the Khmer Rouge regime he was well fed because the community's rice was stored in his house, but now he doesn't have enough food and is often hungry. I think he is being punished by God.

The land around our village is covered with thousands of landmines, small unexploded bombs, grenades, and other military ordnance from the war and bombings. Injuries are common. I felt pity when a six-year-old boy was blinded from an ordnance he was playing with behind my house. In 1993, a de-mining crew came, located some of the buried landmines, and removed them along with other military ordnance. We were pleased because we felt safer and could cultivate more land.

I don't sell firewood any more because it is hard to find. A lot of the forests are gone, and this year the government prohibited cutting trees because the fishing is declining. They said that soil erosion from deforestation fills the rivers with silt, and now there is no place for the fish to lay eggs.

In 1988, one month after we replaced our thatched roof with a tile roof, my husband died at age 78. We had used all our savings for the new roof, so two police officers helped me pay for the funeral ceremony and burial. I have helped a lot of poor people in the past, and sometimes people help me.

My adopted daughter Amara was married in 1990 at age sixteen. I gave her a beautiful wedding that cost $500. I was disappointed when her husband told me they weren't going to live at my house.

Cambodia started preparing for a national election in 1993. I went to get my voting card and I was very surprised when an UNTAC (United Nations Transitional Authority of Cambodia) employee fell in love with me. He took photos for voting cards and was a driver for the United Nations peacekeeping troops from Bangladesh. He asked if he could store the cameras in my house.

For three months he begged me to marry him, but I refused. I had not planned to marry again. He was Khmer, but he loved the Vietnamese people. All of his brothers married Vietnamese women. He told me that a rich Khmer woman with $7,500 wanted to marry him, but he avoided her, saying that if a woman comes to him easily, then she will leave him easily.

After thinking about it for a while, I decided it was a good idea to marry him because I am still afraid of the Khmer Rouge. Our wedding was on March 14, 1993, and many of the Bangladeshi peacekeepers came. My new husband is a good man. He comes with me to Catholic mass, and I go with him to the Buddhist temple. There are about fifty Catholic families that live in this area, and a priest from Phnom Penh comes once a month to give mass.

The Khmer Rouge were as bad as the Nazis. They never stopped murdering the ethnic Vietnamese. I still don't let people know I am Vietnamese because it is dangerous. I am worried because I heard that in the future all ethnic Vietnamese may have to leave Cambodia, even those who speak Khmer. I will wait and see what happens. If I hadn't married a Khmer man, I would move to Vietnam. I feel anxious, and every day I pray for Prime Minister Hun Sen's good health, so he will protect us.

A few hundred feet from Chanthan's house, a girl stands in front of a water-filled crater created by an American bomb during the Vietnam War. Cambodia's landscape is pock-marked with craters; Americans dropped more bombs on Cambodia than all the bombs dropped in World War II. The sign on the tree warns of landmines or other unexploded ordnance. Many poor people disregard the signs and continue to use the land, at risk to their lives, because farming, fishing, and firewood collection are their only means of survival.

A market woman wraps her customer's fish in a banana leaf. Fish is the main staple in the Cambodian diet, next to rice. Chanthan's family, like most ethnic Vietnamese in Cambodia, fished for a living on the big rivers. Today, fishing in Cambodia is declining as deforestation fills the rivers with silt and destroys the fish beds.

In the countryside, a relatively well-off family watches boxing on a TV that is hooked up to a car battery. Chanthan's living situation is similar. Rural Cambodia does not have electricity or running water but does have plenty of exposure to Western culture through television programs from Thailand.

Sovanna takes a break from her administrative duties at the government orphanage to play with four little boys. Snap-together Legos are as popular with children in Cambodia as they are with children in the United States. The orphanage is run almost entirely with international funding.

Sovanna ❦ Orphanage Director

Sovanna, a twenty-five-year-old pre-school teacher, was in labor with her first child on April 17, 1975, the day the Khmer Rouge ousted the Lon Nol government. Soldiers entered her hospital room and ordered her at gun point to leave Phnom Penh, immediately. The street was packed with people and Sovanna had to stop at the first house she came to. Amazingly, the woman who lived there was a midwife, and she delivered Sovanna's baby boy late that night. The baby lived and today is a medical student. Like everyone else in Cambodia, Sovanna struggled to survive the brutal Khmer Rouge regime, but unlike millions who died, Sovanna had many lucky breaks. Perhaps she was divinely protected because in 1979, when the Khmer Rouge regime ended, she went to work at an orphanage and helped raise hundreds of motherless children. Now she is the compassionate and capable director of Phnom Penh's orphanage for infants and young children.

One of the children who grew up in Orphanage Number One fondly remembered Sovanna and suggested that I meet her. As I turned off noisy, dusty Monivong Boulevard and passed through the blue iron gates of the Baby Rescue Center, I was immediately struck by the tidiness of the orphanage. It looked well cared for. I was told, upon inquiring at the office, that Sovanna was away at a meeting, and I would have to come back tomorrow. I had not made an appointment because the phones in Phnom Penh weren't working due to the heavy rains that come almost every day at about three in the afternoon, from May through October. Affluent people bypass the problem with cellular phones.

The Baby Rescue Center staff politely offered to give me a tour and led me to a room full of cribs and sleeping infants. "This baby's mother died in the hospital. This child's mother said she was too poor to raise him and left him here. This baby was found lying in the street," the woman explained as she tenderly touched each little child. Tears filled my eyes as I peered down into the tiny faces of the abandoned babies, victims of poverty. A baby boy with a cleft palate cried on the floor, and a baby girl with one eye reached up toward me. I picked her up and held her.

We returned the following day and met Sovanna. I was immediately struck by how solid yet gentle she was. It was difficult for her to find a time to meet with me because she was so busy, but she graciously accommodated my request. With each interview session I gained more appreciation for Sovanna's fortitude and kindness. The difficulties she has experienced in her life do not show in her face, and instead, she radiates a quality of inner peace and stability. Sovanna moves with the self-assurance of a woman who knows her life purpose, and I could see that she feels fulfilled by her work, even though it entails long hours and low pay. I came to think of Sovanna as a guardian of Cambodian children.

Sovanna:

I was at home, preparing for the arrival of my first baby, when I heard on the radio that the Khmer Rouge had won the war and were marching into Phnom Penh. The announcer said there was a rumor that everyone would have to leave the city for three days, in case the Americans dropped bombs. I didn't pay much attention because I was very busy.

At about five that afternoon, I felt the pain of my first contraction. My husband Sa took me to the hospital on his *moto* (motorbike), winding through the back streets because the Khmer Rouge soldiers forbade driving on the main boulevards. After examining me, the nurse said I would deliver late that night or early the next morning, so Sa went back home to get the clothes and things we needed for the new baby while I settled in at the hospital.

I watched the chaos in the street from the hospital window as my contractions came more frequently. The street was packed with people leaving Phnom Penh, and I saw soldiers carrying guns walking up and down telling people to get out of their houses. I wasn't too concerned because I thought it was just a temporary security measure.

Our house was not far from the hospital, but it took Sa an hour to get home because the streets were so crowded. He returned about eight in the evening, carrying the suitcase I had prepared for the baby. A few minutes later, Khmer Rouge soldiers burst into my hospital room, pointed their guns at us, and told everyone to get out. The guns frightened me, but I had no idea of the horrors that were to come. I couldn't imagine that Khmer would kill Khmer. Since it was my first baby, my labor was taking a long time, and I was able to walk to my husband's motorbike.

It was impossible to go home because the street was a solid slow-moving stream of people, so we had no choice but to walk up to a stranger's house and ask to stay there. The woman who came to the door said she was a midwife and took me in. I was immensely relieved and full of gratitude. All through the night, between my contractions, I heard the noise of horses, cars, and people traveling. I was in a lot of pain at four in the morning when I heard the Khmer Rouge soldiers yell outside the house, "Come out. Come out." I couldn't make any sense out of what was happening.

The midwife's family prepared to leave, but I begged with them to stay until my baby was born. "You can go ahead," the midwife told her family, "I will stay with Sovanna." Just then a man came to the door and asked the midwife to come and help deliver his wife's baby. I grabbed the midwife's arm and held on tightly as I cried with terror, "You can't leave me," knowing I could easily die if I had problems during delivery. The midwife asked her sister to go and help deliver the other baby.

My baby was born at five o'clock in the morning, and immediately afterward we left the house. Sa had gone home again during the night and brought back my nephew's car. He and the midwife's husband carried me out to the car, and the midwife set my new baby boy in my arms. The Khmer Rouge soldiers wouldn't let us drive the car because fuel was being saved, so Sa pushed it in the sea of walking people. It took us from five in the morning until almost nine at night to just travel a few kilometers, from one end of Phnom Penh to the other. I saw people tied up with ropes being taken away by Khmer Rouge soldiers, which made me afraid of this new government.

I was bleeding heavily, had nothing to eat all day, and felt very weak. We asked strangers for water until we came to a stream where we were able to get our own. We spent the first night near the Monivong Bridge, on the south end of Phnom Penh, and the next day we reached Wat Mony in Kien Svey, less than ten kilometers southeast of Phnom Penh. We stayed there a week, and I had the good fortune to meet a doctor who treated me and found a nurse to care for me. I also met my cousin Ath, who felt sorry for me and gave me some money. I was worried for Ath's safety, because he had been an officer in the Lon Nol army, and I knew all the former officers were being executed.

We were told to go to our native province, so we abandoned the car in Kien Svey because it was of no use to us, and we walked to Koke District in Kandal Province. After resting there a few weeks, we continued onward until three weeks later we reached my native province of Prey Veng. Full of anticipation, I walked directly to my family's house in Samke Chong Village. I was overjoyed to see my parents again. We had been separated for the past two years, ever since the Khmer Rouge took over Kompong Travek District in 1973. My parents were very surprised to see me arrive with a baby in my arms. They didn't even know I was married.

I had left Prey Veng in 1970, after General Lon Nol overthrew the king and our country was at war. The Cambodian people loved the king, and we missed him very much. At that time, I was living at home with my parents who were rice farmers. They were afraid the soldiers would kidnap young women in our village, so they sent me to live with my older brother and sister in Phnom Penh. It was impossible to contact my parents after 1973 due to the war, and I worried about them all the time because they were old and all their children lived far away.

When I was living in Phnom Penh in the early 1970s, I was hired as a teacher at the Ministry of Community Development. I trained pre-school teachers to work with children age six months and up, and I had my own pre-school class. I was very happy to have that job because I was trained as an early childhood educator, and it felt great to be financially independent. My parents would have been pleased, if they had known.

Thousands of farmers, government workers, and the wives of soldiers, swarmed into Phnom Penh from the provinces to escape the war. The ministry offered these refugees vocational training programs, and I taught sewing, health education, and child care. We promoted breast feeding, nutrition education, birth spacing, and hygiene.

Sa also worked at the Ministry of Community Development, as an agriculture teacher. I was very surprised when he asked me to marry him because I hadn't even noticed that he liked me. My sympathy for him was greater than my love, but I decided not to refuse because he was kind and hard-working. We followed Khmer tradition and never met privately or spoke together alone before our wedding in 1974. My love for Sa grew after we were married because he was very gentle.

My parents enjoyed getting to know my husband and their new grandson, but our happiness ended abruptly a couple of weeks after we arrived when the Khmer Rouge soldiers took away my husband, brother, and brother-in-law. The Khmer Rouge said they needed to "study," but I was afraid they would be killed. I was very worried and worked as hard as I could, even though I had a tiny baby, because I didn't want the Khmer Rouge to take me too. I labored daily from dawn to dusk, harvesting and threshing rice by hand, since we didn't use machinery under the Khmer Rouge.

While in confinement, Sa attended classes about communist theory, but most of the time he had to carry heavy loads of soil. He was given very little food, and the Khmer Rouge soldiers watched him all the time, even when he went to the toilet. Finally, after five months, my husband, brother, and brother-in-law were released from detention. As they were walking home, a soldier rode up to them on horseback and took away my brother-in-law. We were very sad when we heard he had been killed.

Sa and my brother were assigned hard work and were frequently asked about their personal history. What work did they do? My husband lied and said he used to sell ice. I was careful to tell the Khmer Rouge the same thing each time they asked about him. If we knew how to lie, then we knew how to survive. It was a good thing that my husband had a dark complexion, because dark skin was associated with the working class, whereas light-skinned people were considered members of the educated and wealthy class that the Khmer Rouge wanted to destroy.

We struggled to stay alive. I planted potato, pumpkin, banana, and taro around my parents' house, but the Khmer Rouge came, counted how many vegetables were planted, and returned to take the harvest to the communal kitchen. My effort was still worthwhile because we could secretly pick a few vegetables at night. I traded my jewelry for salt, and when I could not trade for it, I made salty water by burning *pty* (a spinach-like leaf) and pouring water through the ashes. My mother was over seventy years old, but she had to look after my baby because if elderly people didn't work, they couldn't eat.

Luckily for me, one of the Khmer Rouge officials in our village was my former classmate and friend. He came quietly one night asked me if I was hungry, and then he gave me the key to the food storage building so I could get some sugar and *prahok* (fermented fish). "Be patient," he told me, "all of the country is this way." I ate a lot of sugar and got sick. I'm not sure if he made the decision, but I was assigned to work near the village and was able to live at home, which was a great advantage because it was easier to steal rice.

One evening, at a mandatory meeting, a man accused my husband of not looking after the water buffaloes well enough and claimed that they were hungry. Since I knew the Khmer Rouge leader, I was brave enough to declare that it wasn't true, and fortunately, they didn't punish my husband. I don't know if the Khmer Rouge leaders in our village were involved in killings.

My father had influence with another local Khmer Rouge official because they used to work together. Local people like my parents were considered "old people" and were treated better than "new people," the people from the city. My family was more fortunate than most because we had a secret reserve of rice that I had stolen.

In 1976, I became pregnant with my second child. About ninety percent of the women didn't have periods during the Khmer Rouge regime due to lack of food, and I was one of the few women to get pregnant. I wasn't happy because it was a bad time to have a child. I worried that my poor nutrition and hard physical labor would harm my baby. Everyone wished the situation in Cambodia would return to normal, but nothing changed. Early in 1977, one of my relatives who was a mid-wife came over and helped when I gave birth to my daughter.

In 1978, the Khmer Rouge ordered the youth group to dig big holes to be used for mass graves and soon after whole families started disappearing. The Khmer Rouge preferred to hide the killings, but the rainy season had begun and I saw bodies of dead people floating around. I think they intended to murder all of us, but a letter arrived from Angka that told them to stop the killing.

My family and seventeen relatives including my parents, aunt, brothers, sister, nieces, and nephews, were sent to live in Pursat Province. We walked to the ferry at Nakg Loeug and took a boat to Phnom Penh. There the Khmer Rouge gave us new clothes and *kramars*, and put us on the train to Pursat.

When we arrived in Pursat Province, the local people advised us not to use the new clothes because it would identify us as having come from the east. The Khmer Rouge leaders in Pursat killed the people from the east because they thought we were Vietnamese sympathizers. The Khmer Rouge frequently interrogated us about our past, and at night I heard the sound of ox carts carrying more people to the killing fields. I was terrified and thought we were just waiting for our turn. Every day I prayed that we would be spared from being killed, that the Khmer Rouge regime would end, and that our family would not be separated.

During the Khmer Rouge regime, there were two places to work: "in the front" and "in the back." If you were "in the front" then you worked far away and lived at your work site, and if you were "in the back" then you worked locally and went home at night. My husband was sent to the front, working as an ox cart driver. I worked in the back, hauling water in two buckets tied to each end of a wooden pole, which I balanced on my shoulder. I must have walked up and down that steep river bank a hundred times a day as I carried water to the vegetable garden. I felt sorry for myself, but I kept telling myself that this is what I need to do. My old parents looked after my two children and made palm roofing.

The Khmer Rouge murdered a lot of people in Pursat Province at that time, especially Kampuchea Krom, the ethnic Khmer from Vietnam. The Kampuchea Krom had helped Lon Nol troops fight against the Khmer Rouge in the early 1970's. I feared the Khmer Rouge would find out that my husband was Kampuchea Krom and kill him. He was born in South Vietnam, in an area that once belonged to Cambodia, where the Khmer people still live.

The sound of shelling in Phnom Penh during the early 1970s used to scare me. But when I heard shelling and gunfire in Pursat at the end of 1978, I was glad because I hoped it meant independence from the Khmer Rouge. When I learned that the Vietnamese were coming, I became afraid and thought we might be massacred. I had a bad image of the Vietnamese because many years ago they invaded our country and took our territory.

Two weeks before the Khmer Rouge regime ended, my baby daughter became sick with the measles and died. I was heartbroken. Without the Khmer Rouge, she would be alive today because she would have been immunized, we would have had medicine to treat her when she got sick, and I would have been able to take care of her.

As the Khmer Rouge fled from the Vietnamese toward the west, they forced us to go with them, up the Pursat River and deep into the forest. We were so happy when on April 25, 1979, the Khmer Rouge soldiers ran away. We walked back to our village in central Pursat Province, stayed there for a month, and then returned to Phnom Penh.

I was so glad to finally be back in Phnom Penh. I didn't feel greedy or want to be rich; I only wanted to have enough food. This was our lesson from the Khmer Rouge; we just wanted our stomachs full, nothing more than that.

Seven of my family members died under Pol Pot's rule. My brother and three brother-in-laws were killed by Khmer Rouge, my mother-in-law died from starvation, my daughter died of disease, and my sister-in-law drowned herself because she couldn't stand to live in that society.

Many members of my extended family also died. My cousin Ath, the former Lon Nol officer who helped me in 1975, was taken away by the Khmer Rouge for "re-education," wearing only a *kramar* (piece of cloth), after one of his former soldiers reported him. I assume Ath was killed because we never saw him again. His wife and his children also died during the Khmer Rouge regime, except one daughter, whom I took into my home and raised.

During the Khmer Rouge regime I prayed to the spirits of my ancestors, and I believe they helped me survive. As a Buddhist, I know my life is planned by God, and the good deeds I have done in this life have brought me good fortune. This is the law of karma: What we do comes back to us. If I assist you, it doesn't necessarily mean you will turn around and help me, but in the future someone else may. I think the Khmer Rouge leader who was my classmate survived because of his kindness, and today he works for the Ministry of Agriculture.

When I was growing up, my parents taught me to help other people and to have compassion for children. My father let the poor rural children build huts next to our house so that they could live near the regional high school and continue their education. He looked after them and tutored them.

During our first week in Phnom Penh we lived under the broken Chloy Changval bridge that had been blown up in 1973 by the Khmer Rouge and Viet Cong. I managed to find my former boss from the Ministry of Community Development, and he directed me to work at Orphanage Number One, the first orphanage to open in 1979. Vietnamese troops brought hundreds of lost, homeless orphans to Phnom Penh.

I felt sorry for the children and wanted to help them have a good future, so I moved into the orphanage with my husband and four-year-old son. The facility used to be a Catholic girls' school, and after years of disuse, it was dirty and overgrown. We had nearly 500 children who had lost their parents during the Khmer Rouge regime. Many were malnourished and sick with diarrhea, malaria, fever, or jaundice. At first, we didn't have enough rice to feed them, so we had to mix in corn.

I was responsible for a group of thirty-five children and had the role of their parents. I made sure they had clothes, went to school, stayed healthy, and I taught them to be good people. We encouraged the children to do well in school by rewarding the "A" students with toys, clothes, books, pens, or money. Their school had an arts program that taught dance, music, circus, sewing, and knitting. There was also a sports program.

All of the staff considered themselves "second mothers" to the children, and we wanted the children to trust us. I loved them as much as I loved my own children and tried to help them become pillars of the country. They were the young bamboo that would replace the old.

The orphanage never had enough support from the government. We had rice, but not much meat or vegetables. Occasionally, we received medicine, books, milk, or school supplies from aid organizations like the Red Cross, and the Vietnamese donated clothes. The number of children at the orphanage began to drop in the mid-1980s, as some children found relatives to live with, and older children moved out when they got jobs or were married.

My husband worked for the Department of Education, but his salary was too low to support our family, so he also taught a private English class. He always let the orphans join his class for free. I raised pigs and chickens at the orphanage to earn extra money, and at night I embroidered handkerchiefs to sell. We had a little ice business until the government stopped us because ice making uses a lot of electricity.

In the early 1980s my husband and I bought some land in the countryside for $50. We built a pond and raised fish, pigs, garlic, and peppers. In 1987, we sold our little farm so we could buy land closer to Phnom Penh, and in 1989 we built a house. I liked my new house, but I really missed living in the orphanage because it had been my home for ten years.

I hoped I would have another daughter, but I had three more sons, and now I can't have any more children. I am very proud of my sons because they are fine students. My wish is that all my children will complete high school and get good jobs. My son Kunthea, who was born the day the Khmer Rouge evacuated Phnom Penh, is now in medical school.

Cambodia's peace agreement was signed in October 1991, and now we have a government elected by the people. Step by step, things are improving. There is less corruption in the government and in the education system. Recently, Kunthea was one of the few students to pass a final exam at the medical school. Some students accused the teachers of only passing students who paid bribes, but my son didn't pay one. Now that Cambodia has a democracy, students can protest against injustices, and when they did, the medical school agreed to offer the exam again.

I hope my country will stay peaceful, so my sons can avoid military service. Cambodia was divided and at war for many years because of the Khmer Rouge. I thought reconciliation was the best way, but the Khmer Rouge wanted power by military force, not through negotiation. The Khmer people need to stay united, so we can have real security. Women in Cambodia have little influence on public policy.

I worked at Orphanage Number One until December 1992. Then I was transferred to the Baby Rescue Center, which is the orphanage for young children, newborn to six-years-old. We have about seventy-five children, including some handicapped. The center is run by the government, but eighty-five percent of our funds come from foreign organizations. The government gives us 13,000 riels (about $5) each month per child, but baby formula alone costs $60 a month for each child. Recently, one foreign organization gave us a generator, and another gave us furniture, milk, and clothes. The staff felt good because it meant that they trusted us.

We want our children to be adopted, especially by parents who don't have children. I think all couples would like to have children. We investigate the couples who ask to adopt and get verification from their village that they don't have children and really want a child. Cambodians like to adopt girls because they can rely on a daughter for help when they are older, more than a son. Mothers are more likely to give away boys for the same reason, which is why we have more boys than girls here. Cambodian children are taught to respect their parents and to never forget how their parents fed them and raised them. They are expected to help their parents when they become old.

The orphanage staff all work very hard, and on our days off we still come in to see the children. We want what is best for them. Every year we invite a Buddhist monk to come to the orphanage and chant, so our good deeds will be passed on to the ancestors of the children. I enjoy my work, even if I get tired and am paid only $15 per month. I feel pity for orphaned babies because many were abandoned by their parents, and they are so innocent. Often the babies we receive are severely malnourished, and right now we have six in the hospital. It fills me with joy to see them become healthy. I want to help them have as much good fortune in the future as I wish for my own children.

On April 18, 1975, Sovanna gave birth to her first child amidst the mass exodus and commotion created as the Khmer Rouge forced evacuation of the cities. The baby and mother survived four years of brutal treatment by the Khmer Rouge and now, more than twenty years later, Sovanna's son is in medical school. Here he reviews his notes outside a classroom at Phnom Penh University.

A child care worker feeds two orphaned babies and watches two others in the orphanage nursery. Babies are abandoned in the hospital or left on the street because they have birth defects or their mothers are too poor to raise them. Most of the babies at the orphanage are adopted by childless couples. Children comprise half of Cambodia's total population and the birth rate is very high, about four percent. Women in Cambodia have an average of five children, but it is not unusual to find women who have ten or twelve. Most women don't know how to use birth control, and for those who want it, it is either unavailable or too expensive.

This girl is selling grilled spider kabobs on the street to help support her family. Although children living in the orphanage do not have parents, they receive good nutrition, clothes, health care, and an education, which is more than most of Cambodia's children have.

Thavery holds one of her elegant story-picture silk textiles, which is traditionally hung in a Buddhist temple. She carefully tied and dyed the design into the thread before weaving this fabric. Thavery teaches the beautiful art of silk weaving.

Thavery ❦ Traditional Silk Weaver

Thavery grew up on a rice farm, just like eighty percent of Cambodia's children. Her story illustrates a rural child's simple pleasures as well as the struggles of making a livelihood in agriculture. Thavery's experience under the Khmer Rouge began five years earlier than most Cambodians because the Khmer Rouge took over her village in 1970, when she was eight years old. She was subjected to cruel treatment by the Khmer Rouge, including isolation, hunger, and hard labor. Fewer than one out of four children in her work group survived. After Pol Pot was driven out, Thavery became a silk weaver, reviving the ancient tradition of her home village in Takeo Province. Now she is a weaving instructor at Khemara, a community development organization run by Cambodian women.

Weaving is often a source of supplemental income for farm families, and it is common to see looms set up under the stilt houses. Many families weave cotton *kramars*, the ubiquitous uni-sex checkered Cambodian scarf which is used for everything from a head cover to a man's skirt. Khemara is working to bring back Cambodia's traditional art of silk weaving, including silk production, natural dyeing, and fancy classical designs which were nearly lost when the Khmer Rouge destroyed Cambodian society. Today, beautiful hand-woven silk skirts are once again worn by Cambodian women for holidays and weddings.

I met Thavery when I visited Khemara's well-run weaving center, located north of Phnom Penh in Mittapheap Village. She is a shy young woman who conveys both calmness and sadness. Thavery lives far away from home and works hard at a difficult job in order to support her widowed mother and sister. Family is vitally important in Cambodian culture, and Thavery's life illustrates the loyalty and devotion children have for their parents and their willingness to personally sacrifice in order to help the family.

Thavery's sadness may be due to homesickness and also that she believes she is too old for marriage. Rural women in Cambodia typically marry before they reach age twenty, and now Thavery is in her thirties. The Khmer Rouge period interrupted women's lives so dramatically that many missed their opportunity for marriage. Thavery was forced by the Khmer Rouge into a marriage that didn't last. Now Thavery faces the national shortage of men. Most women want to get married and have children so they will have help when they are old. In the absence of any state program, children are Cambodia's social security system.

Thavery is a gentle, kind, and artistic young woman who is helping rebuild the rich classical Khmer culture by teaching traditional weaving.

Thavery:

In my home village of Kdanh in Takeo Province we all knew each other. There were about thirty families and we all farmed rice. My family was poor, but we were happy. We didn't think about being poor. I grew up with four sisters and one brother. My father was very gentle and never beat us. He always gave me pocket money when I asked for it, even if he had to borrow it, because he loved children very much. My mother liked us, but she didn't show it.

My favorite activity as a child was playing with my friends. We played *traes* (pick-up sticks) using chop sticks and a lime, *lort antaik* (jump rope), *buy khom*, a game with ten holes in the ground and snail shells, and *but pune* (hide and seek), which is especially fun to play at night.

Even when I was young I helped with the farming, which I didn't like because it was hard work, but I had to do it. When the first rains came in mid-June, my father plowed, using cows that we rented. Then he chose the best paddy for the first rice planting, plowed that paddy again, and then we planted the rice very thick. A month and a half later, the rice seedlings were ready to pull and transplant into the other paddies, but we had to wait for the rain.

Transplanting was the hardest work because we had to stand in mud and water all day. If our paddies were too dry, we moved water up from our neighbor's lower paddy. After replanting the seedlings, we waited about four months for the rice to grow, and we harvested in January.

Once the rice was planted, my father went to Phnom Penh and worked as a *cyclo* (bicycle taxi) driver, and he made fishing poles to sell in the market to earn extra money. When I was five-years-old there was a drought, and we had to borrow rice. After our harvest the following year, we had very little rice left because people came to our house to collect the debt we owed them. If we borrowed fifteen kilograms of rice, we had to pay back thirty kilograms. It was hard to recover from a bad year because the following year we couldn't afford to buy fertilizer, which meant we produced less rice and had to borrow again.

My mother was not in good health, and she couldn't help with the farming. She and my older sister wove fancy silk skirts, both *hol*, which has a design, and *phamoung*, which is plain. I wanted to help because weaving is much easier than farming, but my legs were too short to reach the pedals on the loom.

In 1970, the Khmer Rouge soldiers presented a letter to our community announcing that they were coming. The Lon Nol soldiers quietly disappeared, and my teacher also left because he knew the Khmer Rouge didn't like teachers, so that was the end of my schooling. The Khmer Rouge organized our village into one class, without poor or rich people, because they wanted equality. They collected all the dishes from each family and established one common kitchen in the village.

In 1972, I was sent to live with the children's group in Sla Bat Village and was put in a work group with twenty-five other kids. I was told to call every adult "father" or "mother," and I saw my parents only twice a month. I wasn't concerned about myself, but I worried about my parents because they were living alone and had to do all the chores without any help from their children. In 1973, my parents were moved to another village because the Khmer Rouge was afraid that people might refuse to obey orders if they knew each other. They isolated people in order to control them.

The Khmer Rouge didn't give us enough food, so I boiled leaves and ate them. I was too skinny, especially during the rainy season when there was a shortage of rice and we only had watery porridge. Under the Khmer Rouge we had to work more and eat less. If they had given us enough rice, they would have gotten better results. The Khmer Rouge forced me to work too hard, planting rice, making fertilizer, digging canals, and building a dam. Even the old people had to work, weaving *kramars*.

There were 450 children in my youth group, and only 100 of us survived. Most were killed by the Khmer Rouge or died from starvation or sickness. We got sick often because we didn't have enough food. If the Khmer Rouge took us to the hospital, we were in a worse situation because then we were accused of pretending to be sick, *"feeling sick"* they called it, and we were given even less food. The Khmer Rouge used traditional medicine, but it didn't cure any illnesses, and five or six people died in the hospital every day.

I was in the hospital with a fever when one of my friends came and told me that in two days all the people in the hospital would be taken away to be killed. At first, I thought I'd like to die, but then I realized I would never see my parents' faces again, so I decided I wanted to live, to struggle, and work. I got up and started cleaning the hospital, and when they saw that I could work, I was sent back to my group.

The next day, the Khmer Rouge told the people in the hospital that they were being moved to a new hospital and proceeded to load more than a hundred patients, including a lot of my friends, into ox carts, horse carts, and trucks, and took them away. I never saw them again. I believed that God could save me, so I always prayed not be killed. Maybe God helped me that day.

In 1976, the Khmer Rouge started a "school" for the children. We sat under a tree for an hour during the mid-day rest time, and they taught us the alphabet and how to read. They included propaganda because they didn't want to waste their time.

In 1978, I turned seventeen and was sent to another work group which was forty to fifty kilometers away, in Sam Rong District. One day, a Khmer Rouge official came up to me as I was working and told me to come with her to a meeting in the next village. When we arrived at the meeting hall I saw two tables facing each other, set with flowers and glasses of water. I was worried and asked if she brought me there to be married. "No, someone older than you will be married," she said.

I waited outside as people started arriving, and an hour later they called me in. As soon as I entered the room I saw my cousin Seng sitting there, and I realized I had been brought there to marry him. I looked down and started crying. When we were growing up, Seng lived in the next village, and we went to school together. Our parents had wanted us to marry ever since we were little children, but at that moment I felt embarrassed and too young to marry.

The leader's wife warned me to be careful because they would take me to be killed if they saw my tears of disagreement. My cousin was older and wiser, and he knew that we wouldn't really have to be husband and wife, we could just act like we were. But I wasn't thinking about how to be flexible at that moment, I just imagined death would be better than living.

The leader gave a speech with advice to everyone who was married, but I didn't hear what he said because I was crying so much. Then we were supposed to speak individually, and when they turned to me, I was speechless. They told us to hold hands and pronounced us married. We were invited to enjoy a special dinner with rice, soup, and meat, and when we finished eating, they gave us our own bedroom in a house.

Later, I learned that our parents believed it was a good idea for us to marry under the Khmer Rouge because they thought it would allow us to live near them in the village, instead of far away in the youth group. But the day after our wedding my new husband was assigned to work far away. I was relieved because I didn't want to be married.

When the Vietnamese came in 1979, the Khmer Rouge left, and I hurried home. It took me two days to walk to my home village, and when I arrived I was very happy to find my parents. Unfortunately, we had to leave right away to escape the Khmer Rouge and the fighting. When we arrived in the next village, we saw that it was still occupied by Khmer Rouge, and as we ran away from the shelling, a crowd of people pushed me ahead and I was separated from my parents.

The Khmer Rouge captured some of us and took us with them to live in the forest. During the day they slept in hammocks while we slept on the ground, and at night they forced us to walk into western Kompong Speu Province. A month later, we heard shelling from the Vietnamese, and the Khmer Rouge ran away. The Vietnamese soldiers came up to us asked if we were Khmer Rouge, and when we said no they let us go.

I was lost and didn't know how to get home, so a kind family invited me to live with them. They loved me like their daughter and didn't want me to work, but I helped with house chores. About nine months later, I was very happy when my father found me and took me home.

My brother never came home. Before 1975, he was a medical student in Phnom Penh, but the Khmer Rouge accused him of being a pilot and killed him. The Khmer Rouge put my sister Wan in prison, and when she didn't come home, we sadly assumed she had been executed.

The women in my village wove silk skirts, and I wanted to learn how to weave, so I volunteered to help them. I liked weaving and wanted to make it my career, but my family was very poor and didn't have enough money to buy the materials to build a loom. So I worked for my cousin who paid me 100 riels (40 cents) for each skirt I wove, which took about three days. That year my family had enough rice and I was able to save my earnings to buy a loom and silk thread.

In 1983, my father became seriously ill, and even though I bought him medicine, he didn't get better. His health had been poor ever since he was badly wounded by a missile that exploded next to our house in 1972, when a Khmer Rouge soldier accidentally fired artillery during training. My father had metal all through his body, including a piece in his head, and my sister Touch was injured too. I was very sad when my father died in 1983. I felt sorry for my mother because now she only had me and my two sisters to take care of her.

In 1985, another cousin asked my mother if he could marry me. Everyone in my family agreed, except me. I didn't want to marry a cousin because they were like brothers to me. My uncle on my father's side of the family kept asking me if I would marry and I kept telling him no, but after a while I got tired of answering him and was silent. He thought my silence meant that I agreed, so he arranged the wedding party. Ten days before the wedding I had a quarrel with my mother and declared that I would not marry my cousin.

I told my mother that if I were married and had children, I would not be able to give her enough attention. I also feared that if my husband didn't have a job, he would stay at home and I would have to support all of us, or he might become a soldier and then I would be separated from him. I did not want to rely on a husband, I wanted to rely on myself, and I thought it was better to live on my own. When my uncle heard that I refused to get married, he beat me until I was bruised and bleeding.

There was a drought in 1985, which meant we couldn't transplant the rice seedlings, so I went to live with another uncle, on my mother's side of the family, in the central part of the province. There I sold cooked rice and snacks to earn money to send to my mother, and my uncle gave me a little gold to buy rice for her.

The next year the rains came, and I went back home to help my sisters Rum and Saven plant rice. My sisters and I also planted rice for a neighbor, in exchange for plowing our fields. During the harvest we had to carry the heavy loads of rice home on our heads, since we didn't have an ox cart. We worked day and night, threshing the rice by hand because we didn't have a threshing machine. When we finally finished, we were disappointed to see that our harvest was only enough to feed us for six or seven months.

About that time, I heard that people were finding work far away from our province. My mother said she didn't want me to go unaccompanied. I told her that whether I was good or bad was up to me, and she finally agreed let me go to the city of Poipet in Battambang Province. There I secretly carried things into Cambodia from Thailand. Several of us walked together across the border, often at night, and then smuggled goods back, like medicine or monosodium glutamate. It was dangerous work, and after six months I quit and moved back home.

In 1990, I was overjoyed to learn that my fourth sister Wan was living at Site Two refugee camp in Thailand. I traded our pig and chickens for gold and paid a guide to take me safely through the jungle and across the border to visit her. We were so happy to see each other. Wan gave me all the gold she had saved, and I came back and paid the debt on my mother's house. Then I returned to Site Two refugee camp and lived with Wan for nearly two years, because it was easier to earn money there than in Cambodia. We wove cotton *sampots* (skirts).

While I was in the camp I learned that my husband, the cousin I married under the Khmer Rouge, had died from a fever in 1987. I felt sorry for him, even though I hadn't seen him in over ten years. Now I was completely free. I wished I could marry a man who had a job and could help support us, and I wanted to have children, but I didn't think anyone would want to marry me because I was too old and not pretty. I moved back home in 1992, when the refugee camp started to close.

196

In 1993, I came to Phnom Penh to teach weaving at Khemara, a community development organization that helps poor women. I like to teach, but I find weaving easier than teaching because teaching requires a lot of thinking. I need to consider: What is the best way to help the students understand? How can I teach everything within three months?

Silk used to be produced in my home province of Takeo, but the Khmer Rouge cut down the mulberry trees that the silk worms fed on, so now I have to buy silk thread from Vietnam. In preparing the thread, I first place it in water with lye made from ashes and boil it for fifteen minutes, then I hang it in the sun to dry. Next, I wrap it around a frame, tie little bundles of thread to make the design, and then I dye it. The yellow color comes from pahoot tree bark, and the red and green are from chemical dyes. We are doing research at Khemara so we can go back to using all natural dyes. Warping the loom is the hardest part of weaving because I have to count the threads exactly, and if I make a mistake, I have to start over.

The *pidan* is the most difficult weaving to do. It is a silk picture that tells a religious story and is hung in the temple for ceremonies, like Ancestors Remembrance Day or the Cambodian New Year. We have to tie 400 tiny bundles of silk to do the whole story and the weaving is six or seven meters long. I've never done the whole story by myself, just parts of it.

The *pidan* picture tells this story: The king had a son named Vesandor who was very kind and intelligent. He studied Buddhism and when people asked him about it, he taught them everything he knew. The king had an elephant, which was an important symbol of the country, and when Vesandor gave the elephant away, the country had a drought. Everyone was so angry that they banished Vesandor.

The next scene shows Vesandor leading his wife and children into the forest. God gave him a palace, Vesandor became a monk, and his wife served him. Then the Buddha flew down as an apsara dancer carrying fruit. When Vesandor's wife went into the forest to look for fruit, the Buddha turned into a tiger and forbade her from going too far. She didn't come home until late, and while she was gone an old man came to the palace and asked for both children. I can't remember the rest of the story because there are so many different parts. Sometimes I depict these tales in my weavings, and other times I just create my own designs.

This kind of weaving is an ancient art. The old woman who taught me learned when she was fourteen years old. She told me that if I do the whole story from beginning to end, I need a spirit to look after me. Once, when I made a *pidan*, I didn't make an offering to the spirit or ask it to guide me, and I became very sick. My mother set out a bunch of bananas, alcohol, cakes, and a glass of water as an offering. Then she lit incense and prayed for the spirit's help in making the *pidan*. After

197

that, my mother advised me to always make an offering before I start weaving, which I did for a while, but later I became lazy and stopped because I didn't think I needed to. When I want to make a *pidan*, I just do it and I don't get sick, but I don't do the whole story.

Sometimes I worry about my teaching ability, because when a student has trouble learning, the family blames me. I am afraid I don't have enough skill and I often get headaches. If I am home, I treat my headache with traditional medicine which takes a while to work, but if I keep taking it, my headache won't come back. When I live at Khemara, I use western medicine, which works very quickly, but my headache usually comes back. If I feel dizzy, I get coined or cupped. Coining is someone rubbing the edge of a coin on your back and chest until it bruises your skin. Cupping is less painful. We put a tiny candle under a two inch glass and set it on the skin, so it creates suction and a red mark.

My body lives in Phnom Penh, but my heart is back home with my family. I worry about my mother because she is seventy-one years old and is in poor health. I go home only twice a year because it is so expensive. If I don't travel, then I can save half my salary to send home. Last year, I saved my earnings for eight months so I could buy my mother a TV and a battery to run it. Now she seems to get sick less often. My older sister still lives with her and weaves silk skirts.

I have met a lot of difficulty in my life, and I often think there is no happiness for me. I think other people have better fortune. I don't blame anyone, only myself. It is due to my sin in my last life.

My love for weaving is as big as my whole life. I enjoy organizing each step, and I feel happy when I finish a piece. When I look at my work and see the bright colors in a good design, I know I can get a good price when I sell it and I feel satisfied. I am glad I can support myself, my mother, and my sister with my job at Khemara.

Bicycle taxis are known as cyclos in Cambodia and are used for hauling people and goods. Many of the cyclo drivers are poor farmers who come to the city to earn extra income, as Thavery's father did.

Two of Thavery's students at Khemara's weaving center prepare colorful natural dyes in a steaming cauldron. Intricate silk weaving, a traditional art of Cambodia, is being revived after the Khmer Rouge almost destroyed it. Mulberry trees are being replanted so Cambodia can once again produce silk thread.

Carefree children swing on a rope, as teenagers sit and talk, and a man in a wheelchair takes his grandchild for a ride. Cambodians live one day at a time and, like Thavery, find joy in their relationships with family and friends.

Saroan, an orphan who came to the United States and worked his way through college, now manages the computer system for a large foreign organization in Phnom Penh. High technology is a novelty in low-tech Cambodia where offices need their own electrical generators because the city's electrical system breaks down frequently.

Saroan ❧
Computer Programmer and US Refugee

The son of an architect, Saroan was taken away from his parents in 1975 at age nine and put in a Khmer Rouge labor camp. When he heard his parents had been killed, Saroan ran away to another district, afraid he would be the next to die since the Khmer Rouge made it a policy to kill whole families. When the Khmer Rouge soldiers came, he hid in the garden. "I read The Diary of Anne Frank twice," Saroan said, "and each time I cried because our stories are exactly the same, except I'm alive today." Saroan, a smart and clever child, escaped to Thailand in 1979, where he lived in a refugee camp before emigrating to America. Next, he lived with several foster families and faced the difficulties of life in a foreign country. Saroan worked his way through college, and after graduation, he returned to Cambodia because he wanted to help his people.

Saroan was teaching word processing at the University of Phnom Penh when I met him in 1991, a couple of months before the peace accord was signed. At that time, the streets of Phnom Penh were quiet, too quiet, and the atmosphere was that of a war-torn society. People were suspicious and afraid to be caught talking with a foreigner. Sadness from losing loved ones during the Khmer Rouge period, and the difficult struggle of daily survival weighed heavily on the Cambodian people. The whole city had a feeling of weariness and despair.

In contrast, I found Saroan, whom I met through friends, to be earnest and good-natured. My friends and I readily accepted his offer to take us to visit Orphanage Number One. This home to several hundred children was in poor condition, with crumbling buildings and peeling paint. We made a donation of $100, imagining it would be spent on toys or books, but were surprised when we learned that it was used to buy firewood for cooking and 300 bottles of soy sauce, which we were told was a real treat for the children because they were tired of eating bland food. In gratitude, the orphaned children performed the beautiful classical Cambodian dance to traditional folk music. They touched our hearts.

During my first encounter with Saroan, I noticed that he frequently looked over his shoulder, hyper-vigilant from living a dangerous life under oppressive regimes. The next time I saw him, a few years later, he was more relaxed. The United Nations had arrived, Phnom Penh's streets were alive and bustling, the beautiful buildings and parks were being restored, and there was a sense of hope among the Cambodian people. Kind-hearted and talented Saroan continued working in Cambodia, and now he has a good job as a computer systems analyst. By a small miracle, he found two of his brothers and is glad to have a family again. Today, Saroan finds himself caught between two cultures, not able to fit well into either one, but he holds fast to his commitment to help Cambodia recover.

Saroan:

When the Khmer Rouge took over we ceased being the children of our parents and became the children of Angka, the government. I was living near the city of Pailin with my father and step-mother. My mother died when I was young, but my stepmother loved me very much. I think I had eight sisters and three brothers, although I don't remember all of them because several died from diseases when they were little.

The Khmer Rouge came and took all of the children, including me, separated us by age, and sent us to live at work camps. My parents had to move out of their house and were given a few tools to build a crude hut to live in. There were about 200 children in my work group, and we slept in long bamboo shacks with the girls on one side and the boys on the other.

We worked every day, from sunrise to sunset, weeding gardens and chasing birds out of rice fields when the grain was ripening. Only children who were very sick didn't have to work. I remember being awakened at three in the morning and walking to a meeting in the rain, slipping and falling in the mud on the way. The Khmer Rouge bosses from Phnom Penh had come to tell us to work hard, and they made promises of more food. I had no energy to listen. I knew they really wanted to keep us half starved so they could control us.

I played a game with the other boys in which we asked each other, "If you were forced to leave your home and could carry only one thing, what would you take?" We all said we would carry rice, since our only thought was food because no one had enough to eat. One night, we were talking before bedtime and an eighteen-year-old boy told us that a child had addressed him as "old man" when he was working in the rice field because he looked so skinny and sickly. We laughed.

Girls were allowed to visit their parents, but they wouldn't let the boys go home, and in a year and a half, I saw my parents only once. I had a friend named Sopheap who knew my family, so whenever Sopheap went home she would visit my mother who gave her a piece of chicken to bring back to me. My mother knew I was hungry and remembered how much I loved chicken.

I was waiting for Sopheap's return one afternoon when a friend came and told me to meet Sopheap under the big tree. I went there and found her crying; she couldn't stop crying. Finally, she said, "You haven't heard? Last night the Khmer Rouge took our parents away." We knew people taken away at night never came back. All of the educated, wealthy, and light-skinned people were killed after the Khmer Rouge was done using them. My father had been trained as an architect, and he owned land and gem mines.

My mind was very sharp and I had good instincts, otherwise I wouldn't have survived. I decided we should leave immediately, so they couldn't kill us next. The Khmer Rouge had a saying that if they cut the grass, they also dug up the roots so the grass wouldn't come back, which meant they had a policy of killing the whole family, including the children.

I told Sopheap of my plan to leave and go to a village on the other side of the river, where no one knew us. She wasn't sure she wanted to go and thought she might prefer to die with her parents. I told her that at seven o'clock that evening I would be in the orange garden waiting for her, and if she didn't show up by dark, I would leave without her.

I put on two pairs of dark pants and two dark shirts, the kind the Khmer Rouge made us wear, and went down near the river to wait in the orange garden for Sopheap. As the sun set and it grew dark, I thought she decided not to come, and I was about to leave when she arrived. I told her we had to make up a story so people wouldn't be suspicious. We would tell them that we were brother and sister, and that our father died from starvation, so they would take pity on us.

We crossed the river and walked all night, to a distant village in another sector, barefoot, because no one had shoes. My plan worked, and we were taken in, fed, and put into another work camp. We felt safe because they didn't know who our parents were, and no one came looking for us. This sector was better because people weren't dying of starvation.

Once a month, the Khmer Rouge at this camp let the children go home to visit their parents for a couple of hours and have a meal with them. Those of us who didn't have parents didn't get any food that day. One orphaned boy named Jong had a small bag of rice. He was starving and hungry like the rest of us, but that day he shared his rice with me and two other boys who had nothing to eat. Soon afterward, we were separated and I never saw him again. Sometimes, when I am lying in bed at night and not able to sleep, I think of his generosity and tears come to my eyes. He is like my angel.

I had lived at the second work camp for almost a year when one day, as I was walking by the river, I saw an old man whom I recognized as Mr. Ngoun, a friend of my family's. When he asked about my father I didn't want to show emotion, but I broke down and started crying and told him that my father had been killed.

The old man took Sopheap and me into his home to live with him and his wife. He taught me how to canoe and catch fish. He said that if anyone asked why we were there, he would tell them we were his grandchildren and were just visiting. Mr. Ngoun was too old to do hard work, so he was given the job of guarding the vegetable garden. When the Khmer Rouge soldiers came, we hid in the garden, like Anne Frank.

In 1978, the Vietnamese started fighting the Khmer Rouge, and everyone living near us fled the war zone, seeking protection in safer villages. Only my "family" and one other stayed behind, which made me feel like I was living in a ghost town. Each day for many months, I took the ox cart and went out to collect food and valuables that had been left behind. I brought back enough to last five years.

I was out scavenging late one afternoon when I heard the blast of artillery. The old man had told me to come directly home if I heard fighting so we would all be together. As I approached our house, I saw flames coming from the roof of our house and people standing outside. I realized it had been shelled, and I left the oxen and ran toward it. "Where's Sopheap?" I asked breathlessly. The old man grabbed me by the arm and said, "Don't go in. You don't want to see. She's a mess." Sopheap was dead, and at that moment, I didn't want to live either.

Mr. Ngoun decided to move to the city of Battambang, and I helped him build a raft of bamboo and load it with food and valuables, such as tobacco. I guided it down the river for three days, by myself, while the old man and his wife walked on the road and waited for me downriver. Floating on the river was so peaceful and beautiful. I knew I wasn't a little boy anymore; I was a man.

We were free now and the Khmer Rouge were gone, but I felt full of despair because I had lost my family. I decided to go to Thailand because I knew my grandparents lived in Bangkok, and my father had always said that if anything happened, we should go there. One night, I slipped away and followed other people who were leaving the country. I had to leave secretly, because the old man wouldn't have let me go. I had no food or gold, but people fed me because we all cared for each other. I felt lucky, as if someone up there were watching me and helping me.

I walked mostly at night, afraid of meeting soldiers. As I was walking, I saw the back of a man who I thought was my father. Full of joy,

I went running up to him crying "Father, father." He turned around and said, "I'm sorry, son. I'm not your father." I kept hoping I would find my father. A guide took us through the jungle and across the border, avoiding the landmines. I reached Thailand, but I didn't know where my grandparents lived. Bangkok was too big to find them in, so I stayed in the refugee camp orphanage.

Orphans had to wait three years before we could be adopted, since our relatives might be found. Mrs. Kun was a Cambodian mother in the refugee camp who had lost her son. She asked my friend if he wanted to go to America with her, in place of her son. My friend didn't want to leave without his brother, so then she asked me if I wanted to go. I did, and I changed my name from Hi to Saroan, which was her son's name, and decreased my age by two years.

I moved to North Dakota with Mrs. Kun and her daughter, where we were sponsored by a Lutheran Church. A few months later, when the weather turned bitter cold, Mrs. Kun decided to move to California where it was warmer. My main reason for coming to America was to get an education, and I didn't want to leave school. I didn't get along well with Mrs. Kun, so a Baptist minister's family, the Millers, invited me to live with them.

The hardest thing to get used to in America was the food. It made me sick at first, and I thought I couldn't live without rice. Mrs. Miller would serve us hamburgers at about five in the evening and a little later I would ask, "When is dinner?" I was still waiting for the rice.

School was difficult. I couldn't keep up for the first two years because I didn't know English. "Mom" Miller took me to a speech therapist who helped me learn how to pronounce English. Mrs. Miller had a good heart and was very nice to me, but I couldn't live by her rules. I felt like I was in prison, having to go to bed at a certain time. I was a boy, but I had the mind of an adult.

Reoundul was a friend of mine from the refugee camp who lived in Longmont, Colorado. When he heard about my situation, he invited me to live with him and sent me a plane ticket. I moved in with Reoundul, his wife, and their two children, into their tiny two-bedroom house. Their sponsor was the Johnson family, and shortly after I arrived the Johnsons said to me, "We have a five-bedroom house, Saroan. Why don't you come live with us?" I accepted. "Mom" Johnson gave me the freedom I needed, so it worked out very well.

By tenth grade, I was getting all As, and after I graduated from high school I went on to study at the university. I attended school from eight in the morning until two in the afternoon and then I would work until two in the morning.

After graduating in computer science, I went back to Cambodia. A friend of mine from the refugee camp had gone back and he suggested that I come too. I had no family left in Cambodia and the thought of returning frightened me. Then I said to myself, "Why should I be afraid of my own country?" I wanted to help the people there.

I arrived in Cambodia in July of 1991, a few months before the peace accord was signed. When I stepped off the plane and saw armed soldiers everywhere I wanted to turn around and get back on the plane. I was afraid when they took away my passport in the airport and told me to pick it up in Phnom Penh, and was very relieved when I got it back. I found a job teaching word processing at the University of Phnom Penh.

Through a friend, I hooked up with Orphanage Number One and Number Four. Getting to know those kids changed my life. I became friends with some of the older orphans who were in their twenties, but still living at the orphanage because they had no money and nowhere else to go. They had lost all of their family as I did.

I took one boy to the hospital. He had lost most of his leg when he stepped on a landmine and now his stump was infected, but the orphanage had no money for medical treatment. Because I spoke English, I was able to help a couple of boys get jobs at American organizations, as a security guard and a driver. To give them some hope means a lot to me, and I feel closer in my heart to them than to anyone else.

I couldn't afford to stay in Cambodia because my salary was $200 per month and my room cost $420 per month, so I returned to the United States to look for a job with an American agency doing work in Cambodia. Living in America was not great for me, and I had many difficulties. I was robbed twice in Los Angeles. I didn't have health insurance and used up my savings when I got sick and had to go to the doctor. I had to use my credit card to survive, and it took me a long time to pay it back.

I met my girlfriend in Los Angeles. She is Cambodian-American and she came to the United States when she was three years old. I was pleased when I was offered a job in Cambodia with Handicap International to develop a computer program to track amputees and landmines. I asked her to come with me to Cambodia but she decided to stay in the United States. While I was overseas, our son was born in Long Beach, California.

The United Nations was hiring people to work in Cambodia in 1992, the year before the national election, and I accepted a job as a computer programmer and supervisor of ten people. One day, Moniroth, one of my employees, came and told me that he met a young man about my age who looked like me, talked like me, and came from the same province as I did. I thought the young man could be one of my brothers, but I was afraid of being disappointed if he wasn't, so I asked Moniroth to interview him for me. When Moniroth returned, he told me that everything matched, and he had brought Hung to meet me.

I was surprised to see that Hung looked older than I, even though he was younger. "If you are my real brother then you will know where I was living when you were young," I said to him. Hung knew I moved to the city of Pailin to live with our aunt while I attended school, which confirmed for me that he truly was my brother. I was glad to find my brother, even though he seemed like a stranger at first; I had felt so lonely without a family for many years.

Hung lives with his wife and two children about thirty-five kilometers from Phnom Penh, where he teaches traditional Cambodian dance. Two years ago, Hung came to the United States on tour and performed at the White House. He earns only $10 - $20 per month, so I try to help him out. I was surprised when he told me that our stepmother and two of our half-brothers are living. Never in the world did I dream I would find them again.

I thought my stepmother was killed when the Khmer Rouge took her away, but she survived and now she lives in Siem Reap. I wanted to visit her, but I didn't have the money to fly to see her and it was too dangerous to go by road. A friend of mine from Los Angeles was robbed and killed on that road, on the way to visit his parents.

I learned that one of my brothers, Sam Nang, was a soldier. I paid $50 to get him out of the military so he could move to Phnom Penh and attend English school. His name means "lucky" in Cambodian. My third brother, Raksmay, lives far away, in a region of Cambodia that the Khmer Rouge occupied until recently.

It was too dangerous to visit him or bring him back, although I wanted to because he is the brother I feel closest to. When I was young and Raksmay was a baby, I loved to carry him around. One afternoon, I took him with me when I went to collect snails in the river and I set him on the bank. The next moment I looked up and saw that he was gone, drowning in the river. He lived, but he developed a high fever which damaged his brain and made one of his eyes crooked. Now I want to find him and help him.

I have a lot of responsibilities, helping support my brothers, girlfriend, and son. My student loans still haunt me and I owe $500 per month. I often can't sleep at night from the stress. I have terrible nightmares of people dying and someone shooting at me, then I wake up with my heart pounding, feeling paranoid.

After my position with the United Nations came to a close I went back to the United States for a while. Then in 1994, I returned to Cambodia to work as a computer programmer. I love just being here, surrounded by my people, speaking my native language, and seeing the countryside. It's exciting and Cambodia makes me feel alive again, although it is a love-hate relationship.

Years ago we couldn't talk openly because Cambodia was communist, and I always had to be conscious of who was behind me. But it's not like that any more, unless you say something bad about the prime minister, and then you could have your head shot off. There are still human-rights violations and corruption. I hate that part, but it won't change overnight. I want to have freedom and security in Cambodia, to be able to get in the car on Friday afternoon and drive off, maybe go to the beach.

I don't have a house here or in America. I feel left out a lot and don't know where to call home anymore. War tears people apart. I can't expect Cambodia to be the same for me, as if I never left. I can live in both worlds because I am flexible. I feel sorry for those who are stuck here, with no chance to leave. If I decide I don't like it here, I always have a way out. Only people with money have the opportunity to leave.

America taught me how to be independent and love freedom. I learned how to stand up for myself, and I can get a job anywhere. The down side is I am in a minority in America, I feel discrimination everywhere I go, and I can't do everything. It doesn't intimidate me, but I feel it inside.

Family bonds are much stronger here than in America. I try to help my relatives as best as I can and will always be here for them, but I tell them not to depend on me. I had to study hard and work my ass off to get where I am. It's hard for people to find jobs in Cambodia, and when they don't have financial resources, they depend on their families. I am glad I met my family, even if it takes time to get to know them and feel close. If my dad were alive it would be different.

I miss my friends in America, but I chose to be here. My job as a systems manager is great and it suits me because I like having contact with people. Sometimes I dream of being an actor or film director. In school I was not very good at writing because English was not my mother tongue, but I was good at math, and computers were popular. I want to be the best at whatever I do.

If I lost everything, I could build up again because I have been down before. Nothing stays the same. We just get old and we die. My dad worked hard and saved all his life, and then communism came, and it was all for nothing. My girlfriend says I spend too much, but I say, "Enjoy it while you can, you only live once. If you have an opportunity, take it." I don't regret my mistakes. If things don't go the way I want, so what?

Cambodia has been down for so long, over twenty-five years. My main goal for this country is to improve the living standard. People need jobs so they won't have to worry about where their next meal is coming from. We need to reduce corruption. Cambodia will take a while to rebuild and it needs industry. I see some changes I like. For example, years ago there weren't any shops for foreigners, and now there are many. The streets are cleaner and there are more gardens, cars, and economic growth, but Cambodia is a hundred years behind America.

The thought "I can't believe I am here today" often passes through my mind. I have been through so much, but these experiences have made me strong. American kids have everything. Sometimes I want to write a book and tell kids to stay in school, even though it is not easy, because afterward you can do anything you want and no one can take away your knowledge. I don't care how poor I am or how down I am, I know I can get by. Each time I go through bad times I know I have nothing to lose. My dad is my hero, and if he could see me now, he would be proud of me.

I came here and saw that Cambodia needs its overseas Khmer to come back and help, especially those of us who have an education or degree. I want to tell my grandchildren that I was a part of rebuilding Cambodia.

Saroan tries his hand at planting rice on a visit to the countryside. The bundled seedlings on the right are transplanted after the rains come and the fields are sufficiently flooded. Eighty percent of the people living in Cambodia are rice farmers. Sugar palm trees tower in the background, creating a typical Cambodian landscape.

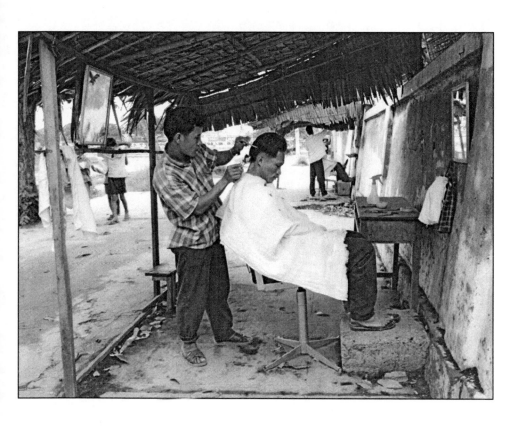

Saroan gets a haircut at an outdoor barber shop. Most people who do not farm earn their living through small businesses, such as selling in the market or offering a service. For many poor people it is very difficult to borrow the capital needed to start a business.

Young men work out in a sweaty Phnom Penh gym. Saroan's "No Limits" t-shirt is a metaphor for his ability to overcome tremendous obstacles with strength. An orphan and refugee in 1975, he now has an education and a successful career, and has found part of his family. The miracle of Cambodia is that after all the decades of war and destruction, people bravely continue the struggle to improve their lives.

SOUL SURVIVORS

Looking back we can see how the US government supported overthrowing the King in 1970, bombed Cambodian villages from 1969 to 1973, supported the Khmer Rouge as Cambodia's representative in the United Nations for twelve years following the genocide, and helped keep the Khmer Rouge fighting the Cambodian government from 1979 to 1991. Yet the Cambodian people do not blame Americans for the immense suffering and losses they have experienced, but instead, focus on rebuilding their lives, step by step.

United States' Role in Cambodia

The United States destablized Cambodia, starting with the bombings in 1969, and helped shape the course of events that led to the Khmer Rouge coming to power. After the Khmer Rouge was ousted in 1979, the United States supported this genocidal regime as Cambodia's official representative in the United Nations and continued to fuel another decade of war in Cambodia. The result has been death and tremendous suffering for the Cambodian people, most of whom live in abject poverty. The majority of the victims of the last three decades of violence have been civilians, including women and children.

The United States used Cambodia as a political pawn in its power struggle against Vietnam and the Soviet Union. In 1969, during the Vietnam-American War, President Nixon secretly ordered the bombing of neutral Cambodia without congressional approval and in violation of international law. The bombing continued for four years until it was halted by congress. The US military claimed to target North Vietnamese bases over the Cambodian border, but the entire country was bombed, killing more than 150,000 civilians, and creating a million homeless refugees. Over half a million tons of bombs, the equivalent of twenty-five Hiroshimas, were dropped on Cambodia.

In March 1970, Cambodia's King Sihanouk was overthrown in a bloodless coup by General Lon Nol. The United States favored removing King Sihanouk because he refused to assist the United States in the Vietnam-American War. The United States poured one million dollars a day into Cambodia in the early 1970s to prop up the corrupt Lon Nol regime as it fought the communist Khmer Rouge. Despite a 1970 congressional ban on aid to the Lon Nol army, US military personnel covertly worked as advisors to the Cambodian military, US helicopters transported Cambodian troops, and the US supplied ammunition.

In April 1970, US and South Vietnamese armed forces invaded Cambodia. Two months later US troops withdrew. The Vietnam-American War ended in 1975, US troops returned home, and North and South Vietnam were reunited under a communist government. Vietnam became an ally of the Soviet Union and enemy of China, the two big players in Asia's political struggle.

The United States held a grudge against Vietnam after losing the war and created policies to punish Vietnam, claiming to "contain Soviet expansion." When Cambodia's new Vietnamese-backed government took office in 1979 the United States used the opportunity to retaliate against Vietnam by supporting Cambodia's counter-revolutionary groups, including the communist Khmer Rouge. United States support for the resistance movement was aimed at engaging the Cambodian government in an exhausting guerrilla struggle that would deplete Vietnam's scarce resources. The United States' objective was to escalate the Cambodian crisis rather than help to find a solution.

The United States was the largest funder of humanitarian relief to the one million hungry Cambodian refugees who fled to Thailand in 1979 and 1980. But keeping the Thai refugee camps open until 1992 instead of repatriating the refugees served to support the guerrilla war against the Cambodian government. The camps were used as bases for the armed resistance coalition of Khmer Rouge, royalists, and Lon Nol supporters.

In 1981, the United States increased its shipments of weapons to Thailand, which were then sold to the resistance coalition. At the same time, China continued to arm and train the Khmer Rouge, with US government knowledge and tacit approval. For five years, the United States provided non-military aid to the Khmer Rouge as well. In 1985, congress stopped overt aid to the Khmer Rouge, but covertly support- ed the Khmer Rouge by giving military and economic aid to the non- communist members of the resistance coalition. The Bush administra- tion admitted there was military cooperation between the non-commu- nist resistance groups and the communist Khmer Rouge.

The United States also channeled $15 million a year to the resist- ance coalition through other countries in the region. A portion of the humanitarian food and medical aid contributed by the United States was sold by the coalition and the funds were used to buy arms from Taiwan and Singapore.

In another geopolitical power move against Vietnam and the Soviet Union, the United States blocked humanitarian and development aid to Cambodia. From 1979 to 1992 the United States led a world-wide eco- nomic embargo against Cambodia which prevented Cambodia from obtaining materials needed to rebuild the country, including farming tools, trucks, irrigation pumps, fishnets, and boats. Equipment pur- chased before 1979 was rendered useless because spare parts and repair manuals could not be obtained.

The United States actively lobbied other western countries to stop providing assistance to Cambodia. Cambodia became the only devel- oping nation to be denied funding from the United Nations. In order to prevent US non-governmental humanitarian organizations from providing development aid to Cambodia, the United States applied its International Emergency Economic Powers Act to Cambodia so that even relief and emergency aid was restricted. When US Representative Chester Atkins (D-MA) was asked in an interview with ABC News in 1990 about US policy toward Cambodia, the Congressman described it as "a policy of hatred."

Adding insult to injury, the United States voted in favor of seating the Khmer Rouge as Cambodia's representative to the United Nations in order to exclude and disempower the Vietnamese-assisted Cambodian government. The genocidal Khmer Rouge officially represented Cambodia in the United Nations between 1979 and 1991 and, at the same time, waged a guerrilla war against the Cambodian government.

The Khmer Rouge maintained power through the late-1990s with help from Thailand. Thai military officials provided sanctuary, weapons and logistical support to the Khmer Rouge. Cambodian gems and timber harvested in Khmer Rouge controlled areas of Cambodia were sold through Thailand with assistance from the Thai military, enabling the Khmer Rouge to feed and arm its troops without foreign aid. The United States, Thailand's military ally and primary foreign aid provider, asked the Thai military to stop cooperating with the Khmer Rouge, but the request went unheeded. The United States chose not to take stronger measures to pressure Thailand, such as cutting aid.

On a more positive note, the United States supported the UN-sponsored Cambodian election in 1992. Afterward, the United States provided development aid to the new government until 1997, when Second Co-Prime Minister Hun Sen ousted First Co-Prime Minister Ranariddh in a coup.

The United States' political motives for supporting the Khmer Rouge disappeared after Cambodia's national election in 1992. Vietnam was no longer backing Cambodia. The US government then reversed its policy and decided to hold the Khmer Rouge accountable for Cambodia's genocide. In 1995, US Congress passed the Genocide Investigation Act which funded the collection of evidence for a trial of the Khmer Rouge. In 1998 the United States attempted to extradite Pol Pot for an international trial, but he died the day before he was to be arrested.

In 1996, twenty-one years after imposing trade restrictions, the United States normalized trade with Cambodia. Prior to granting "most favored nation" trade status, the US customs tax on Cambodian-made products averaged ten times more than the tax on products from other countries, making it impossible for Cambodian goods to compete in the US market.

Before the coup in 1997, the United States was giving Cambodia approximately $40 million in aid per year to support education and health care programs. After the coup the United States stopped all assistance. The United States restored aid at the level of $20 million following Cambodia's national election in 1998. This amount increased over time and in 2007 the U.S. government gave $55 million in assistance.

SOUL SURVIVORS

A child plays with a toy made from a missile fragment. Many curious innocent children have been killed or maimed by exploding military ordnances left over from the war. There are an estimated four to six million landmines buried in the countryside.

Obstacles to Recovery —
Millions of Landmines

"I am an amputee. There is no reason for living found in those words,"
—Hay Loeuth, a thirty-four-year-old double amputee.

There are an estimated four to six million landmines buried in Cambodian soils, planted during the last thirty years by all warring factions, including the Cambodian government and the Khmer Rouge. Millions of mines buried in roads, paths, farms, and forests lie waiting to be stepped on by women planting rice, men gathering firewood, or children tending cows.

Cambodia has the highest percentage of landmine victims of any country in the world. One out of every 236 Cambodians is an amputee. Half of the people who step on a landmine die, often bleeding to death for lack of transportation to medical facilities. Of those who survive, many wish they hadn't because of the difficulties they face as disabled persons in a country without services or support for the handicapped.

Each day, two to three people step on landmines in Cambodia. Most landmine victims are farmers who lose not only their limbs but also their ability to grow food. Cambodia does not have social security or disability pay for landmine victims. Hence, more than 30,000 handicapped people have moved to Phnom Penh in search of work, and many have ended up begging on the streets.

Due to their belief in karma—the concept that our actions have consequences and we eventually get back what we give—Cambodian landmine victims often blame themselves for their accidents, which they consider the result of personal wrong doing in a past life. Besides the ongoing physical pain, amputees experience sorrow and shame. Cambodian society treats amputees as outcasts, seeing them as both morally and physically impaired.

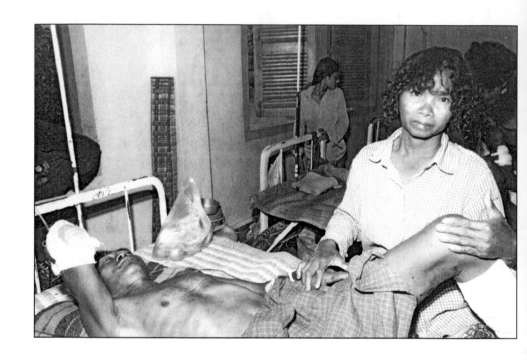

*More than one person's life was shattered when this man stepped on a land-
mine and lost his leg while gathering firewood in Battambang Province.
Cambodia does not have disability insurance nor does it provide government help to landmine victims. How will this family support itself now that
the husband cannot farm?*

"Before, I had many friends, and people liked me. But now, after I've become an amputee, many people look down on me and have nothing to do with me. Please send my leg back to me."
—Choy Li, a woman farmer, wrote in a letter to mine producers.

Landmines were sold in military markets for just a few dollars each and were easy to plant. Removal is much more difficult and expensive. The ground must be gently probed with a knife, inch by inch. The cost to remove one mine averages $1,000. Half of Cambodia has been mined, and de-mining is poorly funded. Forty thousand mines were removed between 1992 and 1995, and at this rate it will take more than 300 years and the deaths of 1,000 de-miners to remove all the mines. Regardless of organized efforts, Cambodia is being de-mined, limb by limb.

Landmines are designed to inflict pain and suffering. They were originally produced with 200 grams of explosives, enough to kill a person. Manufacturers reduced the explosive to 100 grams, so the mines would maim rather than kill the victims because a disabled person is more of a burden on society than a dead person.

Today's landmine technology has created undetectable mines, made from plastic, so de-miners cannot locate them with metal detectors. Furthermore, the plastic fragments in the victims' bodies do not appear on x-rays, which makes removal difficult and causes ongoing infections. Recently, US corporations designed the "smart mine," a landmine that theoretically self-destructs within a few months. But these mines are not as smart as the manufacturer claims, the failure rate is ten to fifty percent.

Thousands of new landmines are manufactured each day. Major producers of landmines over the last quarter century were Belgium, China, France, Italy, the former Soviet Union, United Kingdom, United States, and former Yugoslavia. The United States exported landmines until 1992, when congress enacted a moratorium on their manufacture and sale. However, US businesses continued to export components. For example, one corporation sold a component that caused the mine to detonate when slightly tilted during removal so the de-miner lost his or her eyes and hands.

The curiosity of children increases their chances of injury from landmines, and smaller child-victims are more likely to die. Children's occupations, such as herding livestock and fishing, expose them to higher risks of encountering landmines.

A young Cambodian, Kol Vanna, sent this message to mine manufacturers:

"Don't you have enough capabilities to find another business beside mine production? Your intelligence and your achievement have killed millions of people, especially in my country. If you can find another business, you will become a good friend of the world and a good friend to the children of Cambodia."

Wives who step on landmines are often abandoned by their husbands and left to raise their children alone. Single women amputees are considered inferior and undesirable as wives because they cannot farm or do all the household chores. Similarly, women with disabled husbands have to work twice as hard to support the family.

A worldwide ban on the production, trade, and use of landmines has been proposed as an amendment to the Convention on Conventional Weapons, an international treaty, but there has been resistance from the United States and other nations. The Royal Government of Cambodia ratified the Mine Ban Treaty in July 1999.

International Campaign to Ban Landmines

More than 1400 human rights, humanitarian, medical, development, refugee, arms control and environmental organizations around the world have joined together to form the International Campaign to Ban Landmines and bring a halt to the laying of landmines. Already, 100 million landmines contaminate sixty-four countries, another 100 million mines are stockpiled, and hundreds of thousands of new mines are laid worldwide each year.

The campaign calls for: (1) a total ban on the use, production, stockpiling, sale, transfer, or export of anti-personnel mines; (2) the establishment of an international fund to promote and finance landmine awareness, and clearance and eradication programs worldwide; and (3) the countries responsible for the production and dissemination of anti-personnel mines to contribute to the international fund.

By 2008 one hundred and fifty-five countries had endorsed an international treaty banning anti-personnel landmines, but the United States was not among them. The United States stated that it will continue manufacturing and using landmines until an alternative is developed.

A soldier who stepped on a landmine waits to be fitted with an artificial leg.

Old women with shaved heads bring food to the monks at a Buddhist temple to earn merit so they will suffer less in their next life. Before leaving, the two women add their names to a petition to ban landmines and sign with a thumb print because they cannot read or write. A socially engaged form of Buddhism is emerging in Cambodia in which monks work in community development and lead the peace movement.

Glimmer of Hope — The Peace Movement

"Our journey for peace begins today and every day. Slowly, slowly, each step is a meditation, each step is a prayer, each step will build a bridge."
—Maha Ghosananda speaking to participants
and observers of the Dhamma Yietra

In the cool early morning hours, before sunrise, hundreds of Buddhist nuns, monks, and Cambodian citizens quietly left a temple to begin the first Dhamma Yietra, literally a "pilgrimage of truth." As these peace walkers made their way across the war-torn provinces of Cambodia during the next weeks, tens of thousands of people, including peasants and soldiers, lined the roads with buckets of water, flowers, and incense, holding their hands together in *samphea*, the prayer-like gesture of respect.

The monks used the flowers to sprinkle water on the people and bless them. "May we live in peace and happiness soon," they prayed. Then the monks plunged the incense sticks into the water as a symbol of extinguishing the flames of war.

In the evening, hundreds of people gathered at the local temple to hear the revered monk and leader of the peace walk, Maha Ghosananda, often called the "Gandhi of Cambodia." His main message is more than 2,500 years old and is direct from the Buddha. "Hatred is never overcome by hatred. Only love can overcome hatred. This is the eternal law."

The Buddhist-led walks for peace and reconciliation were an annual event from 1992 to 1999. During the first walk nuns, monks, and lay people accompanied refugees from camps in Thailand as they returned home, many for the first time in seventeen years. The returning refugees feared that the Cambodians at home would mistrust them and associate them with the resistance groups. Fortunately, violence was avoided and tearful reunions occurred daily.

The second peace walk took place just before the UN elections in May 1993, originating in Siem Reap and traversing provinces gripped with the fear of election violence. On the eve of departure, the temple

229

where the peace walkers were staying became a battleground and three peace walkers were killed in cross-fire between government troops and the Khmer Rouge. A grenade was tossed into a room filled with hundreds of peace walkers, but miraculously it did not explode. The walk proceeded, as planned, and during the final days 10,000 people joined in as it passed through the streets of Phnom Penh. The peacefulness and strength of the Dhamma Yietra reassured the Cambodian people and gave them courage to vote.

Two thousand pilgrims embarked on the third Dhamma Yietra in 1994, originating in Battambang and passing through areas controlled by the Khmer Rouge in order to "spread compassion and turn our enemies into our friends." At one point, the Khmer Rouge started firing at the group because government soldiers had joined the walk. A nun and monk were killed and five others were injured. A man who was shot in the leg said from his hospital bed, "I am not angry. I forgive them. If we go on seeking revenge each time it will never end. We are tired of war and violence. That's why we are walking and must continue to walk."

Peace walkers also brought the message, "We need to plant trees, not landmines" as they passed through large tracts of deforested land that had been devastated after the Khmer Rouge granted Thai companies logging and gem-mining concessions in the 1980s and '90s. A tree was planted at each temple as a symbol of rebirth, seeding reconciliation and compassion. Six hundred walkers reached the destination of Angkor Wat. They ranged in age from thirteen to an eighty-nine-year-old nun who had participated in the two previous walks. "People think I am too old to walk," said the nun, "but I tell them we've all got to struggle if we want peace."

At the end of the walk, the venerable monk Yos Hut said in his final address, "Along the route we saw the living conditions of our fellow Cambodians. We witnessed how our compatriots live in constant fear and anxiety due to the endless flames of war, banditry, threats, extortion, rape, and other violations so often occurring in the villages. We also witnessed many displaced persons once again forced to flee their homes without time to gather their belongings.

"All of this suffering encourages us to seek any and all means to end the violence.... Cambodians in every village received the Dhamma Yietra warmly and wholeheartedly. We believe that Cambodians all over the country support the Dhamma Yietra and the call for a non-violent resolution to the conflict through metta-karuna [loving-kindness and compassion] for true lasting peace and reconciliation."

In 1995 the fourth Dhamma Yietra was combined with an international peace walk that originated in Auschwitz, Poland, and passed through Cambodia en route to Hiroshima, Japan. The purpose of the walk, which took place fifty years after the end of World War II, was to remember all the victims of war and to pledge, "Never again."

Maha Ghosananda led the Dhamma Yietras and Cambodia's peace and justice movement. In 1980 he co-founded the Inter-religion Mission for Peace in Cambodia and the Whole World, which launched ecumenical initiatives for peace world-wide. Maha Ghosananda was nominated for the Nobel Peace Prize in 1994.

In his acceptance speech for the prestigious Norwegian Rafto Human Rights Award, Maha Ghosananda said, "All of us must find the courage to leave our temples and enter the temples of human experience, temples that are filled with suffering. If we listen to the Buddha, Allah, Christ, or Gandhi, we can do nothing else. The refugee camps, the prisons, the ghettos, and the battlefields will then become our temples. We have so much work to do."

As soon as the communist government ended in 1991 and it became legal to form local non-governmental organizations (NGOs), many Cambodians started groups to work for peace, human rights, and the alleviation of poverty. Monks initiated development work in rural villages. Khemara was the first organization formed to help women, and now there are many others. Maha Ghosananda is affiliated with the Coalition for Peace and Reconciliation.

Buddhism is revered by the Cambodian people, and the message of peace and non-violence from the nuns and monks shines as a light of hope in Cambodia. Buddhist temples have always served as centers for religious practice, education, as well as community activities. The national movement for non-violence is growing out of the Buddhist tradition.

A valuable aspect of Cambodia's peace movement is that it addresses the emotional needs of a population that has been traumatized by decades of war and violence. Reconciliation efforts are needed to heal the fear, anxiety, pain and suspicion among the Cambodian people.

Buddhist leaders teach that if true peace is to be achieved, each person must realize that she or he has inner spiritual work to do. The Venerable Kim Teng states, "Peace will come not just by throwing away arms. Peace comes from within the soul first, and happens when our heart is calm."

Each time the Khmer Rouge and the government held peace talks, Buddhist monks were present, silently encouraging leaders to end the war. Monks and nuns organized public meditations and prayers for peace in Phnom Penh throughout the negotiations. Although the talks failed, Maha Ghosananda taught, "Peace is always a point of arrival and a point of departure. That is why we must always begin again, step by step, and never get discouraged."

Cambodia's civil war finally ended in 1998, following Pol Pot's death. Pol Pot died the night before he was to be extradited by the United States for crimes against humanity. The cause of his death is unknown. Buddhist monks and nuns continue to teach about non-violence and work to rebuild Cambodia.

Hope for Cambodia's future lies in her children.

How to Help
Women and Children in Cambodia

Cambodia is among the poorest nations in the world and the statistics for children are grim. According to UNICEF (2007), nearly half of the children in Cambodia are malnourished. Because of poverty, only 12% of the children who start school finish high school. One third of the children are not vaccinated. Each year approximately 500,000 children are orphaned due to AIDS and other causes. Over 10,000 children live on the streets of Phnom Penh, the capital city. One out of 10 girls in Cambodia is trafficked, tricked and sold into prostitution. Each day, two to three people step on landmines. Thirty years of war, including genocide, have shattered Cambodia.

In response to the problems in Cambodia, both the author and photographer of this book were moved to start non-profit organizations to help Cambodia. Bhavia Wagner founded Friendship with Cambodia and Valentina DuBasky founded Art in a Box. We are working with several of the people in this book, including Ratha, Chath, Serey Phal, Thavery, Sam Ol, and our interpreter, Kosal.

FRIENDSHIP WITH CAMBODIA

Friendship with Cambodia, provides humanitarian aid to Cambodia, focusing on 1) rural poverty, and 2) people in crisis, including families with AIDS, street children, trafficking victims, and landmine survivors.

Eighty percent of the people in Cambodia are rural and just barely get by. Our programs focus on the poorest people who are lacking education, enough food to eat, a house that keeps them dry, health care, and clean water to drink. Often these families have had a crisis that sent them into debt and extreme poverty, such as a family member who became sick or died. They often feel hopeless and resigned to poverty.

Empowering people through credit or education, with a social worker to provide guidance and encouragement, is a very effective approach to help people overcome poverty. We have micro-credit programs for women, and we help start rice banks, cow banks, and village loan funds. We provide matching grants to families and communities to build houses, schools, community halls, and wells.

For education, we sponsor poor children to attend school and provide vocational training programs to landmine and trafficking survivors. We support an anti-trafficking program, a shelter for street children, and provide assistance to families with AIDS who live in the slums. We give grants to community forestry and fishery associations to protect natural resources from illegal destruction.

Friendship with Cambodia is primarily funded by individuals who make tax-deductible donations. For $360 you can sponsor a student in school for a year, and you will receive a photo and letter from your student. For $250 you can help start a small loan fund for women. A matching grant of $160 will allow a poor family to build a house or buy a cow. Every donation is appreciated and used effectively.

We welcome your support and involvement. Sign up for our free newsletter. You are invited to join one of our trips to Cambodia and visit our humanitarian projects. If you are traveling to Cambodia, contact us for suggestions for making your trip more meaningful.

Friendship with Cambodia
PO Box 5231, Eugene, OR 97405
cambodiaedu@hotmail.com
(541) 343-3782
www.friendshipwithcambodia.org

ART IN A BOX

Art in a Box partners with communities around the world that are facing crisis situations due to war, public health emergencies, natural disasters, or poverty, and assists in their recovery and empowerment through art and art education. We respect the depth and diversity of children, families and communities who are often viewed as representatives of their circumstances rather than as unique individuals.

We work in partnership with local communities to help children and their families—often the least visible, most vulnerable, and poorest people—to find the dignity and beauty of their own self-expression. In Cambodia, we conduct art education programs for children affected by AIDS, AIDS orphans and children with AIDS; silk painting training at the Phnom Penh School for the Deaf, and an income generation project for trafficked girls and women at risk at the Cambodian Womens Crisis Center. We produce children's publication projects and conduct local and international exhibitions of children's art.

Art in a Box
463 West St #G122, NYC, NY 10014
(212) 691-2543
Artpartners@aol.com
www.artinabox.org.

Chronology of Cambodian History

802 AD   The Kingdom of Angkor is established.

900 - 1200   The Angkor Empire covers most of southeast Asia and
                    is known for its beautiful temples and sculpture.

1300 - 1800   Angkor declines due to warfare and loses territory to
                    the Thais and the Vietnamese.

1863   Cambodian King Norodom reluctantly signs a treaty of
                    protectorate with the French, which lasts until 1953.

1930   The movement for independence from foreign imperi-
                    alism in Southeast Asia begins. Ho Chi Minh founds
                    the Indochinese Communist Party.

1941   The French establish nineteen-year-old Prince Norodom
                    Sihanouk as king. The Japanese occupy Cambodia
                    during World War II.

1946   The war for independence in Vietnam begins as Ho Chi
                    Minh's Viet Minh army fights the French. Saloth Sar
                    (Pol Pot) goes to study in France.

1954   Sihanouk wins Cambodia's independence from France.

1963   Saloth Sar (Pol Pot) becomes leader of Cambodia's
                    Communist Party.

1965   US troops arrive in Vietnam. Sihanouk ends diplomatic
                    relations with the United States.

1967   Cambodia loses tax revenues on rice that is smuggled
                    into Vietnam during the war. Sihanouk increases the
                    tax on remaining rice supplies, which spurs a peasant
                    uprising and the armed communist revolution.

Communists seek to eliminate widespread rural poverty and the corrupt ruling elite.

1969 President Nixon begins an illegal secret bombing of neutral Cambodia that continues until August 1973 when US Congress stops the Pentagon.

Mar. 1970 General Lon Nol, with US backing, deposes King Sihanouk. Sihanouk sets up a government-in-exile in Beijing and forms an alliance with the Khmer Rouge, a faction of the Cambodian communist party led by Pol Pot.

Apr. 1970 US and South Vietnamese forces invade Cambodia in an effort to destroy the Viet Cong, then withdraw two months later.

1970-1975 The Khmer Rouge fight the Lon Nol government and gradually take over the rural areas. The Khmer Rouge is seen as the alternative to US bombing and government corruption, and has the support of King Sihanouk. Two million rural residents flee to the cities to escape the war and bombing.

April 17,1975 The Khmer Rouge marches into Phnom Penh, the Lon Nol government surrenders, and the last vestiges of American support are withdrawn.

1975-1979 The Khmer Rouge declares "Year Zero" and proceeds to transform Cambodian society by establishing Maoist, peasant-run, rural cooperatives. City residents are evacuated and the entire population is forced into slave labor: farming rice, digging irrigation canals, and building dams. "Enemies within" are purged from the new society to eliminate all traces of foreign influence. The rich, the educated, former government employees, Buddhist monks, ethnic Vietnamese, Chinese, and Cham are systematically massacred in an act of genocide. An estimated two million people die from torture, execution, starvation, or disease. Other than aid from China, Cambodia is cut off from the outside world.

1976 The Khmer Rouge announces that Pol Pot is Prime Minister of Democratic Kampuchea. Kampuchea is the ancient name for Cambodia.

1977   The Khmer Rouge instigates border clashes with Vietnam and Thailand. Hun Sen and other disenchanted Khmer Rouge officers escape to Vietnam.

Dec. 1978   The National Salvation Front, consisting of Cambodians and 120,000 Vietnamese soldiers, invades Cambodia from Vietnam. Khmer Rouge soldiers escape to Thailand.

Jan. 1979   The Vietnamese install a new communist government led by Cambodians Hun Sen and Heng Samrin. The Thais and Chinese secretly agree to arm and support the Khmer Rouge in a guerrilla war against the new government.

1979   The country is in turmoil as people walk home from their assigned work camps and search the country for their lost family members. Hunger is widespread. Hundreds of thousands of Cambodians flee to Thai refugee camps. The United States imposes an international trade embargo and blocks development assistance. The Khmer Rouge is voted, with US support, Cambodia's official representative in the United Nations.

1982   The three rebel groups opposed to the new Vietnamese-backed Cambodian government form a resistance coalition. By the late 1980s FUNCINPEC, the royalist group loyal to King Sihanouk, has 12,000 soldiers; Khmer People's National Liberation Front (KPNLF), the non-communist former Lon Nol group, has 8,000; and the Khmer Rouge, the communist group, has 40,000.

1985   Vietnamese troops and the Cambodian army attack the resistance coalition camps in Cambodia and push them into Thailand.

1980s   The Khmer Rouge-led resistance coalition shells towns, plants landmines, attacks road transport, kidnaps village chiefs, and kills local administrators and school teachers. Cambodia is the only Third World country denied United Nations development aid.

Sept. 1989   Suffering from internal economic problems, the Soviets cut off aid to Vietnam, causing Vietnam to withdraw its troops from Cambodia. The resistance coalition launches a series of military offensives, displacing tens of thousands of civilians within Cambodia.

July 1990   With the Soviet threat gone, the United States with-
             draws its support for the resistance coalition and initiates
             diplomatic contact with Vietnam and Cambodia.

Oct. 1991   A peace plan agreed upon by the UN Security Council is
             signed by the Vietnamese-backed Cambodian
             government and the three resistance coalition members
             (Khmer Rouge, Lon Nolists, and royalists). The United
             Nations Transitional Authority in Cambodia (UNTAC) is
             established to disarm rebel factions, repatriate refugees,
             and administer democratic elections.

1992   The Khmer Rouge refuses to disarm or cooperate with
             UNTAC. The Khmer Rouge controls about fifteen
             percent of Cambodia and profits from the sale of
             Cambodian timber and gems through Thailand. Buddhist
             monks, nuns, and lay people support the peace process
             and organize the first annual Dhamma Yietra (peace
             walk) led by Maha Ghosananda. The United States lifts
             its trade embargo.

Mar. 1993   To gain popular support, the Khmer Rouge massacres
             ethnic Vietnamese living in Cambodia. Twenty thousand
             ethnic Vietnamese flee to Vietnam.

May 1993   National elections are held and eighty-five percent of
             eligible Cambodians vote. The Khmer Rouge refuse to
             participate. A coalition government is formed between
             FUNCINPEC (the royalists) who won 45% of the vote
             and the Cambodian People's Party (the former
             Vietnamese-backed Cambodian government) who won
             38%. Hun Sen and Prince Ranariddh, King Sihanouk's
             son, become Co-Prime Ministers.

1993   A new constitution is adopted and the Royal Government
             of Cambodia is established, with King Sihanouk as head
             of state. Cambodia is re-admitted to the international
             community. The Khmer Rouge, under the direction of
             Pol Pot, continues to wage war against the government.

1994   The Cambodian government outlaws the Khmer Rouge.
             US Congress passes the Genocide Investigation Act to
             document the killings by the Khmer regime.

1996   The fifth annual Dhamma Yietra (peace walk) is led by
             Buddhist monk Maha Ghosananda, as the fighting

continues. Khmer Rouge leader Ieng Sary is granted a royal pardon and many Khmer Rouge troops defect.

1997   Second Co-Prime Minister Hun Sen ousts First Co-Prime Minister Ranariddh in a coup. The United States cuts aid to Cambodia.

1998   Pol Pot kills his military chief Son Sen. The Khmer Rouge holds a trial of Pol Pot and places him under house arrest. The United States tries to extradite Pol Pot, but he dies the day before he is to be handed over. The Khmer Rouge weakens as thousands of soldiers defect. Cambodia holds a national election and Hun Sen is elected Prime Minister.

1999   Khmer Rouge leaders Khieu Samphan and Nuon Chea declare that the Khmer Rouge doesn't exist and are allowed to re-enter Cambodian society. Ta Mok (a.k.a. the Butcher) and Duch are placed in custody and charged with genocide.

2003   Hun Sen is re-elected Prime Minister. His govern-ment is accused of corruption and suppression of political dissent.

2006   After seven years of negotiations, the United Nations and the government of Cambodia reach an agreement on the International Tribunal to bring the top leaders of the Khmer Rouge to trial for crimes against humanity.

2007   The garment industry accounts for 80% of Cambodia's exports, two-thirds are sold to the US, and support one in five Cambodians. Khmer Rouge leaders Nuon Chea, Ieng Sary, and Khieu Samphan are arrested and charged with mass murder.

2008   The US trade policy that helped created Cambodia's garment industry by giving preferential access to US markets in exchange for high labor standards ends. The genocide trial begins.

Map of Cambodia

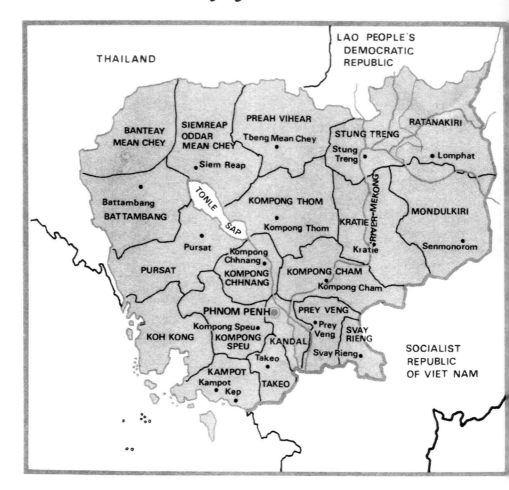

Cambodia is a patchwork of rice paddies and forests, lying between Vietnam and Thailand. It is a hot tropical country about the size of Oklahoma. Of the nearly twelve million people living in Cambodia, ninety percent are Khmer, five percent are Vietnamese, and five percent are other minorities, including Chinese and Cham. Most Cambodians are Buddhist. Cambodia is one of the poorest countries in the world. The average life expectancy of fifty years is the lowest in Asia. The birth rate and infant mortality are the highest in Asia. Eighty percent of the population live on farms, yet malnutrition is twenty percent in the rural areas.

Further Reading

General History

- Chandler, David P. 2000. *A History of Cambodia*. Westview Press.
- Kamm, Henry. 1999. *Cambodia - Report From a Stricken Land*. Arcade Publishing.

Pol Pot and the Khmer Rouge Coming to Power

- Chandler, David P. 1992. *Brother Number One. A Political Biography of Pol Pot*. Westview Press.
- Kiernan, Ben. 1985. *How Pol Pot Came to Power*. Verso.
- Kiernan, Ben, and Chanthou Boua, eds. 1982. *Peasants and Politics in Kampuchea 1942-1981*. Zed Press.

Khmer Rouge Era 1975-1979

- Becker, Elizabeth. 1986. *When the War Was Over: The Voices of Cambodia's Revolution and Its People*. Simon and Schuster.
- Chandler, David. 2000. *Voices from S-21: Terror and History in Pol Pot's Secret Prison*. University of California Press.
- Ponchaud, Francois. 1978. *Cambodia Year Zero*. Holt, Rinehart, and Winston.
- Vickery, Michael. 2000. *Cambodia 1975-1982*. Silk Worm Books.
- Hinton, Alexander Laban. 2004. *Why Did They Kill? Cambodia in the Shadow of Genocide*. University of California Press.

Cambodia in the 1980s

- Chanda, Nayan. 1986. *Brother Enemy: The War after the War: A History of Indochina Since the Fall of Saigon*. Harcourt Brace Jovanovich.
- Mysliwiec, Eva. 1988. *Punishing the Poor: The International Isolation of Kampuchea*. Oxfam.

Cambodia in the 1990s

• Curtis, Grant. 1998. *Cambodia Reborn? The Transition to Democracy and Development.* Brookings Institute.
• Doyle, Michael W. 1995. *UN Peacekeeping in Cambodia: UNTAC's Civil Mandate.* Lynne Rienner Publishers.
• Kiernan, Ben, ed. 1993. *Genocide and Democracy in Cambodia: The Khmer Rouge, the United Nations, and the International Community. Southeast Asia Studies,* Monograph Series No. 41. Yale University.
• Shawcross, William. 1994. *Cambodia's New Deal.* Contemporary Issues Paper No. 1. Carnegie Endowment for International Peace.

US Policy

• Haas, Michael. 1991. *Genocide by Proxy: Cambodian Pawn on a Superpower Chessboard.* Praeger.
• Shawcross, William. 1979. *Sideshow: Kissinger, Nixon and the Destruction of Cambodia.* Simon and Schuster.

Refugees and Relief

• Mason, Linda and Roger Brown. 1983. *Rice, Rivalry and Politics. Managing Cambodian Relief.* University of Notre Dame Press.
• Reynell, Josephine. 1989. *Political Pawns: Refugees on the Thai-Kampuchean Border.* University of Oxford Refugee Studies Programme.
• Shawcross, William. 1984. *Quality of Mercy: Cambodia, Holocaust and the Modern Conscience.* Simon and Schuster.

Women and Children

• Ledgerwood, Judy. 1992. *Analysis of the Situation of Women in Cambodia.* Phnom Penh: UNICEF.
• UNICEF Office of the Special Representative. 1990. Cambodia: *The Situation of Children and Women.* Phnom Penh.

Human Rights

• Human Rights Watch. March 1995. *Cambodia At War.*

Landmines

• Davies, Paul. 1994. *War of the Mines: Cambodia, Landmines, and the Impoverishment of a Nation.* Pluto Press.

• Human Rights Watch. 1993. *Landmines: A Deadly Legacy.*

Peace Movement

• Maha Ghosananda. 1992. *Step by Step.* Parallax Press.

Culture

• Ebihara, May M., Carol Mortland and Judy Ledgerwood, eds. 1994. *Cambodian Culture since 1975. Homeland and Exile.* Cornell University Press.
• Phim, Toni Samantha and Ashley Thompson. 2000. *Dance in Cambodia.* Oxford University Press.
• Poole, Collin. 2006. *Tonle Sap: The Heart of Cambodia's Natural Heritage.* River Books.

Survivors' Stories

• Criddle, Joan D., and Teeda Butt Mam. 1987. *To Destroy You Is No Loss: The Odyssey of a Cambodian Family.* Atlantic Monthly Press.
• Ngor, Haing, and Roger Warner. 1987. *A Cambodian Odyssey.* Macmillan.
• Seng, Vatey. 2005. *The Price We Paid.* iUniverse.
• Szymusiak, Molyda. 1999. *The Stones Cry Out: A Cambodian Childhood, 1975-1980.* Farrar, Straus and Giroux.
• Ung, Loung. 2000. *First They Killed My Father - A Daughter of Cambodia Remembers.* Harper Collins.
• Welaratana, Usha. 1993. *Beyond the Killing Fields: Voices of Nine Cambodian Survivors in America.* Stanford University Press.

Films and VHS/DVD

• *The Killing Fields* is available at many video/vhs/dvd rental stores.
• *Terror in the Mine Fields,* Item Number 2301, Nova, (800) 255-9424, $19.95.

For Youth

• Brown, Ian. 2000. *Cambodia – An Oxfam Country Profile.* Oxfam GB.
• Ho, Minfong. 1993. *The Clay Marble.* Sunburst Book.

Subject Index

Note: *Italic* page numbers indicate *photographs* and their captions. **Bold** page numbers indicate **definitions** or **translations**.

A

adoption, 185–186, 207

aid across borders. *See* humanitarian relief

AIDS (acquired immunodeficiency syndrome)

    education on, *32*, 93, 145, *162*

    inner-city educators and, 51, 59

    women and, 16–17, *162*

air pollution, 88, 169

American Friends Service Committee (NGO), 109, *119*

amputees, 116, 208, 223–*224*, *227*

anesthesiologists, number of, 93, *107*

Angka. *See* Khmer Rouge

Angkor Empire, *164*, 235

Angkor Wat, 9, *31*, 56

apsara dancers, *18*, *31*, 197

artists, 19, 25, 28, 63, 197–198

arts education, 85–86, 184, 197, 203

Atkins, Rep. Chester (D-MA), 219

B

Baby Rescue Center, Phnom Penh, 177, 185, *188*

Baha'i teachings, 59, 62

Battambang Province, 22–23, 34, 39–40, 52

Bours (holiday), **77**

bribes, 43, 88, 103, 155–156, 185

brothels. *See* prostitution

Buddhism

    dietary practices and, 124

    ethical rules of, 130

    kratas, **112**

    monks and, 34, 116, 129, 186, *228*, 229–231

    nuns and, *122*–124, 128, 129–130, 229–231

    silk pictures to illustrate, **197**–198

Buddhist ceremonies

    bay seiy, **25**

    funeral practices, 60–61, 73, 127, *135*

    pakchay buan, **127**

    peace walks and, 229–231

violence
    families and, 57, 196
    institutions and, 85, 111
    roots of, x, 57, 168–169
vocational education, 180
    Maryknoll and, 109, 113–114, *119*
    as women's obstacle, 17, 145, *147*

W

wages, 158, 195
    medical doctors and, 93–94, 103
    orphanage directors and, 178, 186
    teachers and, 41, 208, 209
    trading goods *vs.* paying, 74–75, 77
wats. *See* temples
wealth
    education and, 181, 205, 236
    inequalities of, x, 57, 210
weaving
    dying thread for, 197, *200*
    income from, 191, 193, 195, 198
wedding customs, 26, *82*, 180
    arranged marriages, 75, 117, 125, 155, 195–196
    cost of, 75, 88, 117, 172
widows, *2*, 15, 45, 78, 104
women, 8, 140
    conferences for, 44, 45–46, 144, 145
    higher education and, 138, 145, *149*
    jobs for, 27, 49, 70, 77, 131, *133*, 145, 180, 197, 198
    marriage and, 191–192, 194, 196 (*see also* wedding customs;
        widows)
    men's attitude toward, 27, 89, 145–146
    obstacles faced by, 16–17
    political influence of, 46, 185
women's health, 27, 180, *188*
    care and, 104, 105, 158
    childbirth and, 178–179, 182
    menstruation and, 99, 181
women's organizations, 8, 9, 145
    See also specifics, e.g., Cambodian Women's Development
        Association (NGO)
World College West, California, 58

Epilogue

The roads have improved in Cambodia and now there are nice hotels. Each day 10,000 tourists visit Angkor Wat, and hundreds visit Toul Sleng Genocide Museum. Many Cambodians say they are happy now because their country is finally at peace. However, the daily struggle to survive is the same for the majority of the people in Cambodia. Just getting enough food to eat, living in a house that stays dry when it rains, or being able to send their children to school is beyond the means of millions of people. Although the war is over, the landmines remain and Cambodia is faced with new problems: human trafficking for prostitution, children living on the streets, AIDS, and corruption.

We have stayed in touch with most of the people whose stories are told in this book and want to give you an update. Overall, their lives have improved on a physical level. However, the psychological wounds from genocide will probably never completely heal.

• **Sam Ol** started her own dance company. Her 40 dancers perform at the Angkor Century Hotel in Siem Reap. Her cousin Pov is her administrative assistant.

• **Ratha** continues to be president of Indra Devi Association and her son Sothy is now the program director. Their organization provides home care for families affected by AIDS who live in the slums of Phnom Penh.

• **Chath** worked as a social worker in Lowell, Massachusetts and finished a Masters in Education. His paintings have been on exhibition in Phnom Penh and New York City. He plans to start a school in Cambodia.

• **Halimas** passed away, possibly from heart failure. Her daughter and grandchildren work in a garment factory.

• **Daravuth** immigrated to the US with his wife and two children. He works in a factory in Philadelphia and lives next door to Victor, his friend from the orphanage.

• **Lieng** is semi-retired. She still teaches anesthesiology at the Royal University of Phnom Penh twice a week, but she mainly focuses on being a Buddhist nun, studying vipassana meditation and helping build a Buddhist center in the city of Udong.

• **Maline** married her cousin Seun and they have two children.

• **Aun** developed breast cancer and passed away.

• **Serey Phal** recovered from a brain tumor and continued working as director of the Cambodian Women's Development Association.

• **Bopha** Bopha's wish that her story help other girls avoid being tricked into prostitution was fulfilled. The Genocide Documentation Center of Cambodia translated her story into Khmer, published it in their magazine In Search of Truth, and distributed it throughout the country.

• **Sovanna** continues as director of the government orphanage. Most of the orphaned children are either disabled or HIV positive.

• **Thavery** now teaches weaving to deaf and blind children at a program run by Krousar Thmey, a non-profit organization. Krousar Thmey is directed by Cheam Kosal, the woman who interpreted the interviews for this book.

• **Saroan** is living in Long Beach, California. He has two children and works as a computer systems manager for a non-profit organization.

The genocide survivors have mixed reactions to the trial of the Khmer Rouge. Most are in favor of the trial and say "I want to know why Khmer killed Khmer." Some fear it will create violence. The Khmer Rouge genocide is not included in the school curriculum in Cambodia and many young people don't believe it really happened.

The Eight Stages of Genocide are explained at the website www.genocidewatch.org. They are:

1. Classification	5. Polarization
2. Symbolization	6. Preparation
3. Dehumanization	7. Extermination
4. Organization	8. Denial

It is helpful to become familiar with these stages, so we recognize them and take action to stop genocide at any stage.

A curriculum based on *Soul Survivors* for Grades 8 – 12 can be downloaded from www.friendshipwithcambodia.org It includes nine lesson plans on Cambodian History, Genocide, Human Rights, Sweatshops, War and Peace, Artists and Culture, Powerful Women, Landmines, and Refugees.

Soul Survivors author Bhavia Wagner and photographer Valentina DuBasky invite you to support their latest efforts to help people in Cambodia. Visit their websites www.friendshipwithcambodia.org and www.artinabox.org

Bhavia Wagner dreams of a more kind and compassionate world. She is the former director of an environmental organization in Michigan and a peace center in California. Her first visit to Cambodia was in 1991. Since then she has been leading trips to Cambodia, raising funds for aid, and marketing crafts. She was a UN-trained observer in Cambodia's 1998 election. In 2003 she formed Friendship with Cambodia (www.friendshipwithcambodia.org), a non-profit organization that funds humanitarian projects in Cambodia. Ms. Wagner is currently the Executive Director of Friendship with Cambodia and resides in Eugene, Oregon.

Valentina DuBasky's paintings and prints have been included in over 130 exhibitions nationally and internationally and are represented in numerous public collections. In addition to taking the photographs for *Soul Survivors*, Ms. DuBasky has written and produced visual art projects that address human rights and social justice issues in Southeast Asia, including *Landmines in Cambodia*, a traveling, educational exhibition that documents the impact of landmines on once stable communities in Cambodia, *The Yellow Cloud*, a monograph on Agent Orange and *The Cambodian Journal*, a book of drawings about daily life and recovery from war in Cambodia. Valentina is the Founder of Art in a Box, a nonprofit organization that assists children at risk around the world through art and art education (www.artinabox.org). She resides in New York City.